EASTERN UNITED STATES
Area in which this guide is
especially useful

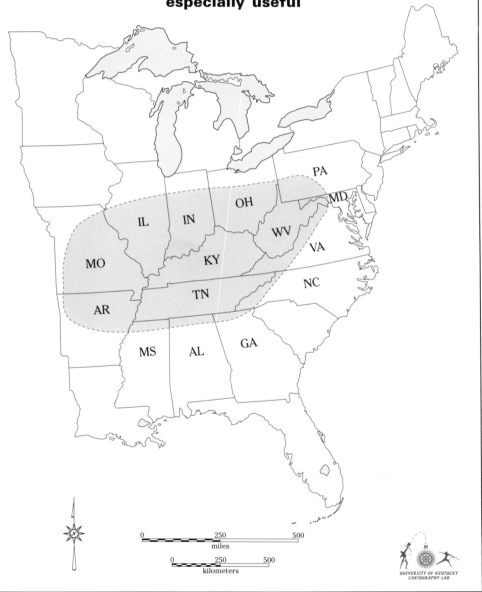

PA

MD

OH

IL

IN

WV

VA

MO

KY

NC

TN

AR

MS

AL

GA

0   250   500
miles

0   250   500
kilometers

UNIVERSITY OF KENTUCKY
CARTOGRAPHY LAB

WILDFLOWERS
and FERNS *of*
KENTUCKY

Proudly funded in part by

Kentucky's Touchstone Energy Partners

Kentucky Natural History Society

Wild Ones: Native Plants, Natural Landscapes

Kentucky Native Plant Society

WILDFLOWERS
and FERNS *of*
KENTUCKY

THOMAS G. BARNES
AND S. WILSON FRANCIS

THE UNIVERSITY PRESS OF KENTUCKY

Publication of this volume was made possible in part by a grant
from the National Endowment for the Humanities.

Editorial and Sales Offices: The University Press of Kentucky
663 South Limestone Street, Lexington, Kentucky 40508-4008
www.kentuckypress.com

20 19 18 17 16   6 5 4 3 2

Maps by Dick Gilbreath.

Library of Congress Cataloging-in-Publication Data

Barnes, Thomas G., 1957-
  Wildflowers and ferns of Kentucky / Thomas G. Barnes and S. Wilson
Francis.
        p. cm.
Includes bibliographical references (p.   ) and index.
  ISBN 0-8131-2319-4 (Hardcover : alk. paper)
  1. Wild flowers—Kentucky—Identification. 2.
Ferns—Kentucky—Identification. 3. Wild flowers—Kentucky—Pictorial
works. 4. Ferns—Kentucky—Pictorial works. I. Francis, S. Wilson. II.
Title.
  QK162.B37 2004
  582.13'09769—dc22   2003020481

This book is printed on acid-free paper meeting
the requirements of the American National Standard
for Permanence in Paper for Printed Library Materials.

Manufactured in China.

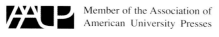 Member of the Association of
American University Presses

CONTENTS

ACKNOWLEDGMENTS

This book has been an enormous undertaking and would not have been possible without the assistance of numerous individuals. To my coauthor, Wilson, I am deeply appreciative of your hard work and efforts in writing text, particularly the family descriptions and taxonomy. I have gained a great friend and respected colleague during this project, and I am thankful for this opportunity we had to work together. I would be remiss if I did not acknowledge my department chair, Don Graves, and the dean of the College of Agriculture, M. Scott Smith, for allowing me the time and financial resources to make numerous trips into the field to obtain photographs. This was no cheap project, and their unwavering support was essential to completing the book. The sources of funding for this part of the book were the Department of Forestry, the College of Agriculture, the Cooperative Extension Service, and the Renewable Resources Extension Act. I am also grateful for financial assistance for production costs from Kentucky's Touchstone Energy Partners, the Louisville Chapter of Wild Ones, the Kentucky Natural History Society, and the Kentucky Native Plant Society.

Because the majority of photographs were taken in a single year, I am deeply indebted to the many individuals who located plants for me. Thanks so much to Ann Longsworth, Howard Murphy, Julian Campbell, Ed Chester, Portia Brown, Mary Carol Cooper, Connie May, Margaret Shea, Steve Elkins, Deborah White, Marc Evans, Susan Wilson, Chris Bidwell, Al Cornett, Christi and Pat Scott, and Karen Maag. Rob Paratley, curator of the University of Kentucky herbarium, was especially helpful in keying out and identifying difficult species. Thanks for all identifications. Vicki Young helped in sorting and labeling slides, and I appreciate her assistance and sense of humor. The original line drawings were done by Dan Dourson, and I am especially grateful for that wonderful artwork. He is a gifted artist and biologist, and his artwork will undoubtedly make field identifications easier. Many thanks to Deborah White and the anonymous reviewers selected by the University Press of Kentucky for commenting on the manuscript prior to publication. Thanks to all the good folks at the University Press of Kentucky, especially Leila Salisbury and Steve Wrinn, who have believed in this project from the start. I am also extremely appreciative of the editorial and marketing staff for their hard work in making this a successful project. I am also grateful to the numerous individuals who contributed photographs for this work, including:

> S. Wilson Francis, *Diphasiastrum digitatum, Triphora trianthophora, Vittaria appalachiana, Deparia acrostichoides, Monotropsis odorata, Huperzia lucidula, Osmunda claytonii, Trichomones boschianum*
>
> James Kiser, *Lycopodium clavatum*
>
> John MacGregor, *Platanthera flava, Malaxis unifolia*
>
> Wally Roberts, *Monotropa hypopithys*
>
> Richard Cassel, *Selaginella apoda, Woodwardia areolata*
>
> Susan Wilson and Chris Bidwell, *Taenidia integerrima*

Finally, and certainly not least important, I need to say thanks to my family for enduring a summer in which I was on the road a great deal and away from them.

—TGB

I express my thanks to Tom Barnes for the opportunity to collaborate on this book and for the friendship and many pleasant conversations and visits that it has entailed. I would also like to thank the staff at the University Press of Kentucky for their kind assistance in the production of this book. Julian Campbell, John Tierney, and Danny Barrett made supportive comments, and Ron Jones was particularly helpful with taxonomic issues. I appreciate and acknowledge my coworkers in the Kentucky State Parks for their support, and in particular my family for their patience, understanding, and the time taken away from them during the preparation of this book.

—SWF

INTRODUCTION

They are all around us and thrive on roadsides, in forests, meadows, wetlands, and, it seems, almost anywhere you travel across the state. They begin their colorful display as early as February or March in the woodlands with hepatica and purple cress and enrich the landscape until the frosts of autumn, when the gentians flower in the prairie patches or woodland edges. There is no time during the growing season that one of more than 2,000 native wildflowers found in Kentucky is not blooming.

The Song of Solomon 2:12 states, "The flowers appear on the earth; the time of the singing of birds has come." Flowers' fleeting beauty and delicacy enrich and enhance our lives. They come in such a diversity of shapes, sizes, and colors that they have inspired artists, musicians, poets, and authors. Even today, as in times past, they provide us with medicines and food. Plants are an essential component of our existence: by converting carbon dioxide into oxygen, they give us our very breath. The relationship between people and plants is a long and fascinating one, providing the historian or biologist an endless, intricate, and fascinating story of interdependence.

Interest, awareness, and inquisitiveness lead to learning. Learning leads to knowledge. Knowledge, a joy in and of itself, leads to appreciation. Appreciation coupled with knowledge about the loss of some of our most precious wildflowers will, one hopes, lead to conservation. We are attracted by wildflowers' beauty, color, or intricate form. We are then moved to find out the plant's name and identify it. Acquisition of this knowledge moves us to protect the wildflower so that we may enjoy it for years to come—perhaps to share it with our children or grandchildren and let them wander through the same wonderful journey and exploration that we experienced in our own youth.

The goal of this book is to spark an interest in, and an awareness of, the incredible beauty and diversity of Kentucky's ferns and wildflowers. It is a further goal that this book may lend assistance to the future conservation of our native flora and wildlands in general. Finally, the book is about enjoying the things you find in the fields and forests and delighting in finding those flowers. The famous naturalist John Burroughs summarizes this purpose well: "Most young people find botany a dull study. So it is, as taught from the text-books in the schools; but study it yourself in the fields and woods, and you will find it a source of perennial delight." Quite simply, this book is about enjoying and appreciating our native wildflowers.

We have become a nation of urbanites, and we seek adventure and recreation in wildlands by hiking, birding, outdoor or nature photography, flower identification, and other outdoor activities. We hope this book serves as an indispensable aid in increasing the enjoyment of the outdoor experience by providing information on some of the most common wildflowers you will encounter in your travels throughout Kentucky and maybe even in your own backyard. It is our further hope that we can provide this information in a nontechnical form.

SCOPE

We have included color photographs or line drawings of 500 species plus descriptions of an additional 134 species that are similar to those depicted by a color plate or drawing. Of the more than 2,000 native species of ferns and seed-bearing wildflowers, the ones included are the most common and likely to be encountered in the field. Our frame of reference for species inclusion in this book was based on three factors: (1) our knowledge of Kentucky's flora, (2) inclusion in *A Guide to the Wildflowers and Ferns of Kentucky* by Mary E. Wharton and Roger W. Barbour (Lexington: University Press of Kentucky, 1971), and (3) the ability of the photographer (a nonbotanist) to locate and photograph the plants. The reasoning behind the third factor was this: if an amateur photographer could find the plants, then other average people could feel reasonably certain that they too could locate and identify the plants. We have also included some rare plants, particularly those that are showy, that an amateur botanist might have a reasonable chance of finding.

WHAT IS A WILDFLOWER?

Surprisingly, this is a very simple question without a simple answer. It is also a very good question because there is much confusion about what actually is denoted by the term *wildflower*. The term itself is a paradox. All flowers are wildflowers somewhere in the world. For instance, tulips growing in the Middle Eastern countries are wildflowers but are ornamental or exotic flowers in Kentucky. Trilliums are wildflowers in North America and ornamental or exotic flowers in Europe. This paradox occurs even within the boundaries of our own nation. Indian blanket *(Gallardia pulchella)* is a native North American wildflower in the Great Plains but is not technically a wildflower in Kentucky.

Dictionaries have fairly simple definitions. *Webster's Unabridged Dictionary* (2nd ed.) defines wildflower as "the flower of a plant that normally grows in fields, forests, etc. without deliberate cultivation." The *New Oxford American Dictionary* defines wildflower as "a flower of an uncultivated variety or a flower growing freely without human intervention." Unfortunately, from a botanical viewpoint these definitions lack some substance, but even professional botanists have a difficult time defining the term. A quick survey of more than 100 wildflower field guides for various regions around North America from 1900 to the present reveals that very few wildflower books actually define the term wildflower! Even those books that define the term appear to be closely aligned to the dictionary definition. Thomas E. Hemmerly, a biology professor at Middle Tennessee State University, in *Appalachian Wildflowers* (Athens: University of Georgia Press, 2000, p. 35) defines a wildflower as "angiosperms (flowering plants) that grow wild." W. H. Duncan and M. B. Duncan (*Wildflowers of the Eastern United States* [Athens: University of Georgia Press, 1997], xv) state, "By wildflowers we mean herbaceous nonwoody plants."

For the purposes of this book, we define wildflowers as **native, herbaceous** (nonwoody plants whose stalk dies back each winter) **flowering plants,** excluding the grasses and sedges. Further, a **native species** is defined as a plant species growing in Kentucky prior to European settlement and adapted to certain habitats in response to specific climatic, geologic, and topographic variables. We chose this definition because we want our fellow Kentuckians and visitors to this commonwealth to have the opportunity to enjoy our unique natural heritage. We also feel this is a tremendous opportunity to bring attention to the ever growing problem of introduced or exotic plants and the impacts they have on natural communities, plants, and animals that are native to Kentucky.

Using this definition of a wildflower, certain plant groups have been omitted, including trees, shrubs, and woody vines. Readers are encouraged to consult Wharton and Barbour's *Trees and Shrubs of Kentucky* (Lexington: University Press of Kentucky, 1973) for assistance in identifying these species. We have also omitted the approximately 350-plus species of grasses, sedges, and rushes. Identifying these plants can be quite difficult for the nonbotanist because they have minute and highly specialized flowers. It might be argued that some "representative" species could be included to show the characteristics of this family. However, the question of which species to include becomes problematic. We avoid the problem by not including any of these species and focusing on easily identified, showier species. The final group of plants that we omitted is the "weeds," or nonnative, exotic, or alien plants. Readers are encouraged to consult *Weeds of Kentucky and Adjacent States,* by Patricia D. Haragan (Lexington: University Press of Kentucky, 1991), for assistance in identifying these plants. All definitions, even those that appear cut-and-dried, present problems because there are plants that occur in the gray area. Is this species a woody vine or a herbaceous one? Some plants, like dittany, might be semiwoody. Therefore, in some instances we have made a judgment call on whether to include that species or omit it.

WHAT IS A WEED?

What is a weed? Is it a plant out of place? Is it a plant growing where it is unwanted? Or is a weed a plant that is "perceived to be undesirable" (Haragan, *Weeds*, p. xi)? Many wildflowers have *weed* as part of their common name and are not weeds at all from the viewpoint of a wildflower, butterfly, or wildlife enthusiast. Examples include joe-pye weed, butterfly weed, star chickweed, jewelweed, sneezeweed, rosinweed, and the milkweeds. Here is the paradox: one person's weed is another person's wildflower. For instance, ironweed is a showy, native wildflower that is considered a weed by the livestock industry because livestock do not eat the plant and it can spread aggressively in pastures and old fields. Haragan includes species like joe-pye weed, partridge pea, and passionflower as weeds, yet these are among some of our "showy" wildflowers. In summary, there is some misconception about what constitutes a weed or "weediness."

From an ecological standpoint, so-called weeds are often plants that can inhabit harsh conditions and are generally the first plants to colonize disturbed sites. Typically, weeds produce large quantities of seeds that can disperse across the landscape. They generally have high germination rates, or can propagate themselves vegetatively, and can quickly dominate the plant community because they can grow rapidly and profusely and are able to compete with and crowd out more "desirable" plants.

Typically, weeds follow humans and their migrations around the globe and often flourish wherever people disturb natural ecosystems and modify the environment to meet human needs. Most noxious weeds arrived from Eurasia, although there are many native weedy species like ragweed *(Ambrosia artemisiifolia)* or annual fleabane *(Erigeron annuus).* To refine the term for this book, we have chosen to use the following terminology to differentiate the term *wildflower* from *weed.*

An **introduced, exotic,** or **alien** plant is a species that has been introduced either accidentally or intentionally from outside its natural geographic range. Some exotic plants escape cultivation or spread from the point of their introduction, become established, and persist in the environment without the assistance of human activities. These plants are said to have become **naturalized** and are a permanent component of our flora. Many people classify these plants as wildflowers, but we have chosen not to include them in this book because they do not meet our definition of a wildflower. Common examples of these species include Queen Anne's lace, chicory, ox-eye daisy, orange or Asiatic daylily, blackberry lily, star-of-Bethlehem, dayflower, mock strawberry, common cinquefoil, common chickweed, deptford pink, corn cockle, dame's rocket, bird's-foot trefoil, crown vetch, moth mullein, dandelion, yarrow—the list goes on and on. It has been estimated that more than 15 percent of our flora is now made up of exotic plants (Edward T. Browne and Raymond Athey, *Vascular Plants of Kentucky* [Lexington: University Press of Kentucky, 1992]).

An **invasive exotic** plant is a species that has escaped cultivation or has spread from its origin and has become a problem or a potential problem in natural biological communities. Examples of invasive plants include Queen Anne's lace, garlic mustard, poison hemlock, lesser and greater periwinkle, ground ivy, Dutch white clover, red clover, yellow and white sweet clover, and Korean, Kobe, and sericea lespedeza. The Kentucky Exotic Pest Plant Council has categorized invasive exotic plants as severe, significant, or lesser threats. Plants listed in the severe category have characteristics that allow them to easily invade native plant communities and displace native vegetation (table 1). Plants in the significant-threat category have some invasive

Table 1. Exotic Plants Listed as Severe Threats by the Kentucky Exotic Pest Plant Council

Common Name	Scientific Name
Tree of heaven	*Ailanthus altissima*
Garlic mustard	*Alliaria petiolata*
Musk thistle	*Cardus nutans*
Oriental bittersweet	*Celastrus orbiculatus*
Poison hemlock	*Conium maculatum*
Crown vetch	*Coronilla varia*
Chinese yam	*Dioscorea oppositifolia*
Autumn olive	*Elaeagnus umbellata*
Winged euonymus or burning bush	*Euonymus alatus*
Winter creeper	*Euonymus fortunei*
KY 31 tall fescue	*Festuca elatior*
Sericea lespedeza	*Lespedeza cuneata*
Privet	*Ligustrum sinense, L. vulgare*
Japanese honeysuckle	*Lonicera japonica*
Bush honeysuckles	*Lonicera maackii, L. morrowi, L. tatarica*
Purple loosestrife	*Lythrum salicaria*
White sweet clover	*Melilotus alba*
Yellow sweet clover	*Melilotus officinalis*
Japanese grass	*Microstegium vimineum*
Miscanthus	*Miscanthus sinensis*
Common reed	*Phragmites australis*
Japanese knotweed	*Polygonum cuspidatum*
Kudzu	*Pueraria lobata*
Multiflora rose	*Rosa multiflora*
Johnson grass	*Sorghum halepense*

characteristics but have less impact on native communities (table 2). They do, however, have the capacity to invade natural areas along disturbance corridors such as roads and spread into natural areas from disturbed sites.

Why worry about the semantics of calling a plant a wildflower or a weed? From our perspective the real issue is the impact that exotic plants have on native plant communities. Exotic plants have shown that they can alter ecosystem processes; displace native species; support popula-

Table 2. Invasive Exotic Plants Listed as Significant Threats by the Kentucky Exotic Pest Plant Council

Common Name	Scientific Name
Akebia	*Akebia quinata*
Mimosa	*Albizia julibrissin*
Common burdock	*Arctium minus*
Hairy jointgrass	*Arthraxon hispidus*
Japanese barberry	*Berberis thunbergii*
Spotted knapweed	*Centaurea biebersteinii*
Ox-eye daisy	*Chrysanthemum leucanthemum*
Queen Anne's lace	*Daucus carota*
Common teasel	*Dipsacus sylvestris*
Goosegrass	*Eleusine indica*
Ground ivy	*Glechoma hederacea*
English ivy	*Hedera helix*
Ivy-leaved morning glory	*Ipomoea hederacea*
Purple morning glory	*Ipomoea purpurea*
Bicolor lespedeza	*Lespedeza bicolor*
Korean lespedeza	*Lespedeza stipulacea*
Mint	*Mentha piperita*
White mulberry	*Morus alba*
Miniature beefsteak	*Mosla dianthera*
Star-of-Bethlehem	*Ornithogalum umbellatum*
Chinese empress tree	*Paulownia tomentosa*
Bluegrass	*Poa pratensis*
Smartweed	*Polygonum cespitosum*
Lady's thumb	*Polygonum persicaria*
White poplar	*Populus alba*
Watercress	*Rorippa nasturtium-aquaticum*
Green foxtail	*Setaria viridis*
Japanese spiraea	*Spirea japonica*
Chickweed	*Stellaria media*
Lesser periwinkle	*Vinca minor*

tions of nonnative animals, fungi, or microbes; hybridize with native species; and alter gene pools. There is also a monetary issue. The U.S. Congress has documented that 15 species of nonagricultural weeds cost the U.S. economy more than $600 million annually. In a potential worst-case scenario, Congress reports that just three species—melaleuca, purple loosestrife, and witchweed—could cause economic losses of more than $4.5 billion.

BOTANY BASICS

Imagine visiting a foreign land with an enormous number of different kinds of plants, none of them familiar. Imagine plants of all sizes and shapes, some with erect stalks, some growing flat along rocks and logs, some with colorful flowers, some without. How could you begin to sort through these plants and group them into meaningful categories?

One traditional starting point for classifying plants distinguishes between those that are vascular and those that are nonvascular. Vascular plants have special tissues that carry water and sugars throughout the body of the plant. They usually, but not always, have stems and stand erect. The important thing is that as a group, vascular plants have the ability to stand erect, which is a great advantage over neighboring plants when there is competition for sunlight. Nonvascular plants, such as mosses and liverworts, lack these tissues to carry water upward and therefore must always be very small, so that water can be absorbed throughout the plant body. All of the plants we will consider in this book are vascular plants.

A second traditional way to classify plants is to separate seed plants from those that are seedless. Seedless plants do not form seeds but reproduce by releasing spores—single cells that are capable of germinating and forming new plants. Most spores consist of a copy of the plant's DNA, a few necessary enzymes, and a protective coat. Since they are so small and each unit is inexpensive in terms of resources required for production, seedless plants can produce and release enormous numbers of spores. The downside is that since spores contain just the basics, the success of each spore is totally dependent upon its chance landing in an optimal environment for germination. Seedless plants include the mosses and liverworts, but we will also examine seedless vascular plants, such as ferns and their allies, including the clubmosses, spikemosses, and horsetails.

THE FLOWERS OF KENTUCKY

Kentucky has been called the "Land of Cane and Clover," but in reality it has an incredible diversity of interesting plants. More than 3,000 species of plants call Kentucky home. We get this diverse flora because the commonwealth is a mixing ground of North and South, East and West. We share many Appalachian species with adjacent states. Some southern Appalachian species extend into our southern tier of counties, and some northern Appalachian species occur only at the highest elevations on Pine, Big Black, and Stone Mountains. Other northern species, relicts of the Pleistocene glaciation when the southern Appalachians provided a refuge from the ice, can be found in localized pockets. At the other extreme, southern species more common in the coastal plain are found in the Jackson Purchase area. We also share a large number of species found in the midwestern tall-grass prairie region. Finally, we have species that are commonly found throughout eastern North America.

The physiographic province or region (see map) is one factor affecting the diversity of wildflowers; many ecological communities are similar throughout an entire physiographic province, and each plant community type has a common flora. The underlying geologic parent material gives rise to unique rocks and soils and outcrops. These geologic features form the unique physiography of any particular region. You are not likely to find Appalachian species like pink corydalis in the coastal-plain flatlands of the Jackson Purchase. Conversely, you are not likely to find copper iris on the Appalachian Plateaus or Cumberland Mountains physiographic province. Because physiography plays such an important part in determining the distribution of any particular plant, we have provided a brief description of the physiographic provinces found in Kentucky.

PHYSIOGRAPHY AND PLANT GEOGRAPHY OF KENTUCKY

The Cumberland Mountains

The true mountains of Kentucky occupy a relatively small part of that region people call the Kentucky Mountains. Kentucky's Cumberland Mountains are part of a rectangular block of land running northeast to

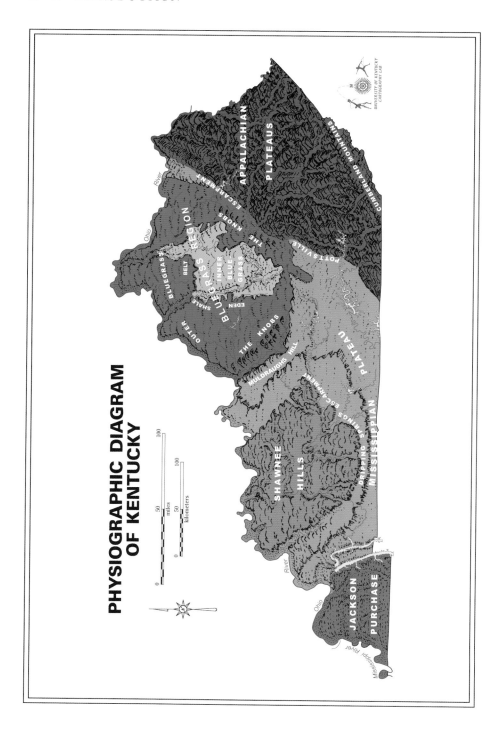

PHYSIOGRAPHIC DIAGRAM
OF KENTUCKY

southwest that was pushed up by geologic forces during the rise of the Appalachian Mountains. This rectangular block is bounded by Cumberland Mountain on the east, Pine Mountain on the west, the Russell Fork Fault on the north, and the Jacksboro Fault on the south.

The backbone of the Cumberlands is Cumberland Mountain, which arises in Virginia, where it is called Stone Mountain. Cumberland Mountain forms the boundary between Kentucky and Virginia from a point near Cawood in Harlan County, southeast to Cumberland Gap National Park near Middlesboro in Bell County, and on toward Jacksboro, Tennessee. Near Cumberland Gap the highest elevations are close to 2,000 ft., but the elevations generally increase to the north, to a maximum of about 3,500 ft. near the White Rock Lookout Tower in Harlan County. The south slope of Cumberland Mountain is quite steep, but the northern slope is much more gentle. Cumberland Mountain forms a watershed between tributaries of the Tennessee River on the east and tributaries of the Cumberland River on the west. Rainfall on both sides of Cumberland Mountain eventually reaches the Ohio River in western Kentucky, but the paths followed by these two streams are quite different.

The eastern boundary of the Cumberland Mountains is formed by Pine Mountain, which begins at Breaks Interstate Park in Pike County and runs southeast to Whitley County and on into Tennessee. The maximum elevation on Pine Mountain is nearly 3,200 ft. The slope of Pine Mountain is just the opposite of that of Cumberland Mountain: the north slope is very steep, while the south is gentle. Between Cumberland Mountain and Pine Mountain lie several shorter mountains, including the Log Mountains, Little Black, and Big Black Mountains. Big Black Mountain near Lynch in Harlan County is the highest elevation in Kentucky, at 4,150 ft.

The Cumberland Mountains as a physiographic region harbor many characteristic southern Appalachian plants. The highest elevations permit the survival of plants that are usually found either north of Kentucky or in other high-elevation plant communities in the Appalachians. Topographic shading provided by the steep mountains creates pockets of cool, moist habitats, even at lower elevations. The soils of the Cumberland Mountains are generally rich in nutrients and somewhat acid, because for the most part they are derived from sandstones and coal-bearing shales. The forests of the Cumberland Mountains are also considered rich in species. Slopes that face toward the south or west tend to be covered with a mixture of white oak, chestnut oak, and yellow poplar, with an understory of mountain laurel. Slopes that face north or east are generally covered with Mixed Mesophytic Forest, the richest forest type in the eastern United States. White oak, northern red oak, American beech, yellow poplar, white basswood, yellow buckeye, and eastern hemlock are all common members of Mixed Mesophytic Forest communities. Rhododendron is a common understory shrub in such communities, especially in sheltered coves and deep hollows.

The Appalachian Plateaus

The Appalachian Plateaus region makes up the bulk of what many people call the Kentucky Mountains. Actually, this region is not mountainous, and part of the confusion results from the definition of true mountains. In the physiographic sense, the true Appalachian Mountains were formed by tectonic events that pushed the mountains above the surrounding country so that the rock layers inside the mountains were tilted away from their original horizontal positions. These diagonally tilted rock layers are typical of road cuts throughout true mountainous areas.

The Appalachian Plateaus were uplifted with the mountains, but the rock layers in the plateaus are still generally horizontal. The vertical relief from the ridge tops to the valley bottoms in plateaus has been formed by erosion, as streams have cut downward through the rock layers, forming the canyons and valleys that are characteristic of the region.

The Appalachian Plateaus region is bordered by the Cumberland Mountains to the southeast, the Big Sandy and Ohio Rivers on the northeast, and the Tennessee state line on the south. The western boundary of the plateaus is one of the most prominent landscape features in Kentucky, the Pottsville Escarpment. The escarpment is a precipitous drop from the higher elevations of eastern Kentucky to the relatively lower elevations of central Kentucky. The change in elevation ranges from about 200 ft. along the northern end of the escarpment to nearly 1,000 ft. at the southern end.

There are actually two Appalachian Plateaus in Kentucky; geographers use the Licking River to distinguish the Allegheny Plateau to the north from the Cumberland Plateau to the south. In terms of plant communities it is difficult to draw distinctions between the two within our state, so we have chosen to use the term *Appalachian Plateaus* to include both.

The Appalachian Plateaus physiographic province is an area of rugged terrain but low elevation. Maximum elevations range from around 1,100 ft. in the north to around 2,000 ft. in the south. The landscape has been carved by tributaries of the Cumberland, Kentucky, Licking, and Big Sandy Rivers and today is characterized by narrow ridge tops, steeply sloping ravines, and, usually, narrow valley bottoms. Around the side slopes are numerous small flat benches that represent erosional remnants of old valley bottoms. The benches accumulate soil that washes down the upper slopes and are often narrow belts of rich wildflower communities.

The soils and underlying rock formations of the Appalachian Plateaus are, for the most part, similar to those of the Cumberland Mountains. However, in addition to the fairly acid soils formed from sandstone and shales, there are extensive regions with belts of exposed limestone. The limestone makes it possible for plants characteristic of neutral soils to exist in close proximity to plants that require acid soils. Soils on the ridge tops tend to be well drained and are exposed to full sunlight throughout the day, while the northern slopes and narrow shaded valleys remain relatively cool and moist. These topographical differences create a wide diversity in habitats in small areas and make the Appalachian Plateaus a province of great interest to wildflower enthusiasts.

The Knobs

The Knobs are a ring of cone-shaped hills that border the Bluegrass Region on three sides. They are sometimes treated as a separate physiographic region, but actually the Knobs represent a transition between the Appalachian Plateaus and the eastern edge of the Bluegrass, and the Mississippian Plateau and the southern and western edges of the Bluegrass.

The isolated hills that make up the Knobs are erosional remnants of the elevated plateaus that surround the Bluegrass. The rock layers within the hills are the same layers that form the plateaus, therefore the soils are similar to those of the adjacent plateaus. What makes the Knobs unique are the wide, flat valleys between the hills, where deep, rich soils have accumulated. Some of Kentucky's most picturesque farmland is in the Knobs region.

From a botanical point of view the Knobs are interesting because a number of plants from different physiographic regions reach their distributional limits in these isolated hills. The valleys between the Knobs often allow species typical of the Bluegrass to radiate out, while up on the slopes of the Knobs isolated populations of plateau species reach toward the Bluegrass.

The Bluegrass

Kentucky's Bluegrass Region is named for a plant that may well be one of the first exotic species introduced to our state from Europe. The Bluegrass sits on a dome of ancient limestones and calcareous shales that have been pushed up from deep within the earth, exposing the oldest surface rocks in Kentucky. This dome is part of a large geologic ridge called the Cincinnati Arch that runs across Kentucky and south into Tennessee.

The Bluegrass Region constitutes northern and central Kentucky. It is bounded on the east by the Appalachian Plateaus, on the north by the Ohio River, and to the south and west by the Mississippian Plateau. A ring of low hills, the Knobs, made up of erosional remnants of the Appalachian and Mississippian Plateaus, forms transitional regions between the provinces.

Most geographers recognize three divisions of the Bluegrass. In the immediate vicinity of Fayette County lies the Inner Bluegrass, an area of little topographical relief but very deep and rich soils. The maximum elevations in the Bluegrass occur here at approximately 1,000 ft. Around the Inner Bluegrass lies a ring of low, rounded hills called the Eden Shale Belt. The underlying rocks here are calcareous shales, and the soils are relatively thin and rocky. The Outer Bluegrass is an area of moderate relief, with soils that are more fertile than the Eden Shale Belt.

The first pioneers recognized the Bluegrass's suitability for agriculture, and practically every acre has been modified from its original state. Historical references suggest that the pioneers found the region to be an open savanna of grassland with an overstory of blue ash, bur oak, and chinquapin oak. Today a rich diversity of wildflower habitats and species survives in the canyons along the Kentucky River Gorge.

The Mississippian Plateau

The area we refer to in this book as the Mississippian Plateau is known by many in Kentucky as the Pennyrile Region. The word *Pennyrile* is a corruption of the word *pennyroyal,* the name for a wildflower in the mint family that can found in the region. The name Mississippian Plateau comes from the underlying rocks formed during the Mississippian Period. The plateau is an elevated limestone plain bordered by the Appalachian Plateaus and the Bluegrass to the east, the Ohio River and Shawnee Hills to the north, the Tennessee state line to the south, and the Jackson Purchase to the west.

Separating the Mississippian Plateau from the Bluegrass is an escarpment called Mulldraugh's Hill, a line of hills formed in shale and capped by resistant limestone. At the top and behind the hills is the elevated, relatively flat surface of the plateau. South of the Bluegrass, the part of the Mississippian Plateau adjacent to the Appalachian Plateaus is a rugged area of steep ridges and narrow valleys. To the west the plateau becomes flatter and drier, as most surface water drains into the numerous sinkholes rather than forming well-developed streams. Maximum elevations in the region range from about 1,000 ft. to over 1,200 ft.

Forests of the region are somewhat similar to those of the Appalachian Plateaus, but with fewer species. Plant geographers recognize this as a transition area between the luxuriant forests of eastern Kentucky and the oak- and hickory-dominated forests of the Midwest. Parts of the western Mississippian Plateau are called the Kentucky Barrens. These are large areas of native grasslands that were not forested in pioneer times. The Barrens appear to have been formed by burning from repeated fires set by Native Americans prior to historic times. Unless these areas are maintained by fires, forest vegetation will slowly reclaim them.

The Shawnee Hills

The name Shawnee Hills has long been applied to a broad area of low hills in southern Illinois and western Kentucky, but many Kentuckians are more familiar with the name Western Kentucky Coal Field. The Shawnee Hills are separated from the Mississippian Plateau on the west, south, and east by the Dripping Springs Escarpment, a line of low hills capped by erosion-resistant sandstone. The region is bounded on the north by the Ohio River.

The soils and underlying rock formations of the Shawnee Hills are similar to those of parts of the Appalachian Plateaus: sandstones, limestones, and acid shales. The landscape of the region resembles a scaled-down version of the Appalachian Plateau, with low hills, steep slopes, and somewhat wider valley bottoms. Maximum elevations in the region are close to 800 ft. The vegetation of the Shawnee Hills is not as diverse as that in the east, however, because the western region is surrounded by the limestone soils of the Mississippian Plateau. Typical forests of the region include white oak, black oak, northern red oak, beech, yellow poplar, and sugar maple. In sheltered valleys there are pockets of white pine, big-leaf magnolia, and mountain laurel.

Jackson Purchase

The Jackson Purchase is that part of Kentucky west of the Tennessee River, added to the state in 1818 as part of a treaty negotiated by Andrew Jackson. It is bounded on the east by the Mississippian Plateau, on the south by the Tennessee state line, on the north by the Ohio River, and on the west by the Mississippi River. Because the region was once covered by an extension of the Gulf of Mexico, it is sometimes called the Mississippi Embayment and considered an extension of the Gulf Coastal Plain. This is primarily a region of low, flat plains; although there are small hills in the vicinity of the Tennessee and Cumberland Rivers, the maximum elevations are below 500 ft. Soils in the region are formed from sands and clays deposited by past flooding. Large areas of the original vegetation have been cleared for agriculture, but forest communities persist along the ridges and waterways. Common trees include black oak, white oak, swamp chestnut oak, pin oak, shagbark hickory, sweet gum, and silver maple.

While geography plays a part, a variety of factors affect the distribution and abundance of plants. The most important is the habitat required by each plant. The habitat contains attributes to which plants are adapted for optimal growth. One is soil chemistry, particularly whether the soil is neutral, basic, or acidic. Soil texture and moisture are also important. Topography, or where the plant grows in the landscape, is yet another factor. A species that grows along a limestone cliff will not be found in a west Kentucky alluvial wetland. Shade tolerance also dictates where a wildflower grows. Many species are adaptable and can flourish in both sun and shade, but others, like many of our native grassland species, cannot tolerate much shade at all. Past vegetational history and plant movements over time also affect plant distributions. This may be why we find some relict coastal-plain species on the Cumberland Plateau. The final factor affecting plant distribution and diversity is human beings. Through our activities we have moved plants to new locations either purposely or inadvertently. Clearing land for development, harvesting timber, plowing grasslands for agriculture, and other human activities have altered, in many cases permanently, the distribution and abundance of our native flora.

WILDFLOWER CONSERVATION

While there is still a great store of wildflower wealth in Kentucky, many species are becoming rare, and many are simply not as abundant as they were in times past. Why? Just like animals, plants have habitat needs, and we are destroying these habitats at an astonishing pace. Kentucky is losing more than 160 acres of rural land each day to development. Other factors, including modern road construction, conversion of wildland to agricultural or industrial development property, and collecting by unscrupulous people (and nurseries), have all had an impact on this decline. The incredible population explosion of some wildlife species, such as white-tailed deer and elk, affect plant populations by eating the foliage or flowers of selected plants, especially monocots, and by trampling areas where the animals are overabundant. Finally, the explosion of invasive exotic organisms has most certainly had an impact on our wildflowers. Many native species are now being crowded out by these pest plants.

Collecting wildflowers from their native habitat is harmful in two ways. First, it eliminates those plants from their natural habitat and impoverishes the local plant community. This will increase the potential for nonnative plants to invade the site. Second, there are no assurances the plants will even live (let alone thrive) if you bring them into the garden. For example, most orchids have a special relationship with fungi in the soil in their native habitat. When you dig these plants and bring them to the garden, they will perish rather quickly unless these fungi are present in the soil. Other plants have exacting soil, pH, or other requirements that your backyard may not meet. For example, the native azaleas and rhododendrons require a sandy, well-drained, acid soil. These plants will not live in the limestone regions unless you modify the soil environment to meet their needs. Also, by adding wildflowers or other plants that were collected from the wild to your yard, you can bring in diseases, fungi, and other pathogens that could harm other plants in the landscape.

HOW TO USE THIS BOOK

This book could very well be a botanist's nightmare and a layperson's dream. Why? It has been organized and arranged to show different species by blooming period and color. Most guides are arranged phylogenetically (from primitive to more advanced plants) or taxonomically by plant family, often beginning with the monocots (those species that have one seed leaf). As any good botanist will freely tell you, the best way to identify plants is to use a taxonomic key. This is certainly true, but the use of these keys is time consuming and requires an intimate knowledge of plant taxonomic terminology. Most people find it simpler and easier to match a flower to a photograph.

To make this guide as user-friendly as possible, we asked ourselves, "How do most people use a field guide with photographs?" The answer came to us immediately: by thumbing through the pages until they find a picture that resembles the plant they are looking at and then reading the text associated with that picture. This book is our solution to the page-thumbing problem. The photographs and associated line drawings and descriptions are arranged by the first time of year a particular plant flowers. Generally, these time periods are spring (March through mid-May), summer (mid-May through mid-August), and fall (mid-August until frost). Within each time frame, the flowers are grouped by color. The color sections are white (gray), yellow, red/pink (includes orange flowers), blue/purple, and green/brown. Within each color group the plants are arranged by flowering period and, when at all possible, grouped by family.

While this arrangement has many obvious advantages, there are several distinct disadvantages to using this system. The first is what to do when a plant flowers in more than one season. In this case, the plant photograph will be found in the time period when the flower first appears; if you cannot locate a plant you have found in the section for the current season, you should search the prior time period. The second problem is what to do with species that produce flowers with different colors. Generally we show the typical color of the flower. For instance, you can often find southern red trilliums that have white flowers. We have chosen to include those species with the most common color form and provide text description for color deviations from the norm. The third difficulty is that the reader does not get a sense of plant families and how the plants are related—hence the botanist's nightmare. To solve this problem, we have included at the back of the book a description of plant families with a listing of species described under each family description.

We have noted the abundance and frequency for each plant described. It is important to note that we are using a habitat-based system, and thus a species "common" in a mature forest and a species "common" along a roadside would differ in their overall abundance. **Abundant** means you are likely to find that particular plant, often in large quantities. **Common** indicates that you will probably find the plant in the appropriate habitat. **Uncommon** means that you may or may not find the plant in the appropriate physical setting and that it will probably not be found in large numbers. **Rare** means that the plant only occurs in limited numbers and there is a good chance you will not see that plant even in the right habitat.

The geographical range for each species is loosely defined by the physiographic provinces we described previously. Within each physiographic region we have indicated the habitat in which the plant grows. To simplify the multitude of plant communities that occur throughout Kentucky, we have provided generalized habitat designations that include:

- Rock Outcrop, Glade, or Cliff: areas with exposed rock and usually thin soils

- Barrens or Prairie Patches: native grasslands with a wide diversity of plant species

- Meadows, Fields, or Old Fields: grasslands that are seeded to exotic grasses and are idle

- Pastures: grasslands seeded to exotic grasses that are grazed by livestock

- Upland Forests: often dry and dominated by oaks, hickories, or pines

- Rich (Mesophytic) Woods: usually moist, with a deep leaf litter and often associated with high plant species diversity

- Streamside, Riparian Forest, or Floodplains: areas close to streams that often have alluvial soil deposits

- Wetlands or Swamps: naturally occurring bodies of water that may be open or forested

- Ponds: shallow bodies of water

- Roadsides: areas adjacent to major roads, not small country lanes

Our reference for indicating habitat, frequency, and geographic range was "An Annotated Catalog of the Known or Reported Vascular Flora of Kentucky," by Max Medley (1993).

SOME NOTES ABOUT WILDFLOWER PHOTOGRAPHY

The vast majority of the photographs were taken during the fall of 2001 and the spring and summer of 2002. For the purposes of this book I have tried to highlight the flower and, where possible, the associated leaves. I have not tried to showcase the entire plant, because in some cases the spectacular flowers may be tiny and "lost" in the image. To solve this problem, we have included line drawings of leaves and/or stalks to aid in the identification of species where it is not possible to show both the plant and the bloom. The original line drawings were created specifically for this book by Dan Dourson.

Documentary photography, or photography designed to assist in plant identification, is quite different from creative or artistic wildflower photography. In creative or artistic photography the entire flower or plant structure may not be in focus, a small part of a flower may be shown, electronic flash is usually not used, and the effects are quite different from documenting the flower in a manner that accurately depicts the plant. Documentary plant photography involves using different techniques to obtain maximum sharpness and detail.

All the images by Thomas Barnes were taken with Nikon camera equipment and a Gitzo tripod with an arca-swiss ball head. The film of choice was Fuji Velvia with Kodak E100VS used as a backup. The primary lens used for photographing the flowers was a 200 micro Nikkor. Supplemental lenses included the 105 Nikkor micro, 85 tilt-shift, and Nikon 3T, 4T, 5T, and 6T Close-up diopters. The other primary piece of equipment used was an SB26 speedlight (flash). This was not used as the primary light source but was used as a secondary source. The use of this flash is what gives many of the photographs the appearance of a "black" or dark background. Close examination reveals the background is not black but is merely underexposed by 1 to 1 1/2 f-stops. The flash exposure guide was set to -2 f-stops.

FERNS &
FERN ALLIES

RUNNING PINE
Lycopodium clavatum

This low-growing plant has a horizontal stem that creeps above ground. Branched stalks, 2 to 4 in. tall, covered with many rows of narrow, pointed leaves, arise from the horizontal stem.

HABITAT: Dry, rocky, disturbed soil

REGION: Appalachian Plateaus

FREQUENCY: Rare

This plant is known from only a few sites.

GROUND PINE
Lycopodium obscurum

This 5- to 7-in.-tall evergreen plant is covered with flattened leaves and grows from an underground stem that forms spreading colonies. The yellow spore-producing cones are found at the tips of higher branches in summer.

HABITAT: Dry ridge tops, acid soil

REGION: Cumberland Mountains, Appalachian Plateaus

FREQUENCY: Common

SOUTHERN GROUND CEDAR
Diphasiastrum digitatum

The 6- to 8-in. stalks grow from a creeping horizontal stem found above ground. The evergreen stem is dark green with scaly leaves, and the branches are spread out parallel to the soil surface. The spore-forming cones occur in clusters of 4 at the tips of erect branches.

HABITAT: Acid soils, dry woods

REGION: Statewide

FREQUENCY: Common

A similar species, wiry ground cedar, *D. tristachyum,* has blue-green stems and upright branches and differs because the horizontal stem is underground. It is an uncommon species found on dry ridge tops in the Cumberland Mountains and Appalachian Plateaus.

SHINING CLUBMOSS
Huperzia lucidula

Note the 4- to 6-in. dark green vertical stems that may or may not be branched midway up the stem. The tiny leaves are called microphylls and are widest near the middle and then taper to a toothed point. The spores occur at the base of short fertile leaves and are interspersed with the longer sterile leaves.

HABITAT: Moist woods

REGION: Cumberland Mountains, Appalachian Plateaus, Shawnee Hills

FREQUENCY: Common

Rock clubmoss, *H. porophila,* is similar, but it is smaller with microphylls that are widest at the base, toothless, and tapered to a sharp point. It is uncommon and found only on sandstone outcrops in the Cumberland Mountains, Appalachian Plateaus, and Shawnee Hills.

SPIKEMOSS
Selaginella apoda

This 1- to 2-in.-high plant appears to be smaller because it grows horizontally along the ground. The leaf arrangement is distinctive with microphylls that are compressed into 4 rows, 2 small rows on the upper side of the stalk and 2 rows of larger microphylls on the lower side. On the upper surface at the base of each microphyll there is a distinctive small scale called a ligule.

HABITAT: Moist openings, disturbed areas

REGION: Statewide

FREQUENCY: Common

This vascular plant could easily be confused with a moss or liverwort.

QUILLWORT
Isoetes butlerii

This is a low-growing, grasslike plant that has a short, fleshy, underground stem surrounded by a spiral of long, narrow leaves with enlarged bases. The leaf bases overlap so tightly that the stem is hidden, causing the plant to look as if it is all leaves and roots.

HABITAT: Glades and open woods

REGION: Mississippian Plateau

FREQUENCY: Rare

I. engelmanii and *I. melanopoda* are the other quillworts that occur in Kentucky; both are rare.

COMMON HORSETAIL
Equisetum arvense

This 12- to 18-in.-tall plant has 2 kinds of stems that grow from an underground rhizome. The sterile stems are green and branched, with tiny leaves in whorls. The fertile stems are short and brown; they appear early in spring and disappear after producing a terminal spore-bearing strobilus.

HABITAT: Wet ditches, damp woods, and fields

REGION: Statewide

FREQUENCY: Common

SCOURING RUSH
Equisetum hyemale

This distinctive species can reach a height of 18 to 36 in. It is unbranched and has dark green stalks. This species spreads by underground stems and is often found in large colonies. The spore-forming strobilus is produced at the tip of the vegetative shoot.

HABITAT: Damp woods, stream banks, wet ditches

REGION: Statewide

FREQUENCY: Common

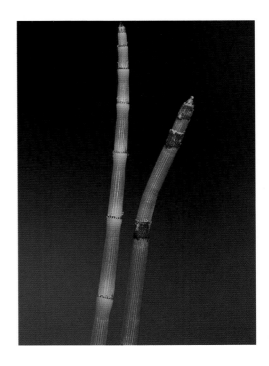

BRADLEY'S SPLEENWORT
Asplenium bradleyi

This is a small, cliff-dwelling fern with 2- to 3-in.-long leaves that are divided into triangular leaflets with toothed edges and lobes at the bases. The lower half of the leaf stalks is dark brown, fading to green in the upper half.

HABITAT: Crevices in sandstone cliffs

REGION: Cumberland Mountains, Appalachian Plateaus, Shawnee Hills

FREQUENCY: Uncommon

This species is a fertile hybrid of mountain spleenwort and ebony spleenwort.

MOUNTAIN SPLEENWORT
Asplenium montanum

This small, evergreen, cliff-dwelling fern has lacy, 2- to 4-in.-long leaves. The brown, cigar-shaped sporangia occur on the undersides of the leaves.

HABITAT: Damp crevices in sandstone cliffs

REGION: Cumberland Mountains, Appalachian Plateaus, Shawnee Hills

FREQUENCY: Uncommon

This is 1 of the 3 original parental species of the Appalachian spleenwort complex.

LOBED SPLEENWORT

Asplenium pinnatifidum

This small evergreen fern has 2- to 5-in.-long triangular leaves with elongated tips and lobed margins. The leaf stalks are brown at the bottom and turn green below the base of the leaf blade. The sporangia are prominent, brown, and elongate, and occur on the undersides of leaves. Occasionally specimens will reproduce vegetatively by forming a plantlet at the tip of the leaf.

HABITAT: Crevices in dry sandstone cliffs

REGION: Cumberland Mountains, Appalachian Plateaus, Shawnee Hills

FREQUENCY: Common

EBONY SPLEENWORT

Asplenium platyneuron

This small, 12- to 18-in.-tall evergreen woodland fern has a dark brown leaf stalk. The leaflets are lobed at their bases and appear to alternate along the leaf stalk.

HABITAT: Open woods

REGION: Statewide

FREQUENCY: Common

BLACKSTEM SPLEENWORT
Asplenium resiliens

This 4- to 6-in.-tall evergreen fern has a dark brown to black leaf stalk. The opposite leaflets have pronounced lobes at their bases.

HABITAT: Limestone cliffs

REGION: Cumberland Mountains, Appalachian Plateaus, Mississippian Plateau, Bluegrass, Shawnee Hills

FREQUENCY: Uncommon

WALKING FERN
Asplenium rhizophyllum

This 2- to 4-in.-tall evergreen fern has pointed, arrowlike leaves with elongated, stringlike tips. The leaf tips usually produce small plantlets that take root. The brown sporangia occur on the undersides of leaves.

HABITAT: Limestone boulders and cliffs

REGION: Cumberland Mountains, Appalachian Plateaus, Mississippian Plateau, Bluegrass, Shawnee Hills

FREQUENCY: Common

Scott's spleenwort, *Asplenium* x *ebenoides,* a related species, can occasionally be found within populations of walking fern, especially in the Bluegrass. This plant is a sterile hybrid of walking fern and ebony spleenwort and looks similar to walking fern except the leaf margins are deeply lobed.

WALL RUE
Asplenium ruta-muraria

This 2- to 4-in.-long evergreen fern is divided into branched leaflets with more or less rounded lobes. The sporangia are found on the undersides of the leaves.

HABITAT: Limestone cliffs and boulders

REGION: Appalachian Plateaus, Bluegrass, Mississippian Plateau

FREQUENCY: Uncommon

MAIDENHAIR SPLEENWORT
Asplenium trichomanes

This small, 2- to 4-in.-long, delicate, evergreen fern has a dark brown stalk with generally opposite, rounded leaflets.

HABITAT: Sandstone and limestone cliffs and boulders

REGION: Statewide

FREQUENCY: Uncommon

NETTED CHAIN FERN
Woodwardia areolata

A thin, delicate-looking, 12- to 18-in.-tall fern. The leaves are broadest near the middle; the leaf stalk is winged, and the upper leaflets appear to be fused. The fertile leaf is separate and taller and has narrower leaflets. The sporangia are arranged in chainlike groups along the center of the fertile leaflets.

HABITAT: Damp woods, wet areas

REGION: Cumberland Mountains, Appalachian Plateaus, Shawnee Hills, Jackson Purchase

FREQUENCY: Uncommon

This species resembles the sensitive fern, from which it may be distinguished by noting the short lower leaflets. The sensitive fern has long lower leaflets with wavy margins. The fertile leaf of sensitive fern is quite different as well.

HAY-SCENTED FERN
Dennstaedtia punctiloba

A light green, 10- to 14-in.-long, lacy fern. The round and black sporangia occur on the undersides of leaves and are arranged near the margins. The leaves turn pale yellow in fall and die back to the ground during winter.

HABITAT: Open woods, along sandstone outcrops and ledges

REGION: Cumberland Mountains, Appalachian Plateaus, Shawnee Hills

FREQUENCY: Common

If you brush your fingers along the leaves, you can smell the scent of a freshly cut lawn.

BRACKEN FERN
Pteridium aquilinum

This is a large, deciduous fern that can reach a height of 18 to 24 in. The fronds have a leathery feel and are divided into 3 distinct leaflets. Each leaflet is further divided into lobed subleaflets. The sporangia occur along the undersides of the leaf margins. This species spreads vegetatively from creeping underground stems into dense clonal stands that in many cases are thought to be several centuries old.

HABITAT: Dry open woods, acid soils

REGION: Cumberland Mountains, Appalachian Plateaus, Shawnee Hills

FREQUENCY: Common

Bracken is an Old English word used for many different kinds of ferns, but over the years the name has become fixed on this species. The bracken fern that is so common in Europe and Asia is the very same species as our native bracken fern, making it one of the most widely distributed species of plants on Earth.

SENSITIVE FERN
Onoclea sensibilis

This is a light green, 12- to 18-in.-tall fern with 2 kinds of leaves. The vegetative leaves are deciduous and broadly triangular with wavy margins. The fertile leaves form in late summer and often last through the winter. They are erect, bare stalks with clusters of sporangia that resemble beads at the tip.

HABITAT: Wet woods

REGION: Statewide

FREQUENCY: Common

This could be confused with netted chain fern. Note that the overall shape of the leaf is triangular in this species whereas it is oval in the chain fern. There is also a striking difference in the appearance of the fertile leaves.

GLADE FERN
Diplazium pycnocarpon

This is a large, delicate, deciduous fern that grows 18 to 30 in. tall. The fronds are divided into simple, distinct alternate leaflets. The leaflets are long and narrow with broad bases and are pointed at the tip. The sori are long and narrow and occur on the lower surfaces of fertile leaves.

HABITAT: Rich, moist woods

REGION: Statewide

FREQUENCY: Common

SILVERY GLADE FERN
Deparia acrostichoides

This 24- to 36-in.-tall deciduous fern has fronds that are divided into long, sharply pointed leaflets that are deeply lobed but not cut to the midrib. The silver-colored sori occur on the undersides of the fronds and show up as a metallic flash when a breeze lifts the fronds.

HABITAT: Rich, moist woods

REGION: Cumberland Mountains, Appalachian Plateaus, Shawnee Hills

FREQUENCY: Uncommon

LADY FERN
Athyrium felix-femina

This is a medium-sized, deciduous fern reaching 18 to 24 in. tall. The fronds are divided into leaflets that are alternate, long, narrow, and tapered to a sharp tip. Each leaflet is cut into finely toothed subleaflets. The lower leaf stalk can be bright green or red; when present, this red color is a distinctive field characteristic. The curved sori are found on the undersides of fertile leaves.

HABITAT: Moist woods

REGION: Statewide

FREQUENCY: Common

BULBLET FERN
Cystopteris bulbifera

This is a medium-sized, 12- to 24-in.-tall, soft-textured, light green, deciduous fern. The fronds are broadest at the base and gradually taper to the tip. They are divided into narrow leaflets, and the leaflets are divided into lobed, rectangular subleaflets with blunt tips. The sori are round and found on the undersides of fertile leaves. The bulblets are small, round structures that form on the undersides of the leaves and are able to break away and grow into clones of the mother plant.

HABITAT: Exposed limestone ledges and crevices

REGION: Cumberland Mountains, Appalachian Plateaus, Bluegrass, Mississippian Plateau

FREQUENCY: Common

The Tennessee bladder fern, *C. tennesseensis*, is similar, but the fronds are smaller and divided into broad triangular leaflets. The leaflets are divided into triangular subleaflets. It is found occasionally on dry limestone cliffs in the Appalachian Plateaus and Bluegrass and is more common on the Mississippian Plateau.

FRAGILE FERN
Cystopteris protrusa

A medium-sized, deciduous fern, 6 to 12 in. tall. The light green, delicate fronds are broadest near the middle and are divided into leaflets, which are divided into toothed subleaflets that are more or less triangular. The sori are round and are found on the undersides of fertile leaves.

HABITAT: Moist soils and around the bases of cliffs and boulders

REGION: Statewide

FREQUENCY: Common

BLUNT-LOBED WOODSIA
Woodsia obtusa

This medium-sized, 8- to 16-in.-tall evergreen fern has fronds that are widest near the middle. These are divided into pinnate leaflets, which are divided into subleaflets with blunt lobes. The rachis is covered with glandular hairs. The sori occur on the undersides of fertile leaves.

HABITAT: Dry, rocky woods

REGION: Statewide, but more common west of the Appalachian Plateaus

FREQUENCY: Common

GOLDIE'S WOOD FERN
Dryopteris goldiana

This is a large, 18- to 30-in.-tall, deciduous fern with broad to almost triangular fronds that are widest just above the base. The sori occur on the undersides of fertile leaves.

HABITAT: Rich, moist woods

REGION: Cumberland Mountains, Appalachian Plateaus, Mississippian Plateau, Shawnee Hills

FREQUENCY: Uncommon

WOOD FERN
Dryopteris intermedia

This large, 18- to 30-in.-tall, evergreen fern has dark green fronds with lance-shaped leaflets. The leaflets are divided into deeply lobed subleaflets, giving the plant a lacy appearance. On the bottom pair of leaflets, note the relative length of the first and second subleaflets on the lower side. The first subleaflet next to the rachis is shorter than the second subleaflet; this is a good field identification characteristic. The sori occur on the undersides of the fertile leaves.

HABITAT: Rich, moist woods

REGION: Cumberland Mountains, Appalachian Plateaus, Bluegrass, Mississippian Plateau, Shawnee Hills

FREQUENCY: Common

This is one of the largest and showiest ferns in Kentucky.

LEATHER WOOD FERN

Dryopteris marginalis

This large (up to 24 in. tall), dark green, evergreen fern has thick, leathery fronds that are cut into lance-shaped leaflets. The leaflets are cut into shallow-lobed subleaflets. The sori are along the margins on the undersides of fertile leaves.

HABITAT: Moist woods

REGION: Statewide

FREQUENCY: Common

CHRISTMAS FERN

Polystichum acrostichoides

This 10- to 14-in.-tall evergreen fern has a leathery texture. The fronds are cut into simple leaflets, and each leaflet has a lobe at the base so that it resembles a boot or Christmas stocking. The sori occur on the undersides of fertile leaflets at the tips of the fronds, giving the fertile fronds a shriveled appearance.

HABITAT: Woods

REGION: Statewide

FREQUENCY: Abundant

This is one of the most common ferns in Kentucky.

FILMY FERN
Trichomanes boschianum

This is a very small evergreen fern with lacy fronds usually only 1 to 2 in. long, although they may occasionally reach 6 in. in length. The fronds are translucent and 1 cell layer thick. The spores are produced in funnel-shaped sori along the margins of the leaves. A short bristle protrudes from each sorus, leading to another common name for this plant, the bristle fern.

HABITAT: Back walls or ceilings of deep, moist, overhanging sandstone rockshelters

REGION: Cumberland Plateau, Shawnee Hills

FREQUENCY: Rare

A member of a tropical family of plants, this species is apparently unable to tolerate current climatic conditions in Kentucky outside of sandstone rockshelters. Another species, *T. intricatum,* occurs in Kentucky only in the gametophyte stage; it resembles a small mass of green thread.

CLIMBING FERN
Lygodium palmatum

This twining, climbing, evergreen fern has a wiry stalk up to several feet long and is often seen climbing over the tops of small, neighboring plants. The palmate leaflets have 4 to 7 lobes that give the appearance of an outstretched hand. The 1- to 2-in.-wide vegetative leaflets occur in pairs along the stalk. The fertile leaflets are at the tip of the stalk and are much smaller, compound, and not evergreen.

HABITAT: Open woods with acid soils

REGION: Cumberland Mountains, Appalachian Plateaus

FREQUENCY: Common to locally abundant

This looks more like a long trailing vine than a fern.

CUT-LEAF GRAPE FERN
Botrychium dissectum

This small evergreen fern, about 6 in. tall, has a single, leathery leaf, which is divided into 3 more or less triangular leaflets. The leaflets are broadest at the base and are cut into irregular segments. The overall appearance varies from blunt lobes to finely cut leaves. This is our common fall species. The new leaves form in summer, turn bronze in fall, and persist through the winter. The spores occur in beadlike sporangia at the tip of a fertile spike that may reach up to 12 in. and develops below the base of the vegetative leaf.

HABITAT: Open woods

REGION: Statewide

FREQUENCY: Common

RATTLESNAKE FERN
Botrychium virginianum

This 6- to 10-in.-tall deciduous fern with 1 thin, lacy leaf appears in the spring and disappears by summer. The leaf is divided into 3 finely cut leaflets that are broadest near the middle. A fertile spike up to 18 in. tall arises right at the base of the 3 leaflets and bears a cluster of bead-shaped sporangia at its tip.

HABITAT: Woods

REGION: Statewide

FREQUENCY: Common

ADDER'S-TONGUE FERN
Ophioglossum pycnostichum

This 6-in.-tall deciduous species doesn't look like a typical fern. The single, 2- to 3-in.-long, thick oval leaf has a blunt tip with veins forming a reticulate pattern. The spores occur at the tip of a fertile spike rising from the base of the leaf blade.

HABITAT: Moist woods, limestone soils

REGION: Statewide

FREQUENCY: Uncommon

O. engelmannii, also called the adder's-tongue fern, is similar, but the leaf has a small, sharp-pointed tip. It is uncommon but widely scattered across the Mississippian Plateau.

ROYAL FERN
Osmunda regalis

This is a large and graceful deciduous fern reaching up to 36 in. tall. The large, compound leaves are divided into opposite leaflets, which are cut into 1- to 2-in. oblong subleaflets. The spores are produced on smaller fertile leaflets at the tip of the frond.

HABITAT: Wet soils around seeps, springs, and along streams

REGION: Statewide except for the Bluegrass

FREQUENCY: Common

This species is found around the world in both the Northern and Southern Hemispheres.

CINNAMON FERN
Osmunda cinnamomea

This is a large, deciduous fern that can grow to 36 in. tall. The frond is divided into lance-shaped leaflets that are deeply lobed but not cut to the midrib. The frond is broadest near the middle and tapers to a fairly sharp point at the tip. There are distinct tufts of brown, woolly hair on the leaf stalk at the points where the leaflets are attached. The spores are produced on a separate, erect, fertile spike that resembles a cinnamon stick.

HABITAT: Wet soils, swamps, seeps, and springs, along stream margins

REGION: Statewide, but rare in the Bluegrass

FREQUENCY: Common

INTERRUPTED FERN
Osmunda claytonii

This species is similar to cinnamon fern except it is a smaller plant and the tip of the leaf is blunt rather than tapering to a sharp point. The leaf is divided into lance-shaped leaflets with broad, rounded lobes. Spores are produced on fertile leaflets about one-third of the way up the stalk. After the spores have dispersed, the fertile leaflets shrivel, giving the fern its "interrupted" look.

HABITAT: Moist woods

REGION: Cumberland Mountains, Appalachian Plateaus, Mississippian Plateau, Shawnee Hills

FREQUENCY: Uncommon, more frequent in eastern Kentucky

ROCKCAP FERN

Polypodium virginianum

This 6- to 12-in.-long evergreen fern has thick, stiff fronds that are divided into leaflets, whose bases appear to be fused to the stalk. The spores are produced on the undersides of fertile leaves.

HABITAT: Top of sandstone boulders and along cliffs and ledges

REGION: Cumberland Mountains, Appalachian Plateaus, Mississippian Plateau, Shawnee Hills

FREQUENCY: Common

RESURRECTION FERN

Polypodium polypodiodes

This species is smaller than the rockcap fern and the undersides of the leaves are gray and scaly. During dry periods the leaves curl up and appear dead, but when they get wet, they open up—hence the name resurrection fern.

HABITAT: Trees and rock ledges, but not in soil

REGION: Appalachian Plateaus, Bluegrass, Mississippian Plateau, Shawnee Hills, and Jackson Purchase

FREQUENCY: Uncommon

MAIDENHAIR FERN
Adiantum pedatum

A delicate and distinctive-looking, 12- to 18-in.-tall deciduous fern. It has a dark brown and wiry stalk, and the leaf blade spreads out horizontally into a fan of leaflets. The leaflets are divided into subleaflets, which occur on individual stalks. The spores are produced along the margins of fertile subleaflets.

HABITAT: Moist woods

REGION: Statewide

FREQUENCY: Common

WOOLLY LIP FERN
Cheilanthes lanosa

This 6- to 12-in.-tall evergreen fern has a reddish brown stalk with rust-colored hairs. The leaf is divided into widely spaced, lobed leaflets, which are covered with light brown hairs. The spores are produced along the margins of fertile leaflets.

HABITAT: Rocky soils and ledges

REGION: Statewide, except for the Bluegrass

FREQUENCY: Uncommon

PURPLE CLIFFBRAKE
Pellaea atropurpurea

This 10- to 18-in.-long evergreen fern is often seen growing flat rather than upright. It has purplish brown, wiry leaf stalks that are covered with fine hairs. The leaves are divided into distinct leaflets, and each leaflet is divided into large, oblong subleaflets. The whole plant has a gray green or purplish color. The spores occur along the margins of fertile subleaflets.

HABITAT: Limestone ledges and outcrops

REGION: Bluegrass, Mississippian Plateau, Appalachian Plateaus

FREQUENCY: Common

NEW YORK FERN
Thelypteris novaboracensis

This light green, 12- to 18-in.-tall deciduous fern grows from a creeping rootstock and can often be seen in thick colonies. The smooth leaf stalk is divided into distinct, lance-shaped leaflets. The leaflets are lobed but not cut to the midrib. The overall shape of the leaf is distinctive: it is widest near the middle and tapers to a point at each end. The spores are produced on the undersides of fertile leaves.

HABITAT: Open woods

REGION: Statewide, most common on the Appalachian Plateaus

FREQUENCY: Common

The marsh fern, *T. palustris,* is a similar species, but the leaves do not taper at each end. The spores occur along the margins of fertile leaflets, and the margins are rolled over to cover the spore-bearing structures. It is uncommon, appearing in wet woods on the Appalachian Plateaus, Mississippian Plateau, Shawnee Hills, and Jackson Purchase.

BEECH FERN
Phegopteris hexagonoptera

This 6- to 12-in. deciduous fern has a triangular leaf that is divided into opposite leaflets, which are fused to the winged leaf stalk at their bases. The lowest pair of leaflets is bent downward. The spores are produced on the undersides of fertile leaves.

HABITAT: Moist woods

REGION: Statewide

FREQUENCY: Common

APPALACHIAN GAMETOPHYTE
Vittaria appalachiana

This fern is known to exist only in the gametophyte stage. The entire plant is only about 1/8 in. in diameter and is ribbon shaped to somewhat triangular, with lobes extending from the tip. There are no leaves because the plant exists as a photosynthetic gametophyte. The plant reproduces by cloning: small vegetative bodies form at the tips of the branches, break off, and are spread to suitable habitat by small animals.

HABITAT: Back walls and ceilings of sandstone rockshelters

REGION: Appalachian Plateaus

FREQUENCY: Uncommon

This species is found in several states in the Appalachians, but always south of the glacial boundary. There is also a species of Trichomanes that exists in Kentucky only as a gametophyte.

SPRING FLOWERS

March–Mid-May

SMALL GLADE CRESS
Leavenworthia uniflora
BRASSICACEAE

A winter annual with 1- to 3-in.-long segmented leaves that look like a ladder. The 1/2-in.-wide flowers have 4 petals and arise on 1- to 2-in.-tall separate stalks in the center of the plant.

HABITAT: Limestone glades, rocky areas

REGION: Mississippian Plateau, Knobs, Bluegrass

FREQUENCY: Rare

Two other species of glade cress, the beaded glade cress, *L. torulosa,* and the pasture glade cress, *L. exigua,* are rare. The beaded glade cress is occasionally found in the cedar glades of the Mississippian Plateau, and the pasture glade cress is only found in southern Jefferson and northern Bullitt Counties.

SMOOTH ROCK CRESS
Arabis laevigata
BRASSICACEAE

A smooth biennial up to 36 in. tall with lightly toothed, oval leaves at the base of the plant. The 4-in.-long leaves with a stalk are narrow and lance-shaped with bases that appear to wrap around the stalk. The small, 1/4-in.-wide flowers have 4 petals and are not showy.

HABITAT: Dry, open woods

REGION: Statewide except rare in Appalachian Plateaus, Cumberland Mountains, Shawnee Hills

FREQUENCY: Common on limestone, rare on sandstone

Four other species of rock cress have been found in Kentucky. Hairy rock cress, *A. hirsuta,* has a shorter stalk and slightly hairy stalk leaves. It is rare and reported from only a few

locations in the Bluegrass. Lyre-leaved rock cress, *A. lyrata,* another rare species, is a much smaller plant with divided basal leaves. It occurs in the Cumberland Mountains, Appalachian Plateaus, and the Bluegrass. Missouri rock cress, *A. missouriensis,* has smooth stalks, lance-shaped leaves, and yellowish-white flowers; it occurs only in the Jackson Purchase. The rock cress *A. perstellata* has a finely haired stalk with toothed oval leaves. The flowers are pink or white. It is found only in the Bluegrass of Kentucky and a few locations in central Tennessee. Accurate identification of these plants requires careful examination of the seeds and seed capsules.

BITTER CRESS
Cardamine pensylvanica
BRASSICACEAE

A biennial reaching 24 in. tall with 2- to 3-in.-long, ladderlike divided leaves at the base of the plant. These leaves usually wither before the plant flowers, so that only a few stalk leaves persist. The tiny flowers are about 1/4-in. wide and have 4 petals.

HABITAT: Moist to wet woods, openings

REGION: Statewide

FREQUENCY: Common

Our native bitter cress should not be confused with the hairy bitter cress, *C. hirsuta,* an exotic species in which the leaves at the base of the plant persist while the plant flowers. Another species, the small-flowered bitter cress, *C. parviflora,* is smaller, with shorter leaves that are divided into very narrow segments. It can be found in disturbed soils statewide.

PURPLE CRESS
Cardamine douglassii
BRASSICACEAE

The leaves at the base of this 8- to 12-in. biennial are rounded and purple beneath and have long stalks. The oblong leaves on the stalk are coarsely toothed and attach directly to the plant stem. The 1/2-in.-wide, 4-petaled flowers occur in a loose cluster at the top of the plant.

HABITAT: Moist woods, especially limestone

REGION: Statewide except rare in Appalachian Plateaus, Cumberland Mountains, Shawnee Hills

FREQUENCY: Common

SPRING CRESS
Cardamine bulbosa
BRASSICACEAE

When growing in a large cluster, this plant is quite showy and is similar to purple cress except it is a taller plant, often with branched stalks. The leaves on the stalk are generally lance shaped.

HABITAT: Springs, seeps, wet meadows, roadsides

REGION: Statewide

FREQUENCY: Common

Another species found in the Cumberland Mountains and Appalachian Plateaus is the mountain or round-leaved bitter cress, *C. rotundifolia*. This small plant can be erect or trailing, with leaves that are rounded to almost heart-shaped, with small lateral lobes on the stalks of the leaves.

CUT-LEAF TOOTHWORT
Dentaria laciniata
BRASSICACEAE

This 10- to 15-in.-tall species has a basal leaf that is cut into 3 narrow, toothed segments that usually wither before the plant flowers. The leaves on the stalk occur in a whorl of 3 with each leaf cut into 3 narrow, deeply toothed segments. The 1/2-in.-wide, 4-petaled flowers occur in a cluster at the top of the plant.

HABITAT: Moist woods

REGION: Statewide

FREQUENCY: Common

WHITE TROUT LILY
Erythronium albidum
LILIACEAE

This is a deep-rooted species with half of the stalk underground, making it appear that the 3- to 6-in.-long, oblong, light green leaves mottled with brown occur at the base of the plant. Nonflowering plants produce 1 leaf whereas flowering specimens produce 2 leaves. The 1 1/2-in.-wide lilylike, showy flowers have 6 segments that close at night and open during the day. When fully open, the segments are recurved to reveal the flower parts. Individual flowers last only a few days.

HABITAT: Moist woods

REGION: Appalachian Plateaus, Bluegrass, Mississippian Plateau, Shawnee Hills, Jackson Purchase

FREQUENCY: Uncommon to locally common

TRAILING ARBUTUS
Epigaea repens
ERICACEAE

Technically, this is a tiny, ground-hugging evergreen shrub with 2- to 4-in.-long, leathery, oval leaves that are rough to the touch. The 1/4- to 1/2-in.-wide tubular flowers have 5 flared petals and occur in small clusters.

HABITAT: Upland, sandstone forests

REGION: Appalachian Plateaus, Cumberland Mountains, eastern Knobs

FREQUENCY: Common

SHARP-LOBED HEPATICA
Hepatica acutiloba
RANUNCULACEAE

The first parts of this plant to appear are the 6-in.-long, hairy flower stalks. At the end of each flowering stalk there is a 3/4-in.-wide flower that may be white, pink, blue, or purple. The flowers have 5 to 12 stamens and 3 green, pointed bracts. The 1- to 3-in.-wide leaves have 3 pointed lobes that resemble the shape of a human liver. The leaves persist through winter; the old leaves are weather-beaten and a darkish bronze color. The young, hairy leaves have not unfurled when the plant flowers in the spring.

HABITAT: Rich woods

REGION: Statewide

FREQUENCY: Common

A less common species also found in rich woods with sandy acid soils is the round-lobed hepatica, *H. americana.*

H. americana

SPRING BEAUTY
Claytonia virginica
PORTULACACEAE

The tiny, 1/2-in.-wide, 5-petaled flowers are streaked with varying amounts of pink. This often overlooked plant has 2 opposite, narrow leaves 3 to 12 in. long. Carolina spring beauty, *C. caroliniana,* looks similar except the leaves are more oblong. It is most frequent in the Appalachian Plateaus and Cumberland Mountains.

HABITAT: Moist woods, lawns, fields, roadsides

REGION: Statewide

FREQUENCY: Abundant

C. virginica   *C. caroliniana*

PUSSYTOES
Antennaria plantaginifolia
ASTERACEAE

A small, inconspicuous, 3- to 10-in. plant that creeps along the ground and often forms large mats or colonies. The oval-shaped, fuzzy leaves, which look woolly or silky, occur at the base of the plant and typically have 3 veins. The 1/2-in.-wide flowers are not showy and have numerous, dense bristles.

HABITAT: Dry, open woods; roadsides; fields

REGION: Statewide

FREQUENCY: Common

Several species of pussytoes are found in the state; most have limited ranges. The 1-flowered pussytoes, *A. solitaria,* is an easily identifiable species because it only has a single flower head on a stalk. It is less common than pussytoes.

> ### THE TRILLIUMS
> *The trilliums are easily recognized spring wildflowers that have a whorl of 3 net-veined (not parallel) leaves with a single flower that has 3 green sepals that are quite different from the petals. This group of plants is often divided into 2 groups: those that have flowers on a stalk with spreading petals* (T. erectum, T. grandiflorum, T. nivale, T. pusillum, T. sulcatum, T. flexipes, *and* T. undulatum) *and those that have flowers with erect petals that sit directly on top of the plant* (T. cuneatum, T. luteum, T. recurvatum, *and* T. sessile).

SNOW TRILLIUM
Trillium nivale
LILIACEAE

This is our earliest-flowering trillium and is also one of the smallest. This 2- to 4-in.-tall, delicate plant has about 1-in.-wide flowers with petals that are from 1 to 1 1/4 in. long. Both the flowers and the leaves have short stalks.

HABITAT: Rich woods

REGION: Inner Bluegrass

FREQUENCY: Rare

This diminutive species is only known from several locations in central Kentucky.

OZARK TRILLIUM
Trillium pusillum
LILIACEAE

This 5- to 8-in.-tall plant has 1- to 3-in.-long, sessile, lance-shaped leaves. The 1- to 1 1/2-in.-wide flower with ruffled edges turns pink with age. The flower sits directly on top of the stem.

HABITAT: Rich, wet woods

REGION: Mississippian Plateau, southern Knobs

FREQUENCY: Rare

This is our other diminutive trillium; it is only known from several locations in several southern counties.

HARBINGER OF SPRING
Erigenia bulbosa
APIACEAE

This small and delicate plant has dark, 6-in.-tall stems. The leaves are divided into 3 pointed, 2-in.-long, oval, coarsely toothed segments. The 1/4-in.-wide, 5-petaled flowers occur in a cluster, and the individual flowers have distinctive reddish-brown anthers.

HABITAT: Rich woods

REGION: Statewide

FREQUENCY: Common in limestone, uncommon in sandstone

EARLY SAXIFRAGE
Saxifraga virginiensis
SAXIFRAGACEAE

This plant has a cluster of up to 2-in.-long, oval leaves with rounded, toothed edges at its base. When the plant first begins flowering, the hairy flowering stalk is quite small, but as the season progresses, it lengthens to 12 in. The cluster of 3/8-in.-wide, 5-petaled flowers with 10 conspicuous yellow anthers is tight in the early season and becomes more open and branched as the season progresses.

HABITAT: Rock outcrops, usually limestone and occasionally sandstone in moist woods

REGION: Statewide except Jackson Purchase

FREQUENCY: Common except in Shawnee Hills

BLOODROOT
Sanguinaria canadensis
PAPAVERACEAE

The flower stalk (up to 6 in. long) is encased by the young, roundish, handlike leaf. The single flower has 8 to 12 petals that can range up to 1 1/2 in. in diameter. The flowers are short-lived; the leaf continues to enlarge after flowering and sometimes reaches a diameter of up to 8 in.

HABITAT: Rich woods

REGION: Statewide

FREQUENCY: Common

The underground stem exudes a bright reddish-orange juice.

TWINLEAF
Jeffersonia diphylla
BERBERIDACEAE

The 2 leaflets, 1 to 3 in. long, resemble elephant ears or kidneys when fully open. The 8-petaled, solitary flowers generally open before the leaves fully emerge. The 2-in.-wide flowers are rarely open for more than a day or two.

HABITAT: Rich limestone woods

REGION: Bluegrass, Mississippian Plateau, rare in Appalachian Plateaus

FREQUENCY: Uncommon to locally common

The genus was named for Thomas Jefferson.

FALSE RUE ANEMONE
Enemion biternatum
RANUNCULACEAE

This is a delicate, 8- to 18-in.-tall plant with largely compound leaves at its base with up to 9 leaflets. The upper leaves are usually 3-lobed and rounded. The 1/2-in.-wide flowers have no petals and 5 sepals.

HABITAT: Rich woods, particularly limestone

REGION: Bluegrass, Mississippian Plateau, rare in Appalachian Plateaus

FREQUENCY: Abundant

RUE ANEMONE
Anemonella thalictroides
RANUNCULACEAE

This is a delicate plant growing to 8 in. tall that superficially resembles false rue anenome. The 1/2- to 1-in.-wide flowers have 5 to 10 sepals with no petals. The earliest flowers are often larger and pink; later flowers are smaller and often white. The compound leaves at the base have stalks whereas the upper leaves do not. The bractlike leaves near the flower resemble 3-lobed leaflets.

HABITAT: Moist woods

REGION: Statewide

FREQUENCY: Abundant

PENNYWORT
Obolaria virginica
GENTIANACEAE

A small, fleshy plant with a greenish or purplish stalk reaching 4 to 6 in. in height. It has 1/2-in.-long, opposite leaves that are purplish underneath. The individual 4-lobed, 1/2-in.-long, tubular flowers occur in small clusters of 1 to 3 at the base of the leaves.

HABITAT: Oak or moist woods

REGION: Statewide except Bluegrass and Jackson Purchase

FREQUENCY: Common

Small size and dull coloration make it easy to overlook this plant in the oak-leaf litter.

EARLY MEADOW RUE
Thalictrum dioicum
RANUNCULACEAE

Plants grow to 2 ft., and the leaves have 3 rounded lobes. The male and female flowers occur on different plants; the male flowers are showier. Like many of the members of this group, the flowers have no petals, the sepals are short-lived, and the stamens are quite conspicuous.

HABITAT: Woods

REGION: Statewide, most abundant on limestone

FREQUENCY: Common

SLENDER TOOTHWORT
Dentaria heterophylla
BRASSICACEAE

The single leaf at the base of the 8- to 12-in. plant is divided into 3 segments that are roundish with rounded teeth. The leaves on the stem look much different and are divided into 3 long, very slender, slightly toothed segments. The 1/2-in.-wide, 4-petaled flowers occur in a loose cluster at the top of the stalk.

HABITAT: Rich woods

REGION: Statewide

FREQUENCY: Common

ALLEGHENY SPURGE
Pachysandra procumbens
BUXACEAE

The 2- to 3-in.-long spikes of flowers on a pale brown stalk occur on an above-ground stem before the large, 3-in.-wide, oval to roundish leaves appear. The male flowers occur on the top of the spike, and the female flowers occur at the bottom. The leaves have long stalks and are coarsely toothed. They are uniform green when they first appear but get mottled as they age.

HABITAT: Rich woods, particularly limestone

REGION: Appalachian Plateaus, Bluegrass, Mississippian Plateau

FREQUENCY: Common in the Mississippian Plateau but uncommon to rare in the Appalachian Plateaus and Bluegrass

EARLY SCORPION GRASS, WHITE FORGET-ME-NOT

Myosotis verna

BORAGINACEAE

This is a 4- to 12-in. plant with a few branches that have linear to oblong, hairy leaves without a stalk. The tiny 1/4-in.-wide, 5-lobed, short, tubular flowers occur in a small cluster at the end of the branches.

HABITAT: Fields, disturbed soil

REGION: Statewide

FREQUENCY: Common

SQUIRREL CORN

Dicentra canadensis

FUMARIACEAE

This plant, up to 10 in. tall, has delicate and feathery gray green, finely cut leaves with rounded edges. The small cluster of 1/2-in. flowers, each resembling a heart, is suspended on a short stalk.

HABITAT: Rich woods

REGION: Statewide

FREQUENCY: Common

The flowers are quite fragrant.

DUTCHMAN'S-BREECHES
Dicentra cucullaria
FUMARIACEAE

Delicate, lacy, fernlike, finely cut leaves closely resemble those of squirrel corn. The 1/2-in.-long flowers are supported on a short stalk and hang upside down, resembling a pair of pantaloons.

HABITAT: Rich woods

REGION: Statewide

FREQUENCY: Common

Unlike those of its cousin, squirrel corn *(D. canadensis),* the flowers of this plant are not fragrant.

STAR CHICKWEED
Stellaria pubera
CARYOPHYLLACEAE

The 3-in.-long, opposite leaves of this 12-in.-tall plant are oblong in appearance with pointed tips. The flowers have 5 petals, but it looks like there are 10 because each petal is deeply cut.

HABITAT: Rich woods

REGION: Statewide except Jackson Purchase

FREQUENCY: Common to abundant

The exotic, abundant common chickweed, *C. meadia,* has smaller flowers and leaves and often forms large mats.

WOOD VETCH, CAROLINA VETCH
Vicia caroliniana
FABACEAE

This slender, sprawling, 15- to 30-in. plant has leaves with 5 to 9 narrow segments. The leaf at the end is modified into a tendril. The slender 3/8- to 1/2-in.-long flowers are arranged in loose clusters.

HABITAT: Moist woods, woodland edge, thickets

REGION: Statewide

FREQUENCY: Common but more abundant in the east

This is our only native vetch.

FALSE GARLIC
Nothoscordum bivalve
LILIACEAE

This plant is similar to the wild onion, but the flowers are bigger, at about 1/2 in. wide, and the plant typically has smaller clusters of flowers. It is a short plant reaching heights up to 8 in. with narrow, stiff, linear leaves. The tall flowering stalk (up to 12 in.) is leafless and supports flowers that have 6 segments.

HABITAT: Open woods, prairie patches

REGION: Bluegrass, Mississippian Plateau, Shawnee Hills, Jackson Purchase

FREQUENCY: Uncommon

This species doesn't have the typical onion odor of other members of the wild onion family.

BEDSTRAW
Galium aparine
RUBIACEAE

This annual, somewhat weedy species is easy to identify because the lance-shaped to linear leaves occur in whorls of 8 around the square stem. The plant can reach heights up to 4 ft. and often is found draping over other vegetation. Both the stem and the leaves have short, stiff hairs or bristles. The small, 1/4-in.-wide, 4-lobed, somewhat tubular flowers occur in clusters of 1 to 3 flowers.

HABITAT: Open, moist woods; fields; disturbed ground

REGION: Statewide

FREQUENCY: Abundant

There are more than a dozen species of bedstraw in the state. They are similar in appearance, and most flower later in the growing season. Most are light, airy plants. The various species have leaves in whorls of 8, 6, or 4.

SWEET WHITE VIOLET
Viola blanda
VIOLACEAE

A delicate, 2- to 4-in.-tall plant whose leaves all occur at the base of the plant. The satiny, circular to broadly heart-shaped leaves are deeply lobed at the base. The 1/2-in.-wide, 5-petaled flowers arise on separate stalks. The 2 upper petals are often twisted, and the lower 3 petals have purple stripes. The flower usually does not have long hairs in the center.

HABITAT: Rich woods with acidic soil

REGION: Appalachian Plateaus, Cumberland Mountains, eastern Knobs

FREQUENCY: Common

CANADA VIOLET

Viola canadensis

VIOLACEAE

This may be our tallest violet, reaching 4 to 8 in. tall, with numerous leafy stems. The lower leaves near the base of the plant are heart-shaped with long stalks, whereas the upper leaves are heart-shaped with shorter stalks. The 3/4- to 1 1/2-in. flowers have yellow centers with purple streaks and purple-tinted backs.

HABITAT: Rich woods

REGION: Appalachian Plateaus, Cumberland Mountains, Knobs, Bluegrass

FREQUENCY: Common

CREAM VIOLET

Viola striata

VIOLACEAE

This species should not be easily confused with the Canada violet because the 1-in.-wide flowers have purple streaks and long hairs near the center of the flower. They do not have yellow at the base, and there is no purple on the back of the flower. The heart-shaped leaves are toothed.

HABITAT: Moist woods

REGION: Statewide

FREQUENCY: Common

PRIMROSE-LEAVED VIOLET
Viola primulifolia
VIOLACEAE

This 3- to 8-in.-tall species has unique leaves that are oblong to elongated oval with long, winged stalks and a rounded base. The 1/2-in.-wide flowers have purple veins and long hairs near their center.

HABITAT: Open or forested wetlands

REGION: Appalachian Plateaus, Cumberland Mountains, Knobs

FREQUENCY: Uncommon

TWO-LEAVED TOOTHWORT, CRINKLEROOT, BROAD-LEAVED TOOTHWORT
Dentaria diphylla
BRASSICACEAE

This 8- to 12-in.-tall plant has a pair of conspicuous, 4- to 6-in.-long, 3-segmented, sharply toothed, narrow oval and sharply pointed leaves. The inconspicuous leaf at the base is divided into 3 toothed segments with a long stalk. The 1/2-in.-wide, 4-petaled flowers occur in a loose cluster at the top of the flower stalk.

HABITAT: Moist rich woods

REGION: Statewide

FREQUENCY: Common

BENT TRILLIUM, NODDING TRILLIUM
Trillium flexipes
LILIACEAE

A large (up to 16 in. tall) species with dark green leaves that appear to be without stalks. The 3/4- to 1 1/2-in.-wide flower on a stalk is typically bent over so that the flower is on or under the leaves. The petals vary from the typically white to maroon and can have varying amounts of maroon in a white flower. The ovary is typically pink or white.

HABITAT: Moist woods on limestone

REGION: Bluegrass, Mississippian Plateau, Shawnee Hills

FREQUENCY: Locally common

LARGE WHITE TRILLIUM
Trillium grandiflorum
LILIACEAE

A large (up to 16 in. tall) species with large, dark green leaves that is often seen in colonies. The

2- to 3-in.- wide, white flower occurs on a stalk above the leaves and turns mottled then dark pink before dropping. The anthers are bright yellow, and the ovary is white.

HABITAT: Moist woods

REGION: Cumberland Mountains, Appalachian Plateaus, Shawnee Hills

FREQUENCY: Common to locally abundant

SHOOTING STAR
Dodecatheon meadia
PRIMULACEAE

The smooth, oblong to spoon-shaped leaves, up to 10 in. long, occur in a cluster at the base of the plant. The cluster of flowers droops at the end of a long stalk. The individual flowers have 5 petals that flare backwards to expose the stamens, which form a beak or cone pointing downward, giving the flower the appearance of a rocket.

HABITAT: Limestone prairie patches, glades, moist woods, bluffs, cliffs

REGION: Statewide

FREQUENCY: Abundant

The pink flowering form is found in several locations but it is uncommon.

SWEET CICELY
Osmorhiza longistylis
APIACEAE

This hairy-stemmed plant, up to 3 ft. tall, has leaves cut into 3 segments; each segment is cut again into 3 toothed parts. The 5 to 20 tiny flowers with the styles noticeably longer than the petals occur in a loose cluster. The roots of this species have the strong odor of licorice.

HABITAT: Moist woods

REGION: Statewide

FREQUENCY: Common

Bland sweet cicely, *O. claytonii,* is similar, but the stems are not hairy, the styles are shorter than the flower petals, and the roots lack the odor of licorice. It is found statewide in similar habitats.

STONECROP
Sedum ternatum
CRASSULACEAE

Note the rounded to spoon-shaped, fleshy leaves that occur in clusters of 3 on this low-growing plant. The flowers occur in flat-topped clusters on 3 forked branches. The 3/8-in.-wide, individual, star-shaped flowers have 4 or 5 petals and conspicuous dark anthers.

HABITAT: Moist woods with rock outcrops

REGION: Statewide

FREQUENCY: Common

WHITE BLUE-EYED GRASS, PALE BLUE-EYED GRASS
Sisyrinchium albidum
IRIDACEAE

This grasslike, leaved species has pale green leaves 4 to 12 in. in length. The flowers occur in small clusters at the tips of winged flowering stalks. The flowering stalks are approximately half as thick as the leaves, and each individual flower has 6 pale segments with a yellow center.

HABITAT: Prairie patches, glades, open woods

REGION: Bluegrass, Mississippian Plateau

FREQUENCY: Common

WILD STRAWBERRY
Fragaria virginiana
ROSACEAE

This is a low-growing, 2- to 6-in.-tall plant that is often seen in large colonies because it has above-ground runners. The coarsely toothed leaves have 3 oval lobes and a hairy stalk. There are small clusters of 3/4-in.-wide, 5-petaled flowers on short stalks. The red fruits are edible.

HABITAT: Fields, meadows, roadsides

REGION: Statewide

FREQUENCY: Common

BISHOP'S CAP, MITERWORT
Mitella diphylla
SAXIFRAGACEAE

Note the 2 opposing sharp-toothed leaves below the spike of widely spaced, 1/3-in.-wide, snowflake-like flowers. Using a hand lens, you can see the cuplike center with 5 fringelike petals. The somewhat heart-shaped leaves at the base of the plant are toothed with a long stalk.

HABITAT: Moist woods

REGION: Statewide except Jackson Purchase

FREQUENCY: Common

DWARF GINSENG
Panax trifolius
ARALIACEAE

A diminutive plant reaching a maximum height of 8 in., this species has whorls of 3 leaves that are divided into 3 toothed, oval segments. The tiny flowers occur in a roundish or dome-shaped 3/4- to 1-in.-wide cluster.

HABITAT: Sandy, rich woods; streamside forests

REGION: Appalachian Plateaus

FREQUENCY: Uncommon

CANADA MAYFLOWER
Maianthemum canadense
LILIACEAE

A small, 2- to 6-in.-tall plant with 1 to 3 dark green, glossy, 3-in.-long, oblong leaves. The tiny, 1/8- to 1/4-in.-wide, 4-segmented flowers occur in a short spike.

HABITAT: Moist woods

REGION: Cumberland Mountains, Jackson Purchase

FREQUENCY: Rare

This species has 4 segments, an unusual characteristic for this group of plants, whose members usually have 3 or 6 segments.

ALUMROOT
Heuchera americana
SAXIFRAGACEAE

Note the heart-shaped leaves, usually with 5 blunt lobes, with long stalks at the base of this 1- to 3-ft.-tall plant. The smooth flowering stalk is 1 to 2 ft. tall and supports a loose, cone-shaped bloom with numerous 1/8-in.-long, widely spaced, 3-petaled, bell-shaped flowers that droop.

HABITAT: Moist woods, especially limestone

REGION: Statewide

FREQUENCY: Common

WOOD ANEMONE
Anemone quinquefolia
RANUNCULACEAE

This is a delicate plant that grows from 4 to 8 in. tall. The lone leaf at the base of the plant is divided into 3 to 5 parts. The edge of the leaf has smooth teeth. The single, 1-in.-wide flower arises from the stalk and has 5 sepals.

HABITAT: Rich woods

REGION: Appalachian Plateaus and Cumberland Mountains

FREQUENCY: Rare

FOAM FLOWER
Tiarella cordifolia
SAXIFRAGACEAE

This low-growing to creeping plant less than 6 in. tall sends up a 6-in.-long flowering stalk that supports a cylindrical or cone-shaped cluster of numerous 1/3-in.-wide, 5-petaled flowers that have 10 conspicuous stamens. Leaf shape can vary tremendously, but the leaves are generally heart shaped to roughly star shaped with 3 to 7 toothed segments.

HABITAT: Rich woods

REGION: Statewide except Jackson Purchase

FREQUENCY: Common to locally abundant

SANDWORT
Minuartia patula
CARYOPHYLLACEAE

This little annual has delicate and wiry stalks with fine, hairlike leaves. The small, 1/2-in. flowers have 5 notched petals. When found growing in large quantities, the plant is quite showy.

HABITAT: Limestone cliffs, rocks, glades

REGION: Bluegrass, Mississippian Plateau

FREQUENCY: Common

CORN SALAD
Valerianella **spp.**
VALERIANACEAE

This 10- to 20-in. smooth and forked-stemmed annual or biennial has opposite, oblong leaves. The 5-lobed, funnel-shaped flowers occur in small, flat-topped clusters. The individual species are separated by technical fruit characteristics.

HABITAT: Moist soil, streamside forests, roadsides

REGION: Bluegrass, Mississippian Plateau

FREQUENCY: Abundant

WESTERN DAISY
Astranthium integrifolium
ASTERACEAE

This 2- to 16-in.-tall, smooth-stemmed annual daisy has smooth-edged, spoon-shaped leaves. The 1- to 1 1/2-in.-wide flower heads have rays tinted with pink and a concave yellow center.

HABITAT: Limestone meadows, prairie patches, open stream banks

REGION: Southern Appalachian Plateau, Knobs, Bluegrass, Mississippian Plateau

FREQUENCY: Uncommon to locally common

Do not confuse this species with the more common and nonnative ox-eye daisy *(Chrysanthemum leucanthemum)*. The ox-eye daisy has large-lobed, blunt-toothed leaves. It is abundant along roadsides and fields throughout the state.

PHILADELPHIA FLEABANE
Erigeron philadelphicus
ASTERACEAE

This 1- to 2-ft.-tall biennial or short-lived perennial has numerous branches; the leaves clasp around the smooth or slightly hairy stem. The 1/2- to 1-in.-wide flower heads have 100 or more rays. The buds typically nod in this species.

HABITAT: Roadsides, fields, meadows

REGION: Statewide

FREQUENCY: Abundant

ROBIN'S PLANTAIN
Erigeron pulchellus
ASTERACEAE

This 1- to 2-ft.-tall plant is quite hairy and soft to the touch. Most of the spoon-shaped leaves are at the base of the plant. There are 1 to several 1-in.-wide flower heads with 50 to 100 rays at the end of each stalk. The flower head has a yellow center that fades over time.

HABITAT: Prairie patches, fields, roadsides, open woods

REGION: Statewide except Shawnee Hills

FREQUENCY: Common

CLIFF RUE
Thalictrum mirabile
RANUNCULACEAE

This delicate plant grows to 18 in. tall and has delicate, 1/2-in.-wide flowers that occur in a loose cluster on long stalks. The leaves are divided twice with each leaflet having 3 shallow lobes. A distinctive characteristic is the curved fruits on the long stalks.

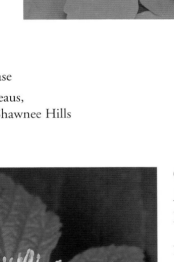

HABITAT: Sandstone cliffbase

REGION: Appalachian Plateaus, Cumberland Mountains, Shawnee Hills

FREQUENCY: Uncommon

GOLDENSEAL
Hydrastis canadensis
RANUNCULACEAE

Note that this plant has only 1 leaf near the base of the plant and 2 large, 6- to 8-in. (or larger) leaves shaped like the palm of your hand with 5 to 7 thickish lobes. The single flower arises from a somewhat hairy stalk. The 1/2-in.-wide flowers have no petals, the sepals drop off early, and the only conspicuous part of the flower is the numerous, showy, feathery-looking stamens. A cluster of very conspicuous red berries will appear between the 2 leaves in late summer.

HABITAT: Rich woods

REGION: Statewide

FREQUENCY: Uncommon

Goldenseal is becoming rare as a result of overcollection of wild specimens.

DOLL'S EYES, BANEBERRY

Actaea pachypoda

RANUNCULACEAE

This plant has long (up to 6 in.), sharply pointed, 2- or 3-times divided leaves on a stem ranging from 1 to 2 1/2 ft. tall. The 1/2-in. flowers occur in a dome-shaped cluster on a 1- to 2-ft.-tall stalk.

HABITAT: Rich woods

REGION: Statewide

FREQUENCY: Common

The round, poisonous berries are white with a black spot, giving rise to the name doll's eyes.

MAYAPPLE

Podophyllum peltatum

BERBERIDACEAE

The flowering plants are up to 2 ft. tall with 2 large, roundish, and umbrella-like leaves that have 5 to 9 lobes on a forked stem. Nonflowering plants have 1 leaf on an unforked stem. A single waxy, 1- to 2-in.-wide flower with 6 to 9 petals arises from the fork via a short stalk.

HABITAT: Open woods, woodland borders, meadows

REGION: Statewide

FREQUENCY: Abundant

The ripe fruit is yellow and pulpy and is edible. The seeds, leaves, and roots are poisonous.

PURPLE ROCKET
Iodanthus pinnatifidus
BRASSICACEAE

A smooth-stemmed plant that reaches 36 in. in height. It has toothed, lance-shaped, and divided lower leaves. The 1/2-in.-long, 4-open-petaled flowers occur in a cone-shaped cluster at the top of the plant. Petal color can vary from purple to white.

HABITAT: Moist woods, streamside forests

REGION: Statewide except rare in Appalachian Plateaus, Cumberland Mountains

FREQUENCY: Common

DEVIL'S BIT, FAIRY WAND
Chamaelirium luteum
LILIACEAE

Look for the 2-in.-wide by 6-in.-long leaves that are widest in the center and taper at each end. The leaves on the stem are few and linear and get progressively smaller as they ascend the stem. Male and female plants are separate. Male plants grow up to 30 in. tall and have a thick, showy flower spike 2 to 5 in. long. The female plants are larger, up to 4 ft. tall, but are not as showy; they have a very slender flower spike that may eventually grow to 12 in. in length.

HABITAT: Dry woods, usually acidic

REGION: Cumberland Mountains, Appalachian Plateaus, Shawnee Hills

FREQUENCY: Uncommon

SPECKLED WOOD LILY, WHITE CLINTONIA
Clintonia umbellulata
LILIACEAE

Note the 2 to 5, large (2 to 4 in. wide by 6 to 10 in. long), smooth, dark green, glossy, oblong leaves. The rounded dome-shaped cluster of 3/8-in.-wide, 6-segmented flowers occurs on a leafless stalk that may reach 16 in. in length. The individual flowers sometimes may have purple spots.

HABITAT: Rich woods

REGION: Cumberland Mountains, Appalachian Plateaus

FREQUENCY: Uncommon to locally common

FALSE SOLOMON'S SEAL
Maiantheum racemosa
LILIACEAE

This plant superficially resembles true Solomon's seal in the vegetative state with an arching flowering stalk that reaches 16 to 30 in. tall. It has alternate, lance-shaped leaves up to 4 in. long that attach directly to the plant stem. The primary difference between the species is that the tiny flowers of false Solomon's seal occur in a cluster up to 4 in. long at the tip of the plant.

HABITAT: Moist woods

REGION: Statewide

FREQUENCY: Abundant

CANCER ROOT
Orobanche uniflora
OROBANCHACEAE

This is a parasite with most of the stalks underground. The slender, leafless, fine-haired flower stalks have a single, somewhat nodding flower at the end. The 3/4-in.-long, tubular flowers have 5 lobes.

HABITAT: Rich woods and stream banks

REGION: Cumberland Mountains, Appalachian Plateaus, Mississippian Plateau, Bluegrass

FREQUENCY: Common in eastern Kentucky, rare in the Bluegrass

FALSE GOAT'S BEARD
Astilbe biternata
SAXIFRAGACEAE

This 3- to 5-ft. plant is similar to goat's beard except this species has an upper hairy stem and the outer leaf segments have 3 lobes. Both species have 2- or 3-times-divided, toothed leaves. The tiny, 1/8-in.-wide flowers occur in a spike arrangement in a large, open cluster at the top of the plant. The individual flowers have 10 stamens and two pistils that produce 2 seedpods per flower.

HABITAT: Rich woods

REGION: Cumberland Mountains, Appalachian Plateaus

FREQUENCY: Common

GOAT'S BEARD
Aruncus dioicus
ROSACEAE

This 3- to 5-ft. plant is similar to false goat's beard except this species has a smooth upper stem and the outer leaf segments have more than 3 lobes. Both species have 2- or 3-times-divided, toothed leaves. The tiny, 1/8-in.-wide flowers occur in a spike arrangement in a large, open cluster at the top of the plant. The individual flowers have 15 stamens and 3 pistils that produce 3 seedpods per flower.

HABITAT: Moist woods, woodland edges

REGION: Statewide except Bluegrass

FREQUENCY: Uncommon

GALAX, BEETLEWEED
Galax aphylla
DIAPENSIACEAE

This evergreen plant has numerous 1- to 3-in.-wide, deep green, round to heart-shaped, shiny or glossy, toothed leaves with long stalks at the base of the plant. The 8- to 16-in.-tall flowering stalks support a tight cylinder of tiny flowers with 5 petals.

HABITAT: Sandy, acidic oak-pine-hemlock woods

REGION: Appalachian Plateaus, Cumberland Mountains

FREQUENCY: Uncommon

GINSENG
Panax quinquefolius
ARALIACEAE

Note the 3 roundish leaves that occur in a whorl of 3 with each leaf divided into 5 pointed, toothed, oval lobes. The 2 lobes closest to the plant are the smallest on this 8- to 18-in.-tall plant. The 1-in.-wide, roundish cluster of inconspicuous flowers occurs in the center of the plant and is not as showy as the red berries produced in late summer.

HABITAT: Rich woods

REGION: Statewide

FREQUENCY: Uncommon

This is becoming rare as a result of overcollection of wild specimens.

MOUNTAIN WOOD SORREL
Oxalis montana
OXALIDACEAE

This 4- to 6-in.-tall northern species can form large colonies and is easy to identify because the 1/2- to 3/4-in.-wide, 5-petaled flowers have dark purple stripes and a purple ring around the center. The flowers usually occur 1 per plant, but sometimes 2 flowers are produced close together. This plant has shamrocklike leaves with 3 heart-shaped segments per leaf.

HABITAT: Cool, damp, and dark hemlock woods

REGION: Cumberland Mountains, Appalachian Plateaus

FREQUENCY: Rare

FOUR-LEAVED MILKWEED
Asclepias quadrifolia
ASCLEPIADACEAE

A slender or delicate plant with thin oval to lance-shaped leaves. Each plant typically has 3 leaf-bearing points of attachment. The lowest and uppermost areas have 2 opposite leaves, whereas the middle area has a whorl of 4 larger leaves. The individual, 1/4-in.-wide flowers look like blunt-nosed rockets with a wide skirt and occur in loose, open, roundish clusters.

HABITAT: Upland woods and woodland edges

REGION: Statewide except Jackson Purchase

FREQUENCY: Common but most abundant in the east

EASTERN BERGAMOT
Monarda bradburiana
LAMIACEAE

This 1- to 2-ft.-tall plant has a mostly smooth stem with 2- to 4-in., toothed, oval leaves that are hairy underneath. The 1- to 3-in.-wide flower head is a rounded cluster of 1-in.-long, 2-lipped, tubular flowers. The lower lip has purple dots, and the stamens are longer than the upper lip.

HABITAT: Moist woods

REGION: Mississippian Plateau, Shawnee Hills

FREQUENCY: Uncommon

WHITE BERGAMOT
Monarda russeliana
LAMIACEAE

This 1- to 2-ft.-tall plant has a smooth stem with 2- to 4-in.-long, toothed, oval, hairy leaves that have a very short stalk or attach directly to the plant stem. The 1- to 2-in.-wide flower heads are clusters of 1-in.-long, 2-lipped, tubular flowers with stamens that are longer than the upper lip.

HABITAT: Open woods

REGION: Knobs, Mississippian Plateau

FREQUENCY: Common

SYNANDRA
Synandra hispidula
LAMIACEAE

The lower leaves of this 1- to 2-ft.-tall biennial are heart-shaped and bluntly toothed with long stalks. Four to 12, 1 1/4-in.-long flowers in an open spike arise at the base of the upper small, oval leaves. The flowers have an upper lip and a 3-lobed lower lip that has purple streaks in the center.

HABITAT: Rich woods, often on limestone

REGION: Appalachian Plateaus, Knobs, Bluegrass, Mississippian Plateau

FREQUENCY: Uncommon

KENTUCKY LADY'S SLIPPER
Cypripedium kentuckiense
ORCHIDACEAE

The 4 to 6 fuzzy, elliptical leaves look a great deal like the large-flowered yellow lady's slipper, except this is a larger, more robust plant that reaches heights of 32 in. or more. The flower is also much larger and may be up to 3 in. long.

HABITAT: Damp woods, floodplains

REGION: Appalachian Plateaus

FREQUENCY: Rare

APPALACHIAN BEARDTONGUE
Penstemon canescens
SCROPHULARIACEAE

A 15- to 30-in.-tall plant uniformly covered with short whitish or grayish hairs. The 1 1/4-in.-long, tubular flower has lines on the inside, and the lower lip projects out farther than the upper lip. The sterile stamen is hairy and yellow and does not extend beyond the edge of the flower.

HABITAT: Dry, rocky open woods; roadsides; prairie patches

REGION: Appalachian Plateaus, Bluegrass, Knobs, Mississippian Plateau

FREQUENCY: Common

THE BEARDTONGUES

These plants are very difficult to tell apart. The species we have included are the most common throughout the state and the easiest to identify in the field. All the species have opposite, lance-shaped leaves. All the members of this genus have 5-lobed, tubular flowers with 2 lobes above and 3 below. There are 4 fertile stamens and 1 large, hairy or fuzzy sterile stamen, which is the source of the name beardtongue.

TALL BEARDTONGUE, FOXGLOVE BEARDTONGUE

Penstemon digitalis

SCROPHULARIACEAE

A smooth and shiny, 2- to 4-ft. plant with a 1 1/4-in.-long, tubular flower. The flower is constricted toward the back and opens wide at the front. It often has purple lines or is tinted lavender on the inside. The lower leaves are more pointed and oval with winged stalks. The upper leaves are more lance shaped and attach directly to the plant, with some even clasping the plant stalk.

HABITAT: Roadsides, fields, open woods

REGION: Statewide except Cumberland Mountains and Shawnee Hills

FREQUENCY: Common except in eastern Kentucky where it is rare

HAIRY BEARDTONGUE

Penstemon hirsutus

SCROPHULARIACEAE

Note that the tubular flower appears to be closed, with the lower lip arching upward toward the upper lip. The stem is finely haired. This species resembles Kentucky beardtongue except the flowers are a light lavender color instead of white.

HABITAT: Limestone cliffs; rocky, exposed soil

REGION: Bluegrass, Knobs, Mississippian Plateau

FREQUENCY: Common

SLENDER-FLOWERED BEARDTONGUE, KENTUCKY BEARDTONGUE

Penstemon tenuiflorus

SCROPHULARIACEAE

A 15- to 30-in.-tall plant with flowers that appear closed. The lower lip arches upward to meet the upper lip. The stalk and opposite, lance-shaped, toothed leaves are hairy.

HABITAT: Prairie patches; dry, rocky, open woods

REGION: Knobs, Mississippian Plateau, Shawnee Hills

FREQUENCY: Uncommon

FRINGED BLUETS

Houstonia canadensis

RUBIACEAE

This species is unique among this group of plants in that there are leaves at the base of the plant when it is flowering. These leaves are oblong or lance shaped, and the stem leaves, which have hairy edges, are linear or narrow. The 4-lobed, 3/8-in.-wide flowers occur in small clusters at the end of the branches.

HABITAT: Dry, open woods; prairie patches; roadsides

REGION: Statewide except Shawnee Hills and Jackson Purchase

FREQUENCY: Common

The long-leaf bluet, *H. longifolia,* is the other spring-flowering species that is common statewide and is found in dry oak or oak-pine woods. It has broad, lance-shaped leaves with a single prominent vein.

VALERIAN
Valeriana pauciflora
VALERIANACEAE

The leaves at the base of this 1- to 2 1/2-ft. plant are 2 to 3 in. long and broadly heart shaped. The opposite leaves have 3 to 7 segments that are pointed oval with the end segment much longer than the side segments. The 5-lobed, tubular flowers occur in loose, open, roundish clusters.

HABITAT: Rich, moist woods

REGION: Statewide except Jackson Purchase

FREQUENCY: Uncommon

PAINTED TRILLIUM
Trillium undulatum
LILIACEAE

One of the smaller, more delicate species. It reaches heights of 8 to 18 in. and has a 1- to 1 1/2-in.-wide flower. The white petals have wavy edges; red, magenta, or rose-

colored spots form a triangle at the center of the flower. The leaves have 1/2-in.-long stalks, and both the leaves and the stem have a purplish-bronze cast.

HABITAT: Moist woods

REGION: Cumberland Mountains

FREQUENCY: Rare

YELLOW TROUT LILY

Erythronium americanum

LILIACEAE

This is a deep-rooted species with half of the stalk underground, making it appear that the 3- to 6-in.-long, oblong, light green leaves mottled with brown occur at the base of the plant. Nonflowering plants produce 1 leaf; flowering specimens produce 2 leaves. The 1 1/2-in.-wide, lilylike, showy flowers have 6 segments that close at night and open during the day. When fully open, the segments are recurved to reveal the flower parts. Individual flowers last only a few days. These plants also reproduce vegetatively from the underground stalk by sending out shoots that terminate in a small bulb, which is why trout lilies often are found in dense colonies.

HABITAT: Moist woods

REGION: Statewide

FREQUENCY: Common

HAIRY BUTTERCUP

Ranunculus hispidus

RANUNCULACEAE

The stalks of this 6- to 18-in.-tall plant are hairy at the base. The leaves are deeply lobed and give the appearance of 3 leaflets. The 1-in.-wide flowers have a glossy, shiny, or waxy appearance.

HABITAT: Moist to wet woods, open woods, woodland edges

REGION: Statewide

FREQUENCY: Common

EARLY BUTTERCUP

Ranunculus fascicularis

RANUNCULACEAE

This buttercup grows up to 12 in. tall and has silky leaves with 3 lobes; the later leaves are often divided into 5 slender lobes.

HABITAT: Prairie, glades, old fields, open woods, usually on limestone

REGION: Bluegrass, Shawnee Hills, Mississippian Plateau

FREQUENCY: Rare

SMALL-FLOWERED BUTTERCUP

Ranunculus micranthus

RANUNCULACEAE

This plant has small, 1/4-in.-wide flowers with 5 shiny, glossy, or waxy petals. The basal leaves of this 18-in.-tall plant are heart shaped, whereas the upper leaves are nearly linear and hairy.

HABITAT: Dry to moist woods, woodland edges, especially on limestone

REGION: Bluegrass, Mississippian Plateau, Appalachian Plateaus

FREQUENCY: Common

Kidney-leaf buttercup, *R. abortivus,* has a hairy stem and leaf margin and the basal leaves are heart shaped. It is common statewide.

R. abortivus

HOOKED CROWFOOT
Ranunculus recurvatus
RANUNCULACEAE

This 10- to 24-in.-tall plant is usually hairy and has 3-part, coarsely toothed leaves. The 3/8-in.-wide flowers are somewhat inconspicuous because they have a large green center surrounded by small yellow petals and green sepals.

HABITAT: Moist woods

REGION: Statewide

FREQUENCY: Common

CELANDINE POPPY, WOOD POPPY
Stylophorum diphyllum
PAPAVERACEAE

The 4-petaled, showy flowers are up to 2 1/2 in. in diameter. The buds and fruits are hairy. The leaves of this tall plant (up to 20 in.) are deeply cut with rounded lobes.

HABITAT: Rich woods

REGION: Statewide except Shawnee Hills and Jackson Purchase

FREQUENCY: Common

The underground stem exudes a yellowish or saffron-colored juice.

YELLOW CORYDALIS, SCRAMBLED EGGS
Corydalis flavula
FUMARIACEAE

This delicate annual has almost fernlike, gray greenish, finely cut leaves with rounded edges. It is a small plant growing to 12 in. tall with 1/2-in.-long flowers.

HABITAT: Moist woods, woodland edges

REGION: Statewide

FREQUENCY: Common

The tall, pale, or pink corydalis, *C. sempervirens,* foliage looks similar, but the small flowers are pink and yellow. It can be found on sandstone outcrops in the Cumberland Mountains and can be locally abundant on Pine Mountain.

YELLOW STARGRASS
Hypoxis hirsuta
AMARYLLIDACEAE

This diminutive plant has a 1/2- to 3/4-in.-wide, 6-segmented, starlike flower that rises several inches from the ground and is overtopped by the linear, grasslike leaves, which may reach 12 to 15 in. tall.

HABITAT: Upland woods, woodland edges, glades

REGION: Statewide

FREQUENCY: Common

ROUND-LEAVED VIOLET
Viola rotundifolia
VIOLACEAE

The 1/2-in.-wide flowers usually appear before the leaves fully expand in the spring. The leaves lie flat and are roundly heart-shaped and about 1 in. in diameter at flowering. The leaves expand up to 5 in. in diameter by summer. The 2 lower petals are streaked with brown at the base, and there are long hairs near the center of the flower.

HABITAT: Moist, rich woods

REGION: Appalachian Plateaus, Cumberland Mountains

FREQUENCY: Uncommon

HALBERD-LEAVED VIOLET
Viola hastata
VIOLACEAE

This 4- to 8-in. plant only has 2 to 4 arrowhead-shaped to long heart-shaped silver mottled leaves. The small, 1/2-in.-wide flowers are usually held above the leaves and have purple streaks near the center.

HABITAT: Upland sandstone open, moist, or dry woods

REGION: Appalachian Plateaus, Cumberland Mountains

FREQUENCY: Common

YELLOW WOODLAND VIOLET, DOWNY YELLOW VIOLET
Viola pubescens
VIOLACEAE

There is occasionally 1 kidney-shaped leaf with a long stalk at the base of this 4- to 12-in.-tall plant; most of the heart-shaped leaves occur near the top of the stalk. The 3/4-in.-wide flowers arise on hairy stalks about as high as the top of the leaves. The petals have brown streaks, and there are long hairs near the center of the flower.

HABITAT: Rich woods

REGION: Statewide

FREQUENCY: Uncommon

LARGE-FLOWERED BELLWORT
Uvularia grandiflora
LILIACEAE

This 8- to 16-in.-tall plant has a few alternate, oblong leaves that are finely hairy on the lower surface. The leaves appear to be pierced by the flowering stalk, which supports 1 to 3 bell-shaped, nodding, 6-segmented flowers that range in size from 1 to 2 in. long.

HABITAT: Moist woods

REGION: Statewide

FREQUENCY: Common

SMALL-FLOWERED BELLWORT
Uvularia perfoliata
LILIACEAE

This plant superficially resembles the much larger and coarser large-flowered bellwort. This is a much more delicate plant. Its leaves are a lighter green with a lustrous sheen and appear to be pierced by the stalk but are smooth on the undersurface. This species typically has 1 to several 1-in.-long flowers per plant.

HABITAT: Moist woods

REGION: Cumberland Mountains, Appalachian Plateaus, Mississippian Plateau, Shawnee Hills

FREQUENCY: Common

The sessile-leaved bellwort, *U. sessilifolia,* occurs infrequently in widely scattered locations from the Appalachian Plateaus westward. It is a smaller plant with narrow leaves that do not appear to be pierced by the stalk.

HOARY PUCCOON
Lithospermum canescens
BORAGINACEAE

This is a very leafy, hairy, and soft-looking 5- to 12-in.-tall plant with narrow, smooth-edged, alternate leaves. The 5-lobed, 3/8-in.-wide tubular flowers occur at the top of the plant in a flat-topped cluster.

HABITAT: Prairie patches, glades, open woods

REGION: Appalachian Plateaus, Knobs, Bluegrass, Mississippian Plateau

FREQUENCY: Common

YELLOW TRILLIUM

Trillium luteum

LILIACEAE

This species looks similar to the sessile or southern sessile trillium, except the 1 1/2- to 2 1/2-in.-long petals are yellow. It is a large species reaching heights up to 16 in. and typically has mottled leaves. The flower has a distinctive lemon scent.

HABITAT: Moist woods

REGION: Appalachian Plateaus, Mississippian Plateau

FREQUENCY: Locally common across southern Kentucky

YELLOW MANDARIN

Disporum lanuginosum

LILIACEAE

This is a 12- to 16-in.-tall plant, usually with forked branches that have pointed, oval, alternate leaves that attach directly to the stalk. The 6-segmented, 1-in.-wide flowers, which look like open bells with the stamens dangling down, hang in clusters under the leaves at the tips of the branches.

HABITAT: Rich woods

REGION: Cumberland Mountains, Appalachian Plateaus

FREQUENCY: Locally common

SPOTTED MANDARIN
Disporum maculatum
LILIACEAE

This is similar to yellow mandarin except the flowers are creamy white with distinctive purple spots.

HABITAT: Rich woods

REGION: Cumberland Mountains, Appalachian Plateaus

FREQUENCY: Uncommon to rare

DWARF CINQUEFOIL
Potentilla canadensis
ROSACEAE

A low-growing plant with above-ground runners that has a hand-shaped leaf with 5 toothed, oval leaves. The teeth on the lobes typically occur in the upper half of the lobe. The 1/2-in.-wide solitary flower has 5 petals.

HABITAT: Open, dry roadsides; fields

REGION: Cumberland Mountains, Appalachian Plateaus, Mississippian Plateau

FREQUENCY: Common

Common cinquefoil, *P. simplex,* is similar except that the leaves are more lance shaped to oblong and the teeth typically extend below the middle of the lobe. It usually flowers several weeks later than dwarf cinquefoil. These plants should not be confused with Indian or mock strawberry, *Duchesnea indica,* which is an Asiatic weed that colonizes disturbed sites, gardens, and lawns. It has a 1/2-in.-wide, 5-petaled flower like the cinquefoils and produces a berry similar to the wild strawberry. The fruits are not juicy or edible.

YELLOW PIMPERNEL
Taenidia integerrima
APIACEAE

This tall plant (up to 32 in.) has smooth, branched stems with alternate leaves. The lower smooth-edged leaves, up to 6 in. long, have long stalks and are divided 3 times. Each 1/2- to 1 1/2-in.-long segment is oval to oblong in shape. The upper leaves are divided once or twice and have a stalk that wraps around the plant stem. The tiny flowers occur in a loose, circular, open cluster.

HABITAT: Rocky woods

REGION: Statewide except Jackson Purchase

FREQUENCY: Common

GOLDEN ALEXANDERS
Zizia aptera
APIACEAE

This is a smooth-stemmed, 18- to 32-in.-tall plant with basal leaves that are rounded to heart shaped with long stalks. The stem leaves are divided into 3 leaflets, and each leaflet is divided into 3 oval to lance-shaped segments. The tiny flowers occur in a loose, circular-shaped, open cluster. A key identifying feature is that the central flower in each cluster does not have a stalk or stem.

HABITAT: Prairie patches, gravel bars

REGION: Appalachian Plateaus, Mississippian Plateau, Bluegrass

FREQUENCY: Uncommon

Two other species of golden alexanders occur in Kentucky. Twice-compound golden alexanders, *Z. aurea,* has a compound basal leaf divided into 3 leaflets and thin, finely toothed stem leaves. It is locally common from the Appalachian Plateaus west. Mountain golden alexanders, *Z. trifoliata*, is quite similar to twice-compound golden alexanders, from which it may be distinguished by its coarsely toothed and leathery stalked leaves. It is uncommon but widely scattered statewide.

Z. aurea

Z. aptera

MEADOW PARSNIP
Thaspium barbinode
APIACEAE

This species is often confused with golden alexanders because it looks so similar. It has a smooth stem and grows up to 39 in. tall, but it has stiff hairs at the base of the leaf. The compound, toothed leaves are oval to lance shaped. The tiny flowers occur in loose, circular, open clusters, and the central flower in each cluster is distinctly stalked.

HABITAT: Moist woods

REGION: Statewide

FREQUENCY: Common

Two other species of meadow parsnip are found in Kentucky. Smooth meadow parsnip, *T. trifoliatum,* has smooth stems, basal leaves that are simple or only once-compound, and stem leaves that are twice-compound. It is common in moist woods statewide. A variety of smooth meadow parsnip with purple flowers occurs in the Cumberland Mountains but it is uncommon. Narrow-leaved meadow parsnip, *T. pinnatifidum,* has compound basal leaves and stem leaves that are divided into narrow linear segments. It is rare on limestone soils in the Appalachian and Mississippian Plateaus.

WOOD BETONY
Pedicularis canadensis
SCROPHULARIACEAE

A low-growing, hairy plant reaching 12 in. tall with deeply cut, fuzzy, fernlike leaves. The 1-in.-long, tubular, hairy flowers have hoods and occur in a whorled cluster. Flower color can vary from yellow to red or brownish purple.

HABITAT: Moist woods

REGION: Statewide

FREQUENCY: Common except in Bluegrass and Mississippian Plateau, where it is rare.

YELLOW HORSE GENTIAN
Triosteum angustifolium
CAPRIFOLIACEAE

The 1/2- to 3/4-in., tubular flowers have 5 lobes and are found at the base of the opposite leaves. The lance-shaped leaves taper at each end and attach to the plant with a short-winged stalk. The stalks have rough hairs.

HABITAT: Rocky dry or moist woods

REGION: Statewide

FREQUENCY: Common

T. perfoliatum

The red horse gentian, *T. aurantiacum,* has purplish flowers and is common in dry woods throughout the state except the Jackson Purchase. Wild coffee, *T. perfoliatum,* is another species that has reddish purplish flowers; it is rare in the Jackson Purchase, Mississippian Plateau, Shawnee Hills, and Bluegrass.

RAGWORT
Senecio spp.
ASTERACEAE

Note the numerous small, yellow, 1/4- to 1/2-in. flower heads that are found in flat-topped clusters. The leaves on the stem are not abundant and have many small leaflets. The basal leaves are much larger.

HABITAT: Woods, fields, meadows

REGION: Statewide

FREQUENCY: Common and abundant

Golden ragwort, *S. aureus,* is common statewide except in the Shawnee Hills and Jackson Purchase. It has large, heart-shaped basal leaves and likes moist soil. Round-leaved ragwort, *S. obovatus,* is another common early-spring-blooming species that occurs in dry woods and woodland edges. It has large, rounded basal leaves that are attached to the plant with a stalk. Butterweed, *S. glabellus,* is a weedy annual or biennial that is found statewide in fields, pastures, and no-till agriculture fields. It is a larger, coarser plant with larger flower heads. It differs from the other species in that the stem leaves are divided into lobed segments and attach directly to the plant. The basal leaves are similar but larger and attach to the plant with a stalk. Appalachian ragwort, *S. anonymus,* is the other common ragwort. It flowers in late spring and early summer. It has narrower, linear leaves and is common statewide but abundant in western and southern Kentucky.

S. aureus   *S. obovatus*   *S. glabellus*   *S. anonymus*

BARREN STRAWBERRY
Waldsteinia fragarioides
ROSACEAE

At first glance, this 2- to 6-in.-tall plant superficially resembles a wild strawberry or mock strawberry in that its leaves are divided into 3 lobes, although the lobes are usually more irregularly rounded and smooth. It is a leafy plant with 1/2-in.-wide, 5-petaled flowers that have 50 or more stamens. The flowers occur on long stalks.

HABITAT: Rich woods

REGION: Appalachian Plateaus, eastern Mississippian Plateau, Bluegrass

FREQUENCY: Uncommon but rare in the Bluegrass

The fruit is dry, not fleshy, and inedible.

YELLOW WOOD SORREL
Oxalis stricta
OXALIDACEAE

Note the 2/3-in.-wide, heart-shaped, cloverlike leaf that is subdivided into 3 segments on this 4- to 6-in. plant. The leaves may have a reddish tint at the base, and the seedpod bends or droops at a sharp angle. This delicate plant has 1/2-in.-wide, 5-petaled, somewhat tubular flowers.

HABITAT: Woods, fields, roadsides

REGION: Statewide

FREQUENCY: Abundant

Yellow wood sorrel is similar to the exotic lawn weed European wood sorrel, *O. europa,* but the latter has erect rather than drooping fruiting stalks.

LARGE WOOD SORREL
Oxalis grandis
OXALIDACEAE

This species is similar to the yellow wood sorrel but is easily identified because the leaves are 2 to 3 times as large and edged in reddish purple. The flowers are about 1 in. wide.

HABITAT: Rich woods

REGION: Statewide

FREQUENCY: Common

YELLOW LADY'S SLIPPER
Cypripedium pubescens
ORCHIDACEAE

The lady's-slipper orchids are among our most prized wildflowers because they have such a unique flower, consisting of 2 united sepals, 1 separate sepal, 2 side petals and 1 petal that is the lip (or forms the pouch). This 18- to 24-in.-tall species has 3 to 5 elliptical and somewhat soft-to-the-touch leaves that sheathe the stem. Each stem usually supports a single 2-in.-long pouch. The slipper usually has purple veins and is wide open at the top rather than slit as in the case of the pink lady's slipper, and the lateral petals are twisted.

HABITAT: Rich woods

REGION: Statewide

FREQUENCY: Uncommon to locally common

The small yellow lady's-slipper orchid, *C. parviflorum,* closely resembles the large-flowered yellow lady's slipper but has a much smaller pouch, usually less than 1 in. long. The slippers are more deeply colored, and individual plants are more likely to bear 2 flowers. Finally, the flowers are produced in mid- to late May, after the large-flowered plants have finished blooming. The other lady's slipper found in the state is the rare white or prairie lady's slipper, *C. candidum.* It has a white slipper about the size of the small-flowered yellow lady's slipper.

SWEET FLAG
Acorus calamus
ARACEAE

The 1-in.-wide, 2- to 5-ft.-long linear leaves resemble those of the common cattail. The tiny flowers occur on a 2- to 4-in.-long cylindrical structure that stands out from the erect flowering stalk at a 45° angle.

HABITAT: Swamps, ditches

REGION: Statewide

FREQUENCY: Uncommon

EARED TICKSEED
Coreopsis auriculata
ASTERACEAE

This is a low-growing species with leaves at the base of the plant reaching 18 in. in height. The oval leaves have a pair of earlike lobes at the base of the stalk that attaches the leaf to the plant. The single, 1 1/2- to 2-in.-wide flower head on top of a long stalk has rays with 4 prominent notches at the tip.

HABITAT: Dry roadsides, field edges, open oak woods

REGION: Appalachian Plateaus, Knobs, Mississippian Plateau, Shawnee Hills

FREQUENCY: Common

CLUSTERED SNAKEROOT

Sanicula gregaria

APIACEAE

This is a 24- to 32-in.-tall, smooth-stemmed plant with leaves that are cut into 3 to 5 lance- to spoon-shaped, toothed segments. The 1/4-in.-wide flower heads have tiny petals with conspicuous yellow anthers.

HABITAT: Rich woods

REGION: Statewide

FREQUENCY: Common

MOSS PHLOX
Phlox subulata
POLEMONIACEAE

This is a creeping, mat-forming, semievergreen species reaching 6 to 8 in. tall with 1/2-in., pointed, linear, smooth leaves. This species has abundant 1/2- to 3/4-in.-wide, 5-notched, lobed flowers with a dark center.

HABITAT: Limestone cliff edges, sandstone ridges

REGION: Appalachian Plateaus, Knobs, Bluegrass, Mississippian Plateau

FREQUENCY: Rare

Lobed phlox, *P. bifida,* looks similar but it is not hairy, has deeply lobed petals, and has longer leaves. It is rare and found only in a few locations in the Bluegrass and Mississippian Plateau. Moss phlox is a widely cultivated species that can be found in a variety of colors.

SWEET BETSY, SOUTHERN SESSILE TRILLIUM
Trillium cuneatum
LILIACEAE

One of the larger species in this group, this plant can reach heights of up to 16 in. It looks like a very large sessile trillium. The large leaves are mottled, and mature plants bear a single flower with 3, 1 1/2- to 2 1/2-in.-long, erect petals that sit directly on top of the plant. The stamens are less than half as long as the petals, and the anthers are blunt. Flower color is typically maroon, although it may sometimes be green. This species smells like a banana.

HABITAT: Moist woods

REGION: Appalachian Plateaus, Mississippian Plateau

FREQUENCY: Locally common across southern Kentucky

RED TRILLIUM
Trillium erectum
LILIACEAE

This large species reaches 16 in. tall and has dark green leaves that appear to be without stalks. The 1- to 2-in.-wide flower occurs on a 1- to 2-in.-long stalk that is usually bent over so that the flower is open to the side of the plant above the leaves. Flower color may vary from maroon to cream or white. You can tell this species from the southern red trillium because the flowers are widely spread from the base so that the dark red ovary is visible when viewed from the side. The flower smells like a wet dog.

HABITAT: Moist woods

REGION: Cumberland Mountains, Appalachian Plateaus

FREQUENCY: Common

SOUTHERN RED TRILLIUM
Trillium sulcatum
LILIACEAE

This species is quite similar to the red trillium, but the petals are broader and form a cup at the base so that the ovary is not visible when the flower is examined from the side. The flower has the smell of rotten mushrooms.

HABITAT: Moist woods

REGION: Cumberland Mountains, Appalachian Plateaus

FREQUENCY: Locally common

SESSILE TRILLIUM

Trillium sessile

LILIACEAE

This is a small species that reaches a height of 4 to 10 in. with rounded, somewhat mottled leaves. It has 1-in.-long, maroon or occasionally green petals. The flower has a faint rotten odor.

HABITAT: Moist woods

REGION: Appalachian Plateaus, Bluegrass, Mississippian Plateau

FREQUENCY: Most common in central Kentucky

PRAIRIE TRILLIUM, RECURVED TRILLIUM

Trillium recurvatum

LILIACEAE

This is a distinctive species that can reach a height of 16 in. The small, mottled leaves have distinctive short stalks. The sepals are bent down between the leaves at flowering, and the 1- to 1 1/2-in. purplish petals are erect but flared out from the base and then recurved together at their tips to form a rounded, open, cone-shaped flower.

HABITAT: Moist woods

REGION: Mississippian Plateau, Shawnee Hills, Jackson Purchase

FREQUENCY: Locally common

CREEPING PHLOX
Phlox stolonifera
POLEMONIACEAE

This is essentially a creeping species that has above-ground runners with most of the numerous spoon-shaped leaves occurring near the base of the plant. The 6- to 8-in. stalk that arises from the base supports 3 to 5 1-in.-wide, 5-lobed flowers in a tight group. Flower color can vary from deep pink to purple.

HABITAT: Moist, rich woods particularly along streams

REGION: Appalachian Plateaus

FREQUENCY: Rare

COLUMBINE
Aquilegia canadensis
RANUNCULACEAE

The red-and-yellow, 1 1/2- to 2-in. flowers are unmistakable. The 5 sepals are brilliant red, and the 5 yellow petals grade backward into red spurs that contain the nectar relished by hummingbirds. The delicate, small, compound leaves are rounded and often have 3 lobes.

HABITAT: Limestone cliffs and rocky woods but occasionally found on sandstone

REGION: Statewide except Jackson Purchase

FREQUENCY: Common

WILD PINK, CAROLINA PINK
Silene caroliniana
CARYOPHYLLACEAE

This 4- to 10-in.-tall plant has up to 5-in. rounded leaves that become narrow at the base and attach directly to the plant. The flower has 5 wedge-shaped, ragged-edged petals. It superficially resembles a phlox, but careful examination will show that the petals are separate, in contrast to the phlox where they are joined to the central corolla.

HABITAT: Dry to moist open limestone woods or cliffs, especially on shale in the eastern and southern Knobs

REGION: Bluegrass, Knobs

FREQUENCY: Uncommon but locally abundant

FIRE PINK
Silene virginica
CARYOPHYLLACEAE

This showy, 1- to 2-ft.-tall species has narrow, 4-in.-long, opposite leaves that are sticky and fuzzy to the touch. The 1- to 2-in.-wide flowers have 5 notched petals.

HABITAT: Moist to dry woods, woodland edges, roadsides

REGION: Statewide

FREQUENCY: Common

DOWNY PHLOX, PRAIRIE PHLOX
Phlox pilosa
POLEMONIACEAE

Note the narrow, sharp-pointed, lance-shaped, opposite leaves on this 12- to 18-in. plant. The 5/8- to 3/4-in.-wide, 5-lobed flowers occur in a more open cluster than in other members of this group.

P. amoena

HABITAT: Grasslands, open woods

REGION: Statewide except Cumberland Mountains

FREQUENCY: Common

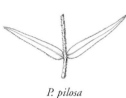

P. pilosa

Hairy phlox, *P. amoena,* is similar but has finely hairy stalks and is uncommon in southern Kentucky.

PINK LADY'S SLIPPER
Cypripedium acaule
ORCHIDACEAE

Note the 2 large, 4- to 8-in.-long, fuzzy, elliptical leaves on the ground that support a leafless flowering stalk up to 16 in. tall. There is a single 2-in.-long flower that looks like an inflated pouch and is folded inward in the center. The upper sepal arches over the flower, and the lower pair of sepals is joined underneath. The "moccasin flower" is white when it first appears and then turns pink.

HABITAT: Dry, acid pine-oak woods

REGION: Cumberland Mountains, Appalachian Plateaus

FREQUENCY: Common

SMALL BLUETS
Houstonia crassifolia
RUBIACEAE

Easy to overlook, this tiny, 2- to 4-in. annual has a few leaves at the base of the plant and sparse, linear leaves on the stem. The tiny, 1/4-in.-wide, 4-lobed, tubular flowers have a very noticeable purple or wine-colored center.

HABITAT: Old cemeteries, roadsides, fields, meadows

REGION: Jackson Purchase, Mississippian Plateau

FREQUENCY: Uncommon

DWARF LARKSPUR
Delphinium tricorne
RANUNCULACEAE

This small plant grows up to 18 in. tall. The leaves range in size from 1 to 4 in. wide and are shaped roughly like the palm of the hand although deeply divided. They usually are found at the base of the plant. The 1-in.-long flowers vary in color from deep purple to lavender or white.

HABITAT: Dry or moist woods often associated with limestone soils

REGION: Statewide

FREQUENCY: Common

This plant is poisonous to cattle.

COMMON BLUE VIOLET, DOORYARD VIOLET

Viola sororia

VIOLACEAE

This is our most common blue violet. It has smooth, broadly heart-shaped leaves that are finely hairy on the lower sides. The 1-in.-wide flowers have a white center and long hairs near the center and are supported on long, slender stalks.

HABITAT: Woods, meadows, roadsides, yards

REGION: Statewide

FREQUENCY: Abundant

BIRD'S-FOOT VIOLET

Viola pedata

VIOLACEAE

This species has the largest flowers of any of our violets. The large, 1- to 1 1/2-in. flowers can vary in color from light lavender to deep purple. A less common variety is bicolored with two satiny, deep purple petals above and light lavender below. The bright orange stamens in the center of the flower are conspicuous in this species. Leaves at the base of the plant are divided into 3 principal divisions, and each division may be divided into as many as 5 linear segments.

HABITAT: Prairie patches; dry, open woods; rocky areas; roadsides

REGION: Statewide

FREQUENCY: Common

FIELD PANSY
Viola rafinesquii
VIOLACEAE

This is a slender, delicate, 4- to 10-in. annual with small round to spoon-shaped leaves. Note that the 1/2-in.-wide flowers arise on leaflike stipules that are deeply lobed or divided. Flower color varies from white to lavender.

HABITAT: Fields, roadsides, disturbed soil

REGION: Statewide

FREQUENCY: Common

The exotic European field pansy, *V. arvensis,* is similar but has pale yellow flowers marked with purple and a slender spur.

ARROW-LEAVED VIOLET, ARROWHEAD VIOLET
Viola sagittata
VIOLACEAE

This small species has distinctive, 2- to 4-in.-long, arrow-shaped leaves with lobes or teeth near the base and long stalks. The 1/2-in.-wide flowers arise on separate stalks, and the lower petals have dark veins against a white center with long hairs.

HABITAT: Wet meadows, fields

REGION: Statewide except Bluegrass

FREQUENCY: Uncommon

LONG-SPURRED VIOLET

Viola rostrata

VIOLACEAE

This 4- to 8-in.-tall species is easy to identify because of the long, 1/2-in. spur at the back of the flower, which has a dark center. The heart-shaped leaves have long stalks and pointed tips.

HABITAT: Dry to moist woods

REGION: Appalachian Plateaus, Cumberland Mountains, Knobs, Bluegrass

FREQUENCY: Common

VIRGINIA BLUEBELLS

Mertensia virginica

BORAGINACEAE

This is a very smooth, 1- to 2-ft.-tall plant with large, 6- to 8-in., smooth, light green, oval leaves. The dangling clusters of 1-in.-long trumpet-shaped flowers have a narrow tube that expands into a bell. They are pink at first and then turn to blue.

HABITAT: Moist rich woods, floodplain forests

REGION: Statewide

FREQUENCY: Common

BLUE PHLOX

Phlox divaricata

POLEMONIACEAE

The 1-in.-wide, 5-lobed flowers occur in a loose cluster at the top of the plant; the lobes are often notched and wedge shaped. This 10- to 18-in., hairy-stemmed plant has few upper stem leaves. The opposite, lance-shaped leaves are widely spaced. Flower color can vary from light blue to lavender or pink.

HABITAT: Moist woods

REGION: Statewide

FREQUENCY: Common

DOG VIOLET

Viola conspersa

VIOLACEAE

This smooth, 8- to 12-in.-tall plant has numerous leafy stems. The leaves at the base of the plant are round to kidney shaped with long stalks. The 1/2- to 3/4-in.-wide flowers are on the same stalks as leaves and have long hairs near their center. The flowers appear to have a very short spur on the back.

HABITAT: Moist woods, streamside forests

REGION: Appalachian Plateaus, Cumberland Mountains

FREQUENCY: Uncommon

MARSH BLUE VIOLET
Viola cucullata
VIOLACEAE

Note the 3/4- to 1-in.-wide flowers that occur on long stalks other than the leaf stems. The flower is darker toward the center, but the bases of the petals are white and there are long hairs near the center. The leaves at the base of the plant are broadly heart shaped. One of the later-blooming species.

HABITAT: Wet soils

REGION: Statewide

FREQUENCY: Common except in the Bluegrass

THREE-LOBED VIOLET, WOOD VIOLET
Viola triloba
VIOLACEAE

This species has a distinctive, 3- to 5-segmented, heart-shaped leaf at the base of the plant with the middle lobe uncut. The side lobes are cut into at least 2 sections. The 3/4- to 1-in.-wide flower does not have hairs near its center.

HABITAT: Dry to moist upland forest

REGION: Statewide

FREQUENCY: Common

The wood violet, *V. palmata,* is similar in appearance, but all of the leaves are cut into 5 to 11 lobes. It is common in rich, moist woods statewide except the Shawnee Hills and Jackson Purchase.

WILD GERANIUM
Geranium maculatum
GERANIACEAE

This 1- to 2-ft.-tall plant has 3-in.-wide leaves with 5 to 7 somewhat pointed segments or lobes that roughly resemble a human hand. The 1- to 1 1/2-in.-wide, 5-petaled flowers have 10 stamens.

HABITAT: Open woods, roadsides

REGION: Statewide

FREQUENCY: Common

JACOB'S LADDER
Polemonium reptans
POLEMONIACEAE

Note the 5 to 9 pairs of opposite leaf segments with smooth edges and a short stalk that has the appearance of a ladder. The 1/2- to 5/8-in.-wide, 5-petaled flowers occur in an open cluster at the top of this 10- to 15-in. plant. Occasionally white-colored flowers can be found on this plant.

HABITAT: Rich woods

REGION: Statewide

FREQUENCY: Common

EARLY SPIDERWORT, VIRGINIA SPIDERWORT

Tradescantia virginiana

COMMELINACEAE

This 12- to 15-in.-tall, smooth plant has 1/2-in.-wide, 6- to 10-in.-long alternate leaves. The leaves are widest at the base where they wrap around the stem. The 3-petaled flowers occur at the top of a stem and are surrounded by bracts that are often larger than the leaves. Color can vary from almost white with a lavender tint to dark blue or reddish purple.

HABITAT: Moist woods, prairie patches

REGION: Appalachian Plateaus, Bluegrass, Mississippian Plateau, Shawnee Hills, Jackson Purchase

FREQUENCY: Uncommon

The glaucous or Ohio spiderwort, *T. ohiensis,* is a similar species that is also uncommon. It is taller and smooth, with a powdery or waxy appearance.

BLUE SCORPION WEED

Phacelia ranunculacea

HYDROPHYLLACEAE

This small (less than 1 ft. tall) annual has 1/4-in. tubular or funnel-shaped flowers with 5 lobes; the stamens do not extend past the petals. The smooth leaves have long stalks and 3 to 7 deeply cut lobes.

HABITAT: Loess bluffs woods, floodplain forests

REGION: Jackson Purchase, Mississippian Plateau

FREQUENCY: Rare

PURPLE PHACELIA
Phacelia bipinnatifida
HYDROPHYLLACEAE

This is a 1- to 2-ft., weak, hairy-stemmed, and sprawling biennial. The leaves are twice divided into 3 to 7 roundish, toothed segments. The 1/2-in.-wide, 5-petaled flowers have a white center with stamens that protrude past the petals.

HABITAT: Moist woods

REGION: Statewide

FREQUENCY: Abundant

QUAKER LADIES, BLUETS
Houstonia caerulea
RUBIACEAE

Often found in large clumps, this delicate, 2- to 6-in.-tall plant has spoon-shaped leaves at its base and a threadlike stalk that supports the 1/2-in.-wide, 4-lobed, yellow-centered, tubular flower.

HABITAT: Less fertile soils in dry woods or wet meadows

REGION: Statewide except Bluegrass

FREQUENCY: Abundant

Mountain or creeping bluet, *H. serpyllifolia,* is another spring-blooming species that looks similar but it is only known from several locations in the Cumberland Mountains.

BLUE-EYED MARY
Collinsia verna
SCROPHULARIACEAE

This small, 6- to 12-in., delicate annual has weak stems. It has triangular, oval-shaped, opposite leaves without a stalk. The 1/2-in.-wide flower occurs in groups of 1 to 3 in whorls at the top of the stem. The 2 upper lobes are white, and the 2 lower lobes are blue. The third lobe is folded between the lower lobes and forms a pouch that encloses the stamens.

HABITAT: Rich woods

REGION: Bluegrass, Knobs, Mississippian Plateau, Jackson Purchase

FREQUENCY: Uncommon but locally abundant in the Inner Bluegrass

DWARF IRIS
Iris verna
IRIDACEAE

The grasslike, narrow, 2- to 4-in.-long leaves of this species are noticeably flattened at ground level and are narrower and longer than those of dwarf crested iris. The large, showy, 2- to 3-in.-wide flowers occur on a long (up to 6 in.) stalk. Individual flowers have 6 purple segments: the 3 narrow petals stand erect, and the 3 wider sepals are bent down and are marked with a smooth, yellow patch.

HABITAT: Dry soils, open upland woods

REGION: Cumberland Mountains, Appalachian Plateaus

FREQUENCY: Uncommon

CRESTED DWARF IRIS
Iris cristata
IRIDACEAE

The 3- to 4-in.-long linear leaves are wide and flat and usually arch over to one side. The 2-in.-wide flowers have 3 small, erect, narrow petals and 3 broad, reflexed sepals. Each sepal has a yellow patch with a fluted texture.

HABITAT: Moist woods

REGION: Statewide

FREQUENCY: Common but rare in the Bluegrass

SHOWY ORCHIS
Galearis spectabilis
ORCHIDACEAE

This is a low-growing, 4- to 8-in.-tall species with 2 elliptical, smooth leaves that are quite thick and deeply veined. In the center of the 2 leaves there is a short, 1- to 6-in.-tall spike of 3 to 8 flowers. Each individual 1-in.-long flower has pinkish to lilac-colored sepals and lateral petals that overlap and form a hood that covers the white lip.

HABITAT: Rich woods

REGION: Statewide, but most common in the Appalachian Plateaus and Cumberland Mountains

FREQUENCY: Common

VIOLET WOOD SORREL
Oxalis violacea
OXALIDACEAE

Note the 3 heart-shaped, shamrocklike leaves that have purplish to brownish linear blotches above and are red-purple underneath. This 4- to 6-in. plant sends up a 2- to 3-in. flowering stalk with the 1/2-in.-wide, 5-petaled flowers occurring singly or in a loose cluster.

HABITAT: Dry open woods, barrens

REGION: Statewide

FREQUENCY: Common

CAROLINA CRANE'S BILL
Geranium carolinianum
GERANIACEAE

This hairy-stemmed annual reaches heights up to 2 ft. with somewhat kidney-shaped leaves, up to 3 in. wide, divided into 3 to 5 linear-to-oblong segments that have

roundish lobes at the tip. The 1/2-in.-wide flowers have 5 petals with slight notches at the tip; the flowers occur singly, in pairs, or in a small open cluster.

HABITAT: Fields, disturbed soil, open woods

REGION: Statewide

FREQUENCY: Common

This plant is often called crane's bill because the long, slender fruits resemble a long beak.

BLUESTAR
Amsonia tabernaemontana
APOCYNACEAE

A 2- to 3-ft.-tall, smooth-stemmed plant that exudes a milky sap when broken. The alternate, lance-shaped leaves attach directly to the plant stem. The starlike, 5-petaled, tubular flowers, which have hairs in the opening, occur in a dense, elongated dome cluster.

HABITAT: Wet meadows, wet open woods

REGION: Mississippian Plateau, Shawnee Hills, Jackson Purchase

FREQUENCY: Uncommon

LYRE-LEAVED SAGE
Salvia lyrata
LAMIACEAE

Most of the leaves occur at the base of this aromatic, 1- to 2-ft.-tall, slightly hairy-stemmed plant. The 2- to 8-in.-long, smooth-edged leaves have irregularly shaped, lobed segments. The upper stem leaves are small and arranged in whorls. The 1-in.-long, tubular flowers grow in whorls in an interrupted spike.

HABITAT: Roadsides, meadows, fields, open woods

REGION: Statewide

FREQUENCY: Abundant

SWEET PINESAP
Monotropsis odorata
MONOTROPACEAE

This plant is similar to pinesap, but it is much smaller and does not grow above 4 in. tall. It is a pale brown or purplish color and is covered with small scales. The flowers are pink or yellowish and occur in a nodding cluster at the end of the stalk. Fresh specimens have a strong odor of violets and may be smelled before they are seen.

HABITAT: Rich woods, acid soils

REGION: Cumberland Mountains, Appalachian Plateaus

FREQUENCY: Rare and easily overlooked

MIAMI MIST
Phacelia purshii
HYDROPHYLLACEAE

Note the fringed edges of the 1/2-in.-wide, 5-petaled flowers with whitish centers. The leaves are deeply cut into 9 to 15 segments, and the lower leaves have stalks whereas the upper leaves do not. Also note the weak stalk and sprawling nature of this 10- to 15-in. annual.

HABITAT: Moist woods, floodplain forests, fields

REGION: Bluegrass, Mississippian Plateau

FREQUENCY: Abundant

LAVENDER WATERLEAF

Hydrophyllum appendiculatum

HYDROPHYLLACEAE

This is a weak-stemmed, softly haired, 1- to 2-ft.-tall biennial with 5-lobed, somewhat star- or maple-shaped leaves. The cluster of 5-lobed, open-bell-shaped flowers have protruding stamens. Small, curved structures alternate with the sepals.

HABITAT: Moist, rich woods

REGION: Statewide

FREQUENCY: Common but locally abundant

WILD HYACINTH

Camassia scilloides

LILIACEAE

This very showy species has a flowering stalk that reaches up to 24 in. tall with a roughly cone-shaped cluster of 1/2-in.-wide, 6-petaled flowers. The 8- to 16-in.-long, grasslike leaves occur at the base of the plant.

HABITAT: Open woods, cedar glades, prairie patches

REGION: Appalachian Plateaus, Bluegrass, Mississippian Plateau, Jackson Purchase

FREQUENCY: Uncommon but locally abundant in the Bluegrass

STOUT BLUE-EYED GRASS
Sisyrinchium angustifolium
IRIDACEAE

This species has medium green, grasslike leaves that reach from 4 to 12 in. in length. It often has several branches. The flowers occur in small clusters at the tips of winged flowering stalks. The flowering stalks are as thick as the leaves, and each individual starlike flower has 6 segments with a yellow center.

HABITAT: Prairie patches, glades, meadows, open woods

REGION: Statewide

FREQUENCY: Common

Eastern blue-eyed grass, *S. atlanticum,* is a similar branching species with light blue flowers. In this species the flowering stalks are less than 1/8 in. wide and much longer than the leaves. It is uncommon to rare in wet meadows and along streams statewide except the Bluegrass.

MEEHANIA
Meehania cordata
LAMIACEAE

This short (less than 8 in. tall) plant trails along the ground and has heart-shaped leaves with a stalk. The 1-in. or larger tubular flowers occur in a short, dense spike on one side of the stalk.

HABITAT: Rich woods, particularly along streams

REGION: Cumberland Mountains, Appalachian Plateaus

FREQUENCY: Common

WILD COMFREY
Cynoglossum virginianum
BORAGINACEAE

Look for large (up to 8 in. long), hairy, oval leaves with a stalk at the base of the 1- to 2-ft.-tall plant. The leaves on the stem are lance shaped and clasp around the stem. The 3/8-in.-wide, short, open tubular flowers occur at the top of the stalk in a loose cluster.

HABITAT: Open woods

REGION: Statewide

FREQUENCY: Common

VEINY SKULLCAP
Scutellaria nervosa
LAMIACEAE

This small, 4- to 10-in., slender, square-stemmed plant has 1/3-in.-long, tubular flowers that arise at the base of the upper leaves. The blunt-toothed leaves are oval to roundish or lance shaped.

HABITAT: Open woods, woodland edges, prairie patches, glades, dry soil

REGION: Statewide

FREQUENCY: Common

The small skullcap, *S. parvula,* is similar except the flower is usually a darker blue color and has smaller, less toothed leaves with fewer veins. It is found in prairie patches and glades throughout the state. These two species are easy to overlook as they are small and blend into the vegetation quite well.

BLUE COHOSH
Caulophyllum
thalictroides
BERBERIDACEAE

When first unfurling, the gray-
greenish leaves have a delicate
appearance. Three 1- to 2-in.
rounded leaflets make up the
compound leaf. The plant
stands up to 2 1/2 ft. tall. The
1/2-in.-wide flowers are
somewhat inconspicuous and
have 6 purplish brownish
sepals, 6 undeveloped petals,
and 6 stamens.

HABITAT: Rich woods

REGION: Statewide

FREQUENCY: Common

WILD GINGER

Asarum canadense
ARISTOLOCHIACEAE

Note the distinctive pair of 3- to 5-in.,
heart-shaped leaves on hairy stalks that
often hide the unusual reddish brown,
1-in.-wide flower. The flower usually lies
on the ground between the leaf stalks and
may be concealed by the leaf litter.

HABITAT: Rich woods

REGION: Statewide

FREQUENCY: Abundant

There is a subspecies known from Pine
Mountain in which the flowers have long,
pointed lobes.

LITTLE BROWN JUG
Hexastylis arifolia
ARISTOLOCHIACEAE

Note the pair of pointed heart- to arrow-shaped, 2- to 4-in.-long leaves above a 1- to 2-in. stalk. The 1-in.-wide flower resembles a brown urn or jug and usually lies on the ground between the leaf stalks, where it may be concealed by the leaf litter.

HABITAT: Upland sandstone woods

REGION: Cumberland Mountains, Appalachian Plateaus, local in Shawnee Hills

FREQUENCY: Common

ERECT CARRION FLOWER
Smilax ecirrhata
SMILACEAE

This species has globelike clusters of small, 3/8-in.-wide flowers that hang under the large, 2- to 6-in.-long, oval leaves with bases that are more or less heart shaped and attached to the plant with a long stalk. Male and female flowers occur on separate plants. The flowers smell like rotten meat.

HABITAT: Damp woods

REGION: Appalachian Plateaus, Shawnee Hills

FREQUENCY: Uncommon

Carrion flower vine, *S. herbacea,* another species found in Kentucky, is similar except that it has twining tendrils.

WILD YAM
*Dioscorea
quaternata*
DIOSCOREACEAE

This is a twining vine that grows up to 6 ft. long. It has heart-shaped leaves, up to 4 in. long, with long stalks in whorls of 4 to 7. Male and female flowers occur on separate plants. The 6-segmented flowers are very small and occur on short flowering stalks that arise from the axils of the clusters of leaves.

HABITAT: Moist woods

REGION: Statewide

FREQUENCY: Common

SPRING CORALROOT
Corallorhiza wisteriana
ORCHIDACEAE

This plant has a 3- to 6-in.-tall, dark red or purplish brown stem that may attain a height of 16 in. Because it is saprophytic— that is, it lives on decaying organic matter and relies on a special fungus to make nutrients available from the soil—it has no green leaves and doesn't feed itself through photosynthesis. It has an open spike of small, 1/8- to 1/4-in.-long, pale flowers. The individual flowers have greenish yellow sepals and petals with an unlobed, white lip dotted with purple spots.

HABITAT: Rich woods

REGION: Statewide

FREQUENCY: Uncommon

Spotted coralroot, *C. maculata,* is rare in the Cumberland Mountains. It is similar to spring coralroot but can be up to 20 in. tall. The lip is white with purple spots and is conspicuously lobed below the middle.

WHORLED POGONIA
Isotria verticillata
ORCHIDACEAE

This is an easily overlooked, 4- to 6-in.-tall species with a soft-textured, purplish green stem. A whorl of 5 to 6, 3-in.-long, oblong leaves is found just below the single flower. The narrow, linear, and widely spaced sepals are purplish brown with greenish yellow petals. Two greenish yellow side petals form the top of the floral tube, and an extended, yellowish, 1/2-in.-long lip forms the bottom.

HABITAT: Dry woods

REGION: Cumberland Mountains, Appalachian Plateaus, Mississippian Plateau, Shawnee Hills, Jackson Purchase

FREQUENCY: Rare

WOOD SPURGE
Euphorbia commutata
EUPHORBIACEAE

This is a smooth-stemmed, 8- to 15-in.-tall, open-branched plant with 2 rounded leaves that appear

to form a circle around the stem. The extremely small flowers, which occur in clusters, do not have petals or sepals. However, they are surrounded by a crescent-shaped gland with short spikes that is easily identifiable.

HABITAT: Rocky, dry to moist woods

REGION: Bluegrass and Mississippian Plateau

FREQUENCY: Common

JACK-IN-THE-PULPIT
Arisaema triphyllum
ARACEAE

This is an easily recognized, 6- to 18-in.-tall plant that normally has 2 compound leaves divided into 3 sections. The unique vaselike structure with a flap on top has tiny flowers at the base of the center cylinder-like structure. The plants are unisexual; the larger plants tend to be females, whereas the smaller ones tend to be males.

HABITAT: Moist woods

REGION: Statewide

FREQUENCY: Abundant

GREEN DRAGON
Arisaema dracontium
ARACEAE

This 6- to 18-in.-tall plant has 1 compound leaf divided into 7 or more sections. The tiny green flowers occur on a green cylinder-like structure inside a green sheath.

HABITAT: Damp woods, floodplains

REGION: Statewide

FREQUENCY: Uncommon; more common in the Bluegrass and Mississippian Plateau

GREEN VIOLET
Hybanthus concolor
VIOLACEAE

At first glance this plant doesn't look like other violets because it is a coarse plant growing up to 3 ft. tall. It has long (up to 6 in.), oval, finely hairy leaves with long, tapering tips. The flowers hang from long stalks in clusters at the base of the leaves. The individual pale green flowers are cupped and have 5 nearly equal petals, quite unlike typical violet flowers.

HABITAT: Moist woods

REGION: Statewide

FREQUENCY: Uncommon

SQUAWROOT
Conopholis americana
OROBANCHAECEAE

This plant is a parasite on oak trees and has a 1-in.-thick, unbranched stalk with numerous overlapping leaf scales. The tiny whitish flowers are found in the upper half of the plant.

HABITAT: Oak woods

REGION: Statewide

FREQUENCY: Common

INDIAN CUCUMBER ROOT

Medeola virginiana

LILIACEAE

This plant, which grows up to 24 in. tall, has a hard, wiry texture and lance-shaped leaves that occur in whorls of 5 or more. Plants that will bloom have an upper whorl of 3 or more pointed oval leaves. The 1/2-in.-long, spiderlike, 6-segmented flowers with 3 brown, threadlike stigmas dangle from delicate stalks beneath the upper leaves.

HABITAT: Moist woods

REGION: Cumberland Mountains, Appalachian Plateaus, Shawnee Hills

FREQUENCY: Common

SMOOTH SOLOMON'S SEAL

Polygonatum biflorum

LILIACEAE

This tall (up to 24 in.), delicate, and gracefully arching plant has smooth, alternate, lance-shaped leaves that are up to 4 in. long and attach directly to the plant. The 1/2-in.-long, tubular flowers hang in pairs below the arching stalk.

HABITAT: Moist woods

REGION: Statewide

FREQUENCY: Abundant

Downy Solomon's seal, *P. pubescens,* is similar, but the stem can be up to 36 in. tall and the plant often stands more erect. The veins on the undersides of the leaves are finely hairy rather than smooth, and the flowers are smaller. It is locally common statewide.

PUTTYROOT
Aplectrum hyemale
ORCHIDACEAE

For most of the year this plant consists of a single, 4- to 6-in.-long, light green leaf with prominent white veins lying flat on the forest floor. In late

spring the leaf withers, and a slender pale green to brown flowering stalk supports an open spike of 7 to 15, 1/2- to 1-in.-long flowers that are purplish near the base and brown near the tips; the lip is greenish white with purple spots.

HABITAT: Rich woods

REGION: Statewide

FREQUENCY: Uncommon and rare in the Bluegrass

LILY-LEAVED TWAYBLADE
Liparis liliifolia
ORCHIDACEAE

Note the two dark green, broad oval, 6-in. leaves on the ground that are smooth and shiny. The 8-in.-tall flowering stalk is leafless and supports an open-spike arrangement of interesting flowers. Each flower has 3 widespread sepals and 2 side petals that are linear and hang to either side of the pale purple lip.

HABITAT: Moist woods of medium age

REGION: Statewide

FREQUENCY: Uncommon to common

Loesel's twayblade, *L. loeselii,* is similar to the lily-leaved twayblade except that the basal leaves are narrower and pale green. The flowers are similar, but the lip of the flowers is yellowish green. It is rare and found in wet seeps in the Cumberland Mountains and southern Appalachian Plateaus.

SUMMER FLOWERS

Mid-May–August

STRAP-LEAVED VIOLET, LANCE-LEAVED VIOLET
Viola lanceolata
VIOLACEAE

Note the long, smooth, narrow, lance-shaped leaves that taper to a reddish-colored stalk. The 1/2-in.-wide flowers have 3 lower petals with purple veins without hairs near the center of the flower.

HABITAT: Wet meadows, swamps, wet woods

REGION: Statewide except Bluegrass

FREQUENCY: Uncommon

PARTRIDGEBERRY
Mitchella repens
RUBIACEAE

This is a small, trailing, evergreen plant that often forms large colonies carpeting the ground. It has 1/2-in.-long, oval, opposite leaves. At the end of the branches, 2, 1/2-in.-long, 4-lobed, tubular, hairy flowers appear like twins. A pair of flowers will produce a single red berry that often lasts through the winter.

HABITAT: Rich woods, often in acidic soil

REGION: Statewide

FREQUENCY: Common and locally abundant

DOCKWEED
Rumex verticillatus
POLYGONACEAE

This 2- to 4-ft., unbranched plant has smooth-edged, lance-shaped leaves. The small, 1/8-in.-wide flowers have 6 lobes and occur in small whorls. This plant stands out more when the reddish brown seed heads appear in mid- to late summer.

HABITAT: Wetlands, stream banks, ponds, moist meadows

REGION: Statewide except Appalachian Plateaus and Cumberland Mountains

FREQUENCY: Uncommon but locally abundant

This native species should not be confused with the other numerous species of weedy, exotic docks like curly dockweed, *R. crispus.*

ANNUAL FLEABANE
Erigeron annuus
ASTERACEAE

There are many branches on this 1- to 4-ft.-tall, hairy-stemmed annual. The coarsely toothed, oval leaves attach directly to the stem. The leaves at the base of the plant are oval and have stalks. The 1/2- to 3/4-in.-wide flower heads have 50 or more rays.

HABITAT: Roadsides, fields, meadows

REGION: Statewide

FREQUENCY: Abundant

The daisy fleabane, *E. strigosus,* is similar except it is shorter and not as hairy and has more linear, smooth-edged leaves.

INDIAN HEMP
Apocynum cannabinum
APOCYNACEAE

This 3- to 5-ft.-tall, smooth- and fibrous- stemmed plant exudes a milky sap when broken. It has 2- to 5-in.-long, opposite, rounded, lance- shaped leaves. The 1/4-in.- wide, urn-shaped flowers occur in a loose cluster.

HABITAT: Roadsides, meadows, woodland edges

REGION: Statewide

FREQUENCY: Abundant

This is one of the best butterfly-attracting plants in Kentucky. The Native Americans used the plant to treat various ailments, but it is considered poisonous and should not be eaten.

COLIC ROOT
Aletris farinosa
LILIACEAE

The 3- to 6-in.-long, lance-shaped, dull green, and very stiff leaves occur at the base of the plant in a circular arrangement radiating from the center. The numerous 1/4- to 1/2-in.-wide, tubular flowers occur on a 12- to 18-in. spike.

HABITAT: Wet meadows, damp open woods

REGION: Cumberland Mountains, Appalachian Plateaus

FREQUENCY: Common

WILD GARLIC
Allium canadense
LILIACEAE

Note the relatively short, 12- to 15-in.-long, flat, narrow leaves of this native species. The abundant and exotic field garlic, *A. vineale,* is a much taller and coarser plant with hollow, round leaves. The 2 to 5, 1/4- to 3/8-in.-wide, 6-segmented flowers occur in loose clusters with several bulblets. Flowers may appear pink because of the heavy pinkish stripes and pinkish stamens.

HABITAT: Moist woods, wet soils, prairie patches

REGION: Appalachian Plateaus, Bluegrass, Mississippian Plateau

FREQUENCY: Uncommon to locally common

AMERICAN IPECAC
Porteranthus stipulatus
ROSACEAE

This 2- to 3-ft., airy, and open-branched plant has long flower stalks with 5 narrow, spreading and somewhat twisted, delicate petals that often droop. The leaves have 3 sharp, toothed segments. However, there appear to be 5 segments because there are 2 toothed stipules at the base of the leaf.

HABITAT: Dry to moist woods, woods edges

REGION: Statewide except Bluegrass

FREQUENCY: Common

Indian physic, *P. trifoliatus,* is a similar species, but the leaves are not nearly as toothed and it does not have the large stipules. It also has a reddish cup at the base of the flowers that makes the flower appear pinkish from a distance. It is uncommon to rare on the southern Appalachian Plateaus and in the Cumberland Mountains. It typically flowers several weeks before American ipecac.

AVENS
Geum canadense
ROSACEAE

This multibranched, 1 1/2- to 2 1/2-ft.-tall, smooth- or somewhat hairy-stemmed plant has lower leaves that are divided into 3 pointed oval, sharply toothed lobes. The narrow upper leaves are typically not divided and attach directly to the plant. The 1/2-in.-wide flowers occur at the tip of a branch and have 5 petals, 5 downward-curving sepals, and numerous stamens.

HABITAT: Woods, woodland edges, fields

REGION: Statewide

FREQUENCY: Common

WHITE FALSE INDIGO
Baptisia leucantha
FABACEAE

This is a large, showy plant reaching 2 to 3 ft. tall with a smooth stem and leaves. The 1-in.-wide flowers have 5 petals; the outer and largest one is often tinged with blue. The flowers occur in a tall, open spike. The modified leaves under the flowers fall off early. The leaves have 3 round, blunt, or oblong segments.

HABITAT: Dry, open woods; prairie patches; grasslands

REGION: Mississippian Plateau, Shawnee Hills, Jackson Purchase

FREQUENCY: Uncommon

The blue false indigo, *B. australis,* is rare and found on several prairie patches in the Mississippian Plateau and on the banks of streams and rivers. The cream false indigo, *B. bracteata,* is rare and found primarily in the western Mississippian Plateau. The yellow false indigo, *B. tinctoria,* is rare and found only in the Cumberland Mountains.

SENECA SNAKEROOT
Polygala senega
POLYGALACEAE

This 10- to 18-in.-tall, unbranched plant has alternate, lance-shaped, pointed leaves with smooth edges that attach directly to the plant. The 1-in. or longer spike has numerous tiny flowers that have 3 petals. Two of the 5 sepals are colored and look like petals; these are called "wings."

HABITAT: Woodland edges, open woods

REGION: Statewide except Shawnee Hills and Jackson Purchase

FREQUENCY: Common

PALE-SPIKED LOBELIA
Lobelia spicata
CAMPANULACEAE

This is a usually smooth, unbranched, 1- to 2-ft.-tall plant with narrow, linear leaves. The leaves near the base of the plant are more oval. The flowers attach to the plant with a short stalk in a single open spike arrangement. The individual 3/8-in., tubular flowers have 5 unequal lobes.

HABITAT: Limestone prairie patches, glades, roadsides

REGION: Statewide except Cumberland Mountains, Shawnee Hills, Jackson Purchase

FREQUENCY: Common in Knobs and Mississippian Plateau but uncommon in other parts of its range

WHITE MILKWEED

Asclepias variegata

ASCLEPIADACEAE

This is a thick-stemmed plant with 6-in.-long, broad oval, opposite leaves that can reach a height of 36 in. The individual, 1/2-in.-wide flowers occur in a ball or globelike cluster at the end of the stalk or from axils of upper leaves.

HABITAT: Open upland oak or oak-pine forests, woodland edges

REGION: Statewide except Bluegrass

FREQUENCY: Uncommon

Another white milkweed is smooth-seed milkweed, *A. perennis*. It has thin, lance-shaped, alternate leaves that gradually taper to the base. It is common in wet areas in the Mississippian Plateau, Shawnee Hills, and Jackson Purchase. It flowers in mid- to late summer.

BROADLEAF WATERLEAF

Hydrophyllum canadense

HYDROPHYLLACEAE

Note the large, 3- to 10-in., 5- to 9-lobed, star-shaped leaves on this 1- to 2-ft.-tall plant. The small cluster of 5-lobed, somewhat open, bell-shaped flowers with protruding stamens hangs below the leaf.

HABITAT: Moist woods

REGION: Statewide

FREQUENCY: Common

HEDGE NETTLE
Stachys nuttallii
LAMIACEAE

The lower leaves of this 1- to 4-ft.-tall, hairy-stemmed plant are heart shaped to oval with stalks. The flowers are whorled clusters of 1/2-in.-long flowers in a somewhat interrupted, 6- to 8-in. spike. The individual flowers have lobes, and the upper part arches over to cover the 4 stamens.

HABITAT: Rich woods, streamside forests

REGION: Cumberland Mountains, Appalachian Plateaus, Knobs, Bluegrass, eastern Mississippian Plateau

FREQUENCY: Common in eastern Kentucky but uncommon to rare in the remainder of its range

NARROW-LEAVED HEDGE NETTLE
Stachys tenuifolia
LAMIACEAE

The leaves of this 1- to 4-ft., smooth-stemmed plant are toothed and lance-shaped with points. The flowers are clusters of 6, 1/2-in.-long flowers in an interrupted spike that arises at the base of the upper leaves.

HABITAT: Wet woods, streamside forests, wet meadows

REGION: Statewide

FREQUENCY: Common in Jackson Purchase but uncommon to rare in the remainder of its range

WILD QUININE

Parthenium integrifolium

ASTERACEAE

This is a sturdy, 1- to 4-ft.-tall plant with thick, alternate, lance-shaped leaves that are rough to the touch. The upper leaves often attach directly to the plant. The flower heads are not showy and are found in small, dense, flat-topped clusters. There are usually 5 relatively tiny rays evenly spaced around the edge of the flower.

HABITAT: Prairie patches; dry, open woods

REGION: Jackson Purchase, Shawnee Hills, Mississippian Plateau, southern Appalachian Plateaus

FREQUENCY: Uncommon to locally common

PALE-FLOWERED LEAFCUP

Polymnia canadensis

ASTERACEAE

This is a coarse plant, up to 5 ft. tall, with large, 10-in. leaves that are somewhat arrow shaped with sharp edges and a short stalk. There are few flowers, and the 1/2-in.-wide flower heads have a yellow center and white rays that have 3 lobes.

HABITAT: Moist or dry woods

REGION: Cumberland Mountains, Bluegrass, Mississippian Plateau, Jackson Purchase

FREQUENCY: Abundant

INDIAN TOBACCO
Lobelia inflata
CAMPANULACEAE

Note the inflated "capsules" that appear after blooming on this 1- to 2-ft.-tall, branched, hairy annual. The toothed, oval leaves attach directly to the plant. A single, 3/8-in.-long flower arises at the base of each upper leaf in a loose, open, 2- to 4-in. spike.

HABITAT: Fields, roadsides, open woods

REGION: Statewide

FREQUENCY: Common

BIENNIAL GAURA
Gaura biennis
ONAGRACEAE

This tall, spindly, and much branched biennial reaches 5 ft. tall and has narrow, lance-shaped leaves. The long, branched flowering stalks have many 1/2-in.-long, tubular flowers with 4 spoon-shaped, spreading petals, a cross-shaped stigma, and 8 drooping stamens.

HABITAT: Prairie patches, meadows, fields, open woods

REGION: Statewide

FREQUENCY: Common

Three other species of Gaura occur in the state. Slender gaura, *G. filipes,* is common in prairie patches across western Kentucky. The other two species, the small-flowered gaura, *G. parviflora,* and southern gaura, *G. longiflora,* are both rare.

WINTERGREEN, TEABERRY, MOUNTAIN TEA
Gaultheria procumbens
ERICACEAE

This small (up to 6 in. tall) evergreen plant can often be seen in large colonies. The 1-in.-long, oval leaves have short stalks and smell like oil of wintergreen when crushed. The white, 1/4-in.-long, barrel-shaped flowers hang in small clusters below the leaves. The red berries often persist throughout the winter.

HABITAT: Upland forests in sandstone

REGION: Appalachian Plateaus, Cumberland Mountains, Shawnee Hills

FREQUENCY: Abundant

SPOTTED WINTERGREEN, PIPSISSEWA
Chimaphila maculata
PYROLACEAE

This is a small, 4- to 6-in.-tall, evergreen plant with 2-in.-long, toothed, lance-shaped leaves. The leaves usually have a pale stripe down the center. The flowers usually hang upside down in pairs. Each 3 1/4-in.-wide flower has 5 white petals and 10 conspicuous stamens.

HABITAT: Dry to moist woods

REGION: Statewide except Bluegrass

FREQUENCY: Common

POKEWEED
Phytolacca americana
PHYTOLACCACEAE

This is a large, coarse or stout plant with numerous branches, red stalks, and 4- to 10-in., oblong leaves growing up to 8 or 9 ft. tall. The numerous 1/4-in. flowers grow in a cone-shaped cluster and have no petals and 5 greenish white sepals. Reddish purple fruits can often be seen developing in a flower cluster while other individual flowers are still blooming.

HABITAT: Fields, thickets, fencerows, disturbed ground

REGION: Statewide

FREQUENCY: Abundant

Mature or older leaves, stalks, roots, and seeds are poisonous, although the young leaves are eaten as a spring salad after cooking with at least two changes of water.

BASIL BEE BALM
Monarda clinopodia
LAMIACEAE

Look for pointed-oval leaves with stalks on this 2- to 3-ft.-tall, smooth-stemmed plant. The flower heads are a rounded cluster of 1-in.-long, fragrant, 2-lipped flowers. The upper lip of each flower is hairy.

HABITAT: Rich woods

REGION: Cumberland Mountains, Appalachian Plateaus

FREQUENCY: Common

RAGGED FRINGED ORCHID

Platanthera lacera

ORCHIDACEAE

This species has several elliptical leaves that get progressively smaller as they ascend the flowering stalk, which may reach up to 32 in. tall. The individual flowers occur in a loose and open spike. Note that the lip of the individual 1-in.-long flower has 3 distinctive lobed segments that are fringed or look like hairlike filaments.

HABITAT: Damp woods, wet meadows

REGION: Statewide except Bluegrass

FREQUENCY: Uncommon

AMERICAN WATER WILLOW

Justicia americana

ACANTHACEAE

A 1- to 3-ft.-tall plant that has long, lance-shaped leaves that may have a short stalk. The small cluster of 1/2-in. flowers occurs at the end of long stalks. The opposite flowers are 2-lipped with purple markings on the lower lip.

HABITAT: Shallow water in streams, pond margins, wet or muddy soil

REGION: Statewide

FREQUENCY: Common

GLADE BLUETS

Houstonia nigricans

RUBIACEAE

This is a short plant, reaching a maximum height of 18 in. It has 1-in.-long, linear, rough, opposite leaves. The 4-lobed, tubular, 3/8-in.-long flowers appear on very short stalks or they appear to have no stalks at all.

HABITAT: Glades; rocky, dry, exposed soil; cliffs

REGION: Knobs, Bluegrass, Mississippian Plateau

FREQUENCY: Common

SOUTHERN WATER PLANTAIN

Alisma subcordatum

ALISMATACEAE

This 12- to 36-in.-tall aquatic plant has 3- to 6-in.-long, pointed oval leaves with long stalks at the base of the plant. The small, 1/8- to -1/4-in.-wide, 3-petaled flowers occur in a very loose cluster above the leaves.

HABITAT: Wet soils, ditches

REGION: Statewide

FREQUENCY: Common

AMERICAN BUR REED
Sparganium americanum
SPARGANIACEAE

This 12- to 36-in.-tall aquatic plant has narrow, cattail-like leaves that may reach up to 36 in. long. The 1-in.-wide, roundish, globe-shaped flower heads occur in a spike, with the male flower heads at the top of the stalk and the female flower heads in the axils of leaves along the stalk.

HABITAT: Edges of ponds, shallow streams

REGION: Cumberland Mountains, Appalachian Plateaus, Mississippian Plateau, Jackson Purchase

FREQUENCY: Uncommon

Another species of bur reed, *S. androcladum* (branched bur reed), is uncommon but does occur in Kentucky in the Cumberland Mountains, the Shawnee Hills, and the Jackson Purchase. The species are distinguished by carefully examining the size, texture, and color of the fruit.

ILLINOIS BUNDLEFLOWER
Desmanthus illinoensis
FABACEAE

This 1- to 4-ft. plant has 2- to 3-in.-long, alternate leaves that have numerous finely textured, oblong segments. The flowers have minute petals and 5 stamens and look like fuzzy Koosh balls. The seedpods are unique. They are strongly recurved and twisted into a ball-like cluster.

HABITAT: Prairie patches, grasslands, rocky open areas, stream banks

REGION: Outer Bluegrass, Knobs, Mississippian Plateau, Jackson Purchase

FREQUENCY: Uncommon

WHITE PRAIRIE CLOVER
Dalea candidum
FABACEAE

This is a tall, slender or linear-type plant reaching 3 ft. in height. Each leaf has 5 to 9 narrow, spoon-shaped segments. The 1- to 2-in.-long, cylinder-shaped flower heads have numerous flowers and occur at the tip of the flowering branches.

HABITAT: Prairie patches, glades, open woods

REGION: Western Knobs and Mississippian Plateau

FREQUENCY: Uncommon

Purple prairie clover, *D. purpurea,* is a similar plant with lavender flowers that is rare in the western Knobs and Mississippian Plateau.

GOAT'S RUE, RABBIT'S PEA
Tephrosia virginiana
FABACEAE

Note the soft, silky, grayish to green appearance of the leaves, stems, and buds. This upright, unbranched plant is covered with soft hairs. The leaves have 15 to 25 oblong segments. The bicolored flower is quite distinctive.

HABITAT: Dry, open woods; prairie patches; gravel bars; roadsides with noncalcareous soil

REGION: Statewide except Bluegrass

FREQUENCY: Common

RATTLESNAKE MASTER
Eryngium yuccifolium
APIACEAE

This plant may be up to 3 1/2 ft. tall and has succulent, long, narrow leaves that are sharp tipped with spinelike serrations along the margins. The upper leaves look similar and gradually get smaller up the stem. The 1-in.-wide flower heads are green or white and sharp to the touch.

HABITAT: Prairie patches, grasslands, glades

REGION: Statewide except Bluegrass, Cumberland Mountains

FREQUENCY: Uncommon

HAIRY ANGELICA
Angelica venenosa
APIACEAE

Note the slender stalks that have fine gray hairs on this tall (up to 6 ft.) plant. The leaves on the stem are the largest and can reach 8 in. in length. The leaves taper to the top and are doubly compound with elongated oval to lance-shaped, toothed leaflets, which may be up to 2 in. long. The small flowers are found in slightly rounded to flat, 6-in.-wide clusters.

HABITAT: Dry, open woods; woodland edges; roadsides

REGION: Statewide

FREQUENCY: Common

LOPSEED
Phryma leptostachya
PHRYMACEAE

This 1- to 3-ft.-tall plant has large, toothed, 6-in.-oval, opposite leaves with stalks. The sparse, 1/4- to 3/4-in.-long, somewhat tubular flowers occur opposite one another in a loose spike arrangement. The flowers stick straight out and wilt over time, giving rise to the name lopseed.

HABITAT: Moist woods, woodland edges

REGION: Statewide

FREQUENCY: Common

HOARY MOUNTAIN MINT
Pycnanthemum pycnanthemoides
LAMIACEAE

Note the conspicuous whitish or grayish upper leaves around the flowers. This aromatic, 1- to 3-ft.-tall plant has oval to lance-shaped, toothed leaves with stalks that are white underneath. The small, 1/4-in.-wide, tubular flowers with purple spots on the lower lip occur in clusters at the top branches.

HABITAT: Fields, meadows, open woods, roadsides

REGION: Statewide except Bluegrass

FREQUENCY: Common

P. incanum looks the same and is distinguished by technical characteristics. It is also common statewide in the same habitat.

SLENDER MOUNTAIN MINT
Pycnanthemum tenuifolium
LAMIACEAE

This 1 1/2- to 2 1/2-ft.-tall, smooth-stemmed plant has numerous linear, sharp-pointed leaves on many short branches. The flower heads are clusters of small, 5-lobed, tubular flowers in a compact or dense arrangement at the top of the branches.

HABITAT: Fields, meadows, open woods, roadsides

REGION: Statewide except Inner Bluegrass

FREQUENCY: Common

AMERICAN GERMANDER
Teucrium canadense
LAMIACEAE

This 1- to 3-ft.-tall, primarily unbranched plant has 2- to 5-in.-long, toothed, lance-shaped, opposite leaves with a stalk. The individual 1/2- to 3/4-in.-long flowers occur in a 2- to 8-in., crowded spike. The stamens stick out through an opening between the 2 upper lips and bend downward toward the larger lower lip in each flower.

HABITAT: Moist woods, woodland edges, meadows, fields

REGION: Statewide

FREQUENCY: Common but locally abundant in the Bluegrass

ENCHANTER'S NIGHTSHADE

Circaea lutetiana

ONAGRACEAE

This 1- to 2-ft.-tall plant with a loose spike of 1/4-in.-wide flowers is not showy. Close inspection with a hand lens reveals that the individual flowers have 2 petals, 2 sepals, and 2 stamens. The wide, lance-shaped. pointed, alternate leaves with stalks are irregularly toothed.

HABITAT: Moist woods

REGION: Statewide

FREQUENCY: Common

The small enchanter's nightshade, *C. alpina,* looks similar except it is 4 to 6 in. tall. It is rare and widely scattered in the Appalachian Plateaus, the Mississippian Plateau, and the Shawnee Hills.

PALE INDIAN PLANTAIN

Cacalia atriplicifolia

ASTERACEAE

This is a large, coarse plant with a whitish-looking, smooth stem that reaches a height of up to 7 ft. The broad, roundish leaves with sharp points have a whitish appearance underneath. The flowers occur in flat-topped clusters and are not showy.

HABITAT: Open woods, woodland edges, fields

REGION: Statewide

FREQUENCY: Uncommon

GREAT INDIAN PLANTAIN

Cacalia muhlenbergii

ASTERACEAE

This large, coarse plant is similar to pale Indian plantain except that the stem is grooved and angled and does not have a whitish appearance. The large, rounded, toothed leaves attach to the plant with a short stalk and are not as sharply pointed as those of pale Indian plantain. The flowers occur in flat-topped clusters and are not showy.

HABITAT: Moist, open woods; woodland edges

REGION: Appalachian Plateaus, Knobs, Bluegrass, eastern Mississippian Plateau

FREQUENCY: Uncommon to locally common

NODDING WILD ONION

Allium cernuum

LILIACEAE

This 12- to 16-in.-tall plant has numerous 1/4- to 3/8-in.-wide, narrow, flat leaves. The 1/2-in.-wide flowers occur in a rounded cluster at the tip of the nodding flowering stalk. The flowers are not replaced with bulblets as in wild garlic.

HABITAT: Prairie patches, glades, cliff lines, limestone soils

REGION: Statewide

FREQUENCY: Common

WILD LEEK, RAMP
Allium tricoccum
LILIACEAE

In early spring, this plant has clusters of 2-in.-wide, 12-in.-long flat, smooth, lance-shaped leaves that taper at each end; these disappear before the flowers develop in midsummer. The leaves have a very strong onionlike odor when crushed. The flowering stalk is up to 6 to 18 in. tall with a roundish cluster of 1/4-in.-long, 6-segmented flowers.

HABITAT: Rich woods

REGION: Cumberland Mountains, Appalachian Plateaus, Bluegrass, Mississippian Plateau

FREQUENCY: Uncommon to locally common

FALSE BUGBANE, TASSEL-RUE
Trautvetteria caroliniensis
RANUNCULACEAE

This tall and robust plant with large, 6- to 10-in.-wide leaves reaches a height of up to 4 ft. The lobed, toothed leaves are in the shape of a human hand. The basal leaves have a stalk. The flowers are about 1/2 in. across. The petals are absent, and the numerous white stamens are very conspicuous.

HABITAT: Moist or wet woods, stream banks

REGION: Southern Appalachian Plateau and Cumberland Mountains with isolated populations in the Knobs and the Mississippian Plateau

FREQUENCY: Uncommon

BLACK SNAKEROOT, BLACK COHOSH
Cimicifuga racemosa
RANUNCULACEAE

This is a tall yet delicate plant that can reach 6 ft. tall. The sharp-pointed and toothed compound leaves are divided twice into groups of 3. The 1/2-in.-wide, white flowers lack petals, and the sepals fall off early, leaving a striking linear flower cluster up to 1 ft. long that resembles a white candle.

HABITAT: Rich woods, woodland borders

REGION: Statewide except Inner Bluegrass

FREQUENCY: Common

American bugbane or summer cohosh, *C. americana,* is similar to black snakeroot except that it flowers in late summer instead of midsummer. It is uncommon in the Appalachian Plateaus and Cumberland Mountains.

THIMBLEWEED, TALL ANEMONE
Anemone virginiana
RANUNCULACEAE

This 3-ft.-tall plant has both basal and stem leaves. The compound leaf has 3 to 5 sections, and each section has sharp points. The 1-in.-wide, solitary, greenish to white flower has 5 sepals and no petals. The flowers are found on top of a 1-ft. or longer stalk.

HABITAT: Prairie patches, glades, and open woods, preferably on limestone

REGION: Statewide

FREQUENCY: Common

The fruit after flowering resembles a thimble, giving rise to the common name.

TALL MEADOW RUE
Thalictrum pubescens
RANUNCULACEAE

This plant, which may be up to 7 ft. tall, has delicate, 3-times-compound leaves, and each leaflet is more than 1/2 in. long. It has groups of wispy, delicate, loose, globelike clusters of 1/2-in. flowers. Like other members of this family, the flowers do not have petals and the stamens are quite conspicuous.

HABITAT: Wet meadows, streamsides, floodplains

REGION: Statewide except Jackson Purchase

FREQUENCY: Common

The waxy meadow rue, *T. revolutum,* looks similar but has fine, gland-tipped hairs on the lower leaflet surface and drooping stamens. It is common statewide in prairie patches, various types of woods, and woodland borders, and adjacent to streams.

STARRY CAMPION
Silene stellata
CARYOPHYLLACEAE

This 4-ft.-tall plant has a finely haired, stiff stem and 4 whorled, 2- to 4-in.-long, pointed oval leaves. The 3/4-in.-wide flowers have 5 fringed petals. Note the greenish, bell-shaped outer flower parts.

HABITAT: Rich woods

REGION: Statewide

FREQUENCY: Uncommon

CLIMBING FALSE BUCKWHEAT

Polygonum scandens

POLYGONACEAE

This is a very large (up to 17 ft. long), twining vine that has a sharply angled and rough stem. It has 2- to 5-in.-long, somewhat heart-shaped leaves. The outer flower parts of the 1/4-in.-wide flowers are wavy or tattered, and the fruits have wings.

HABITAT: Roadsides, fencerows, woodland edges, streamsides

REGION: Statewide

FREQUENCY: Abundant

VIRGINIA KNOTWEED

Polygonum virginianum

POLYGONACEAE

This plant has 6-in.-long, oval leaves with short stalks on the lower 18 in. of the plant. The flower stalk may reach an additional 18 in. in height with widely spaced, 4-lobed, 1/8-in.-long flowers.

HABITAT: Woods

REGION: Statewide

FREQUENCY: Common

INDIAN PIPE
Monotropa uniflora
MONOTROPACEAE

This plant feeds itself entirely through interactions with root fungi; it has no green leaves and does not carry out photosynthesis. The waxy stems are usually 3 to 4 in. tall with a few small scales. Each stalk supports a single, nodding flower at the tip. After the plant has been pollinated, the flower and developing seed capsule stand straight up and do not nod.

HABITAT: Rich woods

REGION: Statewide except Bluegrass

FREQUENCY: Uncommon

FLOWERING SPURGE
Euphorbia corollata
EUPHORBIACEAE

This slender-stemmed, 1- to 3-ft. tall plant exudes a milky sap when the stem is broken. The alternate, oblong leaves taper at each end and attach directly to the plant. The 1/3-in.-wide flower heads have clusters of minute flowers with no petals or sepals inside the 5 white, petal-like appendages or bracts.

HABITAT: Prairie patches, roadsides, open woods

REGION: Statewide

FREQUENCY: Common

WHORLED MILKWORT
Polygala verticillata
POLYGALACEAE

This is an easy-to-overlook, 6- to 12-in. annual with
a 1/2- to 1-in. spike of tiny 1/8-in.-wide or smaller
flowers that have a pinkish tint and yellow center.
The lower, linear leaves attach to the plant in whorls
of 3 to 6, and the plant is branched above.

HABITAT: Prairie patches, meadows, fields, barrens

REGION: Statewide

FREQUENCY: Common

RATTLESNAKE PLANTAIN
Goodyera pubescens
ORCHIDACEAE

Note the reticulated pattern of white veins
on the dark bluish green, elongated oval
leaves on the ground. In midsummer, the
plant sends up an 8- to 16-in.-tall, leafless
flowering stalk that has a 2- to 4-in., dense column of small,
greenish white flowers.

HABITAT: Rich woods

REGION: Cumberland Mountains, Appalachian
Plateaus, Bluegrass, Mississippian Plateau, Shawnee
Hills

FREQUENCY: Common

FREQUENCY: Common

SPIKENARD
Aralia racemosa
ARALIACEAE

This is a large, multibranched, 3- to 6-ft.-tall, coarse plant. The twice-divided leaves have numerous heart-shaped segments. The tiny flowers are found in large, open clusters and are followed by purple berries.

HABITAT: Rich woods

REGION: Statewide

FREQUENCY: Common in the Cumberland Mountains and Appalachian Plateaus but uncommon to rare further west in state

WATER HEMLOCK
Cicuta maculata
APIACEAE

Note the distinctive thick stalks with purple blotches on this aquatic plant that grows up to 6 ft. tall. The leaves are 2 or 3 times divided into coarsely toothed, lance-shaped segments. The small flowers occur in slightly rounded to flat, 4-in.-wide clusters.

HABITAT: Wetlands, wet meadows, stream banks

REGION: Statewide

FREQUENCY: Common

The root is highly poisonous.

WHORLED MILKWEED
Asclepias verticillata
ASCLEPIADACEAE

This is a delicate, slender plant that may reach 20 in. tall. It has numerous narrow or linear, 2-in.-long leaves in whorls of 3 to 6. The individual 1/4-in.-wide flowers occur in a widely spaced, domelike cluster at the end of the stalk and from the upper nodes.

HABITAT: Limestone prairie patches, grasslands, fields

REGION: Statewide except Appalachian Plateaus, Cumberland Mountains

FREQUENCY: Common

WILD POTATO VINE
Ipomea pandurata
CONVOLVULACEAE

The large, 2- to 3-in., funnel-shaped flower of this plant has a purple or crimson center. This trailing or twining vine has pointed, heart-shaped leaves and can reach lengths of 10 to 15 ft.

HABITAT: Prairie patches, fencerows, roadsides, riverbanks

REGION: Statewide

FREQUENCY: Abundant

This plant is sometimes called man-of-the-earth because it has an enormous tuberlike root.

HEDGE BINDWEED
Calystegia sepium
CONVOLVULACEAE

This is a trailing vine reaching 10 ft. or more in length. The arrow-shaped leaves have pointed lobes at the back of the leaf. The 2- to 3-in.-long, funnel-shaped flower may have a pinkish tint.

HABITAT: Fields, roadsides, open woods

REGION: Statewide

FREQUENCY: Common

FOGFRUIT
Phyla lanceolata
VERBENACEAE

The stems of this plant creep along the ground with multiple erect, 15-in.-long branches. The plant has 3-in.-long, opposite, sharply toothed, lance-shaped leaves. The 1/2-in.-wide by 3/4-in.-long flower heads have many small, 4-lobed flowers with a purple center.

HABITAT: Wet fields, pond and stream banks

REGION: Statewide

FREQUENCY: Common

GIANT HYSSOP
Agastache nepetoides
LAMIACEAE

This 3- to 5-ft.-tall, coarse, multibranched plant has a flower head that resembles a candelabra. The individual 1/4-in. flowers with 4 stamens occur in a dense spike. The oval, toothed leaves are up to 6 in. long and have a stalk.

HABITAT: Woodland borders, open woods, mostly on limestone

REGION: Bluegrass, Knobs, Mississippian Plateau, Jackson Purchase

FREQUENCY: Uncommon

WHITE VERVAIN
Verbena urticifolia
VERBENACEAE

The stem of this 3- to 5-ft. annual is square or 4 angled and has fine hairs. At the end of each of the multiple branches is a spike of small, 5-lobed, tubular flowers. The plant has toothed, opposite, pointed lance-shaped leaves.

HABITAT: Open woods, woodland edges, fields, roadsides

REGION: Statewide

FREQUENCY: Common

CULVER'S ROOT
Veronicastrum virginicum
SCROPHULARIACEAE

Note the toothed, lance-shaped leaves that occur in whorls of 3 to 6 on this 2- to 6-ft. plant. At the top of the usually unbranched plant are spikelike clusters of 1/4-in.-long, tubular flowers with 2 stamens protruding from each flower.

HABITAT: Moist, open woodland edges, prairie

REGION: Statewide except Cumberland Mountains

FREQUENCY: Uncommon and rare in the Appalachian Plateaus

LIZARD'S TAIL
Saururus cernuus
SAURURACEAE

This is a 12- to 24-in.-tall aquatic plant that has up to 6-in.-long, pointed oval leaves with a heart-shaped base and a long stalk. The tiny flowers occur in a dense cluster on a spike up to 6 in. long that droops at the tip. The flowers do not have petals or sepals, but the 8 stamens are quite showy.

HABITAT: Wetlands, wet ditches and roadsides, pond edges

REGION: Statewide

FREQUENCY: Common

VIRGINIA BUTTONWEED
Diodia virginiana
RUBIACEAE

This 1- to 2-ft.-tall annual has stems that often recline and lie on the ground. It has 2-in.-long, thin, opposite, lance-shaped leaves. The 4-petaled, 3/8-in.-wide, tubular, hairy flowers arise directly at the base of the leaves.

HABITAT: Wet meadows, roadsides, ditches, stream banks

REGION: Statewide

FREQUENCY: Common

ROSE MALLOW
Hibiscus laevis
MALVACEAE

This large, 3- to 5-ft. plant has 2- to 4-in.-wide, 5-lobed flowers with a dark purplish or red tubelike structure in the center. The arrow-shaped leaves have 2 pointed lobes at the back. Flower color can vary from pure white to dark pink or rose.

HABITAT: Wetlands, swamps

REGION: Statewide

FREQUENCY: Common

Wild cotton, *H. moscheutos,* has similar large flowers, but the leaves are lance shaped and hairy underneath.

WHITE TURTLEHEAD
Chelone glabra
SCROPHULARIACEAE

This is a smooth-stemmed, 1- to 3-ft.-tall plant with opposite, toothed, pointed, lance-shaped leaves with little or no stalk. The flowers occur at the top of the plant in a short, dense, 3-in. spike. The 1- to 1 1/2-in.-long tubular flowers have 2 lips, with the upper lip forming a hood over the lower one.

HABITAT: Wet meadows, springs, seeps

REGION: Cumberland Mountains, Appalachian Plateaus, Bluegrass, Mississippian Plateau

FREQUENCY: Common in eastern Kentucky but rare in the rest of its range

The pink turtlehead, *C. obliqua,* is uncommon to rare in the Jackson Purchase and Shawnee Hills.

PENNSYLVANIA SMARTWEED
Polygonum pennsylvanicum
POLYGONACEAE

This widely branched annual can reach heights of 4 ft. or more. It has smooth, alternate, pointed, lance-shaped leaves. The 1/8-in.-long, 5-lobed flowers occur in a dense, cylindrical cluster. The leaves form a sheath around the plant stem, which is somewhat bristly or hairy.

HABITAT: Wetlands, stream banks, ponds, moist meadows and fields

REGION: Statewide

FREQUENCY: Abundant

CORNEL-LEAF ASTER

Aster infirmus

ASTERACEAE

This is a medium-sized plant, up to 2 ft. tall, with a more open appearance than the other asters. The 3/4-in. flower heads have 5 to 10 rays on top of a leafless stalk. The leaves are not toothed, have hairs on the edges and in the veins underneath, and attach directly to the plant stalk.

HABITAT: Dry, open woods

REGION: Cumberland Mountains, Appalachian Plateaus, eastern Knobs

FREQUENCY: Common

The flat-topped aster, *A. umbellatus,* is a larger plant with a similar flat-topped cluster of flowers with approximately a dozen rays in each 3/4-in.-wide flower head. It grows in moist or wet ground.

A. infirmus   *A. umbellatus*

WHITE-TOP ASTER

Aster paternus

ASTERACEAE

A key characteristic of this 1- to 2-ft.-tall plant is that the 1/2-in.-wide flower heads only have 4 or 5 rays in a flat-topped cluster. The modified leaves under the flower heads are also a creamy white color. The leaves are somewhat spoon shaped and toothed near the tip.

HABITAT: Dry, open woods; woodland edges; roadsides

REGION: Statewide except Bluegrass

FREQUENCY: Common

The narrow-leaved white-top aster, *A. solidagineus,* has linear leaves. It is also common statewide except in the Bluegrass and can be found in similar habitats.

A. solidagineus   *A. paternus*

SWEET EVERLASTING, PEARLY EVERLASTING
Gnaphalium obtusifolium
ASTERACEAE

Look for the whitish, felt- or cottonlike appearance of the stem and the underside of the leaves of this 1- to 2-ft.-tall annual. It has 1- to 2-in.-long, narrow, alternate leaves. The flowers occur at the top of the branches. There are thin, almost scalelike, whitish modified leaves under the flowers.

HABITAT: Fields, prairie patches, roadsides

REGION: Statewide except Shawnee Hills and Jackson Purchase

FREQUENCY: Common

Purple cudweed, *G. purpureum,* is similar, but it is smaller, less branched, and has a spikelike cluster of flowers.

WHITE CROWNBEARD, FROSTWEED
Verbesina virginica
ASTERACEAE

This large, coarse plant with winged stems may reach 6 ft. tall. The large, alternate leaves have winged stalks near the base of the plant, and the upper leaves attach directly to the stem. The 3/4-in.-wide flower heads are in a flat-topped cluster at the top of the plant, and each individual flower has no more than 5 notched rays. The disk flowers are also white.

HABITAT: Open, moist woods; woodland edges; fields; roadsides

REGION: Knobs, Bluegrass, Mississippian Plateau, Jackson Purchase

FREQUENCY: Common

HOG PEANUT

Amphicarpaea bracteata

FABACEAE

This is an annual or short-lived perennial twining vine that has a slender, hairy stem; the leaves have 3 distinct segments. The oval leaf segments are 1/2 to 3/4 in. across and 1 to 2 in. long. The pealike flowers are slender and occur in small dangling clusters.

HABITAT: Moist woods, woodland openings, meadows

REGION: Statewide

FREQUENCY: Abundant

SPIDER LILY

Hymenocallis caroliniana

AMARYLLIDACEAE

This aquatic plant has a large, 3- to 5-in.-wide, distinctive flower that has a rounded tubular center with 6 narrow, 3- to 4-in.-long segments. The 24- to 30-in.-tall plant has thick, linear, swordlike leaves that reach 24 in. in length.

HABITAT: Wetlands, open wet or dry woods

REGION: Mississippian Plateau, Shawnee Hills, Jackson Purchase

FREQUENCY: Locally common

SPRING LADIES' TRESSES
Spiranthes vernalis
ORCHIDACEAE

This species has linear, rigid leaves, up to 5 in. long, on the ground that persist during flowering. The flowering stalk may reach 24 in. tall and has a few small stem leaves with small, tubular flowers with a 1/4-in. lip and yellow center in a single spiral.

HABITAT: Prairie patches, meadows, old fields

REGION: Cumberland Mountains, Appalachian Plateaus, Bluegrass, Mississippian Plateau, Jackson Purchase

FREQUENCY: Uncommon but rare in the Appalachians

CLUB-SPUR ORCHID
Platanthera clavellata
ORCHIDACEAE

This 12- to 16-in.-tall species has a single oblong leaf that clasps around the base of the stem. It appears to have more leaves, but these are small bracts below the open cluster of 1/4- to 1/2-in.-long flowers. The lip of each individual flower has an elongated, 1/4- to 1/2-in. spur that projects from the back of the flower.

HABITAT: Wet woods, ditches, wet meadows

REGION: Cumberland Mountains, Appalachian Plateaus, Mississippian Plateau, Jackson Purchase

FREQUENCY: Uncommon

FRAGRANT WATER LILY

Nymphaea odorata

NYMPHACEAE

This is a showy aquatic plant that has 6- to 8-in.-wide, roundish leaf blades floating on the water; the blades are often red or purple beneath. The multiple-petaled flowers float on the water and range in size from 3 to 8 in. in diameter.

HABITAT: Shallow wetlands and ponds

REGION: Appalachian Plateaus, Bluegrass, Shawnee Hills, Jackson Purchase

FREQUENCY: Rare

HAIRY WATERLEAF

Hydrophyllum macrophyllum

HYDROPHYLLACEAE

Note the large, often bicolored, leaves with 7 to 13 sections that have toothed points at the tip. The stem of this 1- to 2-ft. plant is quite hairy. The cluster of dull, 1/2-in.-wide, somewhat open, bell-shaped flowers with protruding stamens is found at the top of a stem that occurs above the leaves.

HABITAT: Moist woods

REGION: Statewide

FREQUENCY: Uncommon

SPATTERDOCK, YELLOW POND LILY

Nuphar advena

NYMPHACEAE

Note the large, roundish, 4- to 12-in.-wide leaves that are either floating on, or raised slightly above, the water. The small, 1- to 2-in. flower heads resemble little yellow bowls and are raised just slightly above the water.

HABITAT: Shallow wetlands and ponds

REGION: Statewide

FREQUENCY: Common except in the Bluegrass and Cumberland Mountains

PRICKLY PEAR
Opuntia humifusa
CACTACEAE

This is our only native cactus. The stems are modified into greenish, flattened pads, and the leaves are modified into small spines. The large, 2- to 3-in.-wide showy flowers only last 1 day. The reddish purple fruits are edible.

HABITAT: Dry rocky cliffs, glades, road-sides, or other areas with thin soil, usually limestone

REGION: Bluegrass, Knobs, Mississippian Plateau, Shawnee Hills

FREQUENCY: Common

LANCE-LEAF COREOPSIS
Coreopsis lanceolata
ASTERACEAE

Note the 2-in.-wide flower head with 6 to 10 rays that have 4 or 5 distinctive notches at the tip of this 12- to 18-in.-tall plant. The lance-shaped, smooth-edged leaves on the upper stem do not have stalks, whereas the lower stem leaves have short stalks and may have 1 to 3 rounded lobes.

HABITAT: Dry, open woodland; roadsides

REGION: Statewide

FREQUENCY: Common

The native populations are uncommon in the Jackson Purchase, Mississippian Plateau, and southern Kentucky. The species has been widely planted by the highway department across the state.

TICKSEED
Coreopsis major
ASTERACEAE

The leaves of this plant appear to encircle the stem in a whorl. Close examination reveals that 2 leaves with 3 segments each are attached to the smooth stem. The 2-in.-wide flower heads have 6 to 9 rays with a yellow center. The plant grows 2 to 3 ft. tall.

HABITAT: Dry, open woods; woodland edges

REGION: Statewide

FREQUENCY: Common

HAWKWEED
Hieracium venosum
ASTERACEAE

Note the distinctive field characteristic of this plant: the reddish purple veins in the oval leaves at the base of the plant. The 1/2- to 1-in.-wide flower head at the end of each branch superficially resembles a dandelion.

HABITAT: Dry, open pine-oak woods; pine woods; roadsides

REGION: Statewide except Bluegrass

FREQUENCY: Most common in Appalachian Plateaus and Knobs

DWARF DANDELION
Krigia biflora
ASTERACEAE

The distinctive field characteristic of this 12- to 18-in.-tall plant is the smooth, bluish to bluish green leaves and stems. Most of the leaves are at the

base of the plant. The few leaves clasp around the stem. At the end of each stem is a 1- to 1 1/2-in.-wide dandelion-like flower head.

HABITAT: Open woods, fields, roadsides

REGION: Statewide except Bluegrass

FREQUENCY: Common

BLACK-EYED SUSAN
Rudbeckia hirta
ASTERACEAE

This is a very hairy, 1- to 3-ft. annual with alternate leaves that are soft and fuzzy. The leaves do not have lobes, and they are longer than wide. The large, 2- to 3-in. flower heads have 10 to 20 rays with a dark brown center.

HABITAT: Roadsides, fields, prairie patches

REGION: Statewide

FREQUENCY: Abundant

GRAY-HEADED CONEFLOWER
Ratibida pinnata
ASTERACEAE

This plant has a distinctive flower head with 5 to 10, 3-in.-long rays that droop from a central conelike column. The cone is gray but turns brown with age. The plant, which reaches a height of up to 4 ft., is hairy with leaves that have 3 to 7 deeply cut segments.

HABITAT: Prairie patches, fields, roadsides

REGION: Appalachian Plateaus, Bluegrass, Mississippian Plateau

FREQUENCY: Common

ST. ANDREW'S CROSS
Hypericum hypericoides
CLUSIACEAE

This low-growing, 4- to 8-in.-tall plant has 1-in.-long, oval leaves that taper toward the back and form a short stalk. This multibranched plant looks like a cluster of plants because of the branches and reclining stems. The 1/2-in.-wide, 1-in.-long flowers have 4 petals that form a cross.

HABITAT: Sandy, open woods; sandstone outcrops; fields; meadows

REGION: Statewide

FREQUENCY: Common except uncommon in Bluegrass, Mississippian Plateau, and Jackson Purchase

A related species, St. Peter's wort, *H. stans,* is a rare species that is similar but has shorter, more rounded leaves and wider petals.

ROUGH-FRUITED ST. JOHN'S WORT
Hypericum sphaerocarpum
CLUSIACEAE

This 1- to 2-foot-tall, 4-angle-stemmed plant is somewhat woody at the base and has oblong, opposite leaves. The 5-lobed, 1/2- to 5/8-in.-wide flowers do not have black spots on them.

HABITAT: Glades; dry, rocky ledges; cliffs; stream banks

REGION: Bluegrass, Mississippian Plateau, Appalachian Plateaus

FREQUENCY: Uncommon

The common St. John's wort, *H. perforatum,* is an introduced species that is similar in appearance except the flowers have black dots at the edge of the petals.

STRAGGLING ST. JOHN'S WORT
Hypericum dolabriforme
CLUSIACEAE

The 1-in.-wide, showy, 5-lobed flowers are large for the size of this small, 8- to 15-in.-tall plant. The stems are somewhat woody at the base, and the opposite leaves are widely linear to lance shaped.

HABITAT: Limestone glades, rocky soil

REGION: Knobs, Bluegrass, Mississippian Plateau

FREQUENCY: Uncommon, but where found, it is common

FRINGED LOOSESTRIFE
Lysimachia ciliata
PRIMULACEAE

Note the 1-in.-wide, 5-lobed, downward-hanging flowers with a single point or fringe at the tip. The flowers arise at the base of the broad, opposite, lance-shaped leaves supported by a hairy stalk on this 1- to 3-ft.-tall plant.

HABITAT: Wet meadows, forests, roadsides, stream banks

REGION: Statewide except rare in the Appalachian Plateaus and Cumberland Mountains

FREQUENCY: Uncommon to locally common

LANCE-LEAVED LOOSESTRIFE
Lysimachia lanceolata
PRIMULACEAE

The long, linear to lance-shaped leaves of this 1- to 2-ft.-tall plant taper at both ends but do not have a stalk. The 5-lobed, 3/4-in.-wide flowers hang downward and have sharp points at the tips of the petals. The flowers arise at the base of the opposite leaves.

HABITAT: Dry, open woods; grasslands; wet meadows

REGION: Statewide

FREQUENCY: Common

WHORLED LOOSESTRIFE
Lysimachia quadrifolia
PRIMULACEAE

Note the 4 lance-shaped leaves without stalks that occur in a whorl on this 1 1/2- to 2 1/2-ft.-tall, smooth-stemmed plant. The 1/2-in.-wide, 5-petaled, star-shaped flowers have a red center and occur at the end of long stalks that arise at the base of the leaves.

HABITAT: Dry to moist open woods

REGION: Statewide except Jackson Purchase

FREQUENCY: Common

RATTLEBOX
Ludwigia alternifolia
ONAGRACEAE

This is a 2- to 3-ft., smooth-stemmed plant with linear to somewhat lance-shaped, alternate leaves, up to 4-in. long, with short stalks. The 1/2- to 3/4-in. flowers occur by themselves at the base of the leaf and have 4 petals, which drop off easily, revealing a square-shaped capsule.

HABITAT: Wet soils in meadows, roadsides, and open woods

REGION: Statewide

FREQUENCY: Common

SUNDROPS
Oenothera tetragona
ONAGRACEAE

This is a highly variable 1 1/2- to 2 1/2-ft. species that usually has smooth and slender stems with smooth-edged, lance-shaped leaves. The delicate 1- to 2-in.-wide, 4-petaled flowers have a cross-shaped stigma. The flowers open during the day, in contrast to those of other members of this group, which primarily open in the morning and evening.

HABITAT: Moist wooded slopes, stream banks, woodland edges, grasslands, open woods

REGION: Statewide

FREQUENCY: Uncommon

Southern sundrops, *O. fruticosa,* an uncommon species or subspecies of sundrops, is found in grasslands, meadows, fields, and open woods statewide. It is similar and usually has very thin, narrow leaves.

VIRGINIA YELLOW FLAX
Linum virginianum
LINACEAE

This 12- to 18-in., slender-stemmed plant has branches at the top with alternating lance-shaped to oblong leaves that taper at each end. The 1/3-in.-wide, 5-petaled flowers occur in a widely spaced, flat-topped cluster at the end of the branches.

HABITAT: Dry or moist open woods, meadows, stream banks

REGION: Statewide except Bluegrass and Jackson Purchase

FREQUENCY: Common

COMMON YELLOW FLAX
Linum medium
LINACEAE

This is a slender-stemmed, 1- to 2-ft.-tall plant with stiff, erect branches. The 1/2-in.-wide, 5-petaled flowers occur in a widely spaced and open, flat-topped cluster. The narrow, lance-shaped leaves oppose each other and attach directly to the plant.

HABITAT: Prairie patches, barrens, disturbed soil

REGION: Knobs, Mississippian Plateau, Jackson Purchase

FREQUENCY: Common

PENCIL FLOWER
Stylosanthes biflora
FABACEAE

This is a short, 1- to 1 1/2-ft.-tall, wiry plant with bristle-tipped leaves that have 3, 1-in.-long segments. The small, 3/8-in.-wide flowers are found at the end of the stems and have an almost circular appearance.

HABITAT: Prairie patches, roadsides, dry fields

REGION: Statewide except Bluegrass

FREQUENCY: Common

DOWNY FALSE FOXGLOVE
Aureolaria virginica
SCROPHULARIACEAE

This 4-ft.-tall, hairy, whitish-stemmed plant is a parasite on the roots of oak trees. The lower lance-shaped to oval leaves have 1 or 2 lobes, whereas the upper leaves are unlobed and get smaller as they ascend the stem. The 1 1/2- to 2-in.-long, tubular flowers have 5 lobes.

HABITAT: Dry, open woods

REGION: Western Appalachian Plateaus, Knobs, Mississippian Plateau, eastern Shawnee Hills

FREQUENCY: Common

The Appalachian false foxglove, *A. laevigata,* has a smooth stem and the leaves do not have lobes. It is common in dry, rocky woods in the Cumberland Plateau, Appalachian Plateaus, Knobs, and Mississippian Plateau. The smooth false foxglove, *A. flava,* has more deeply lobed, smoother leaves. It is common in dry, open woods in the Mississippian Plateau, Knobs, and Jackson Purchase. Two other species in this genus, the fernleaf false foxglove, *A. pectinata,* and the annual false foxglove, *A. pedicularia,* are rare.

YELLOW CROWNBEARD
Verbesina occidentalis
ASTERACEAE

The 2-in. flower heads with 8 to 15 rays look like a sunflower, but this species can be easily identified by the 4 wings on the hairy stem. The toothed leaves are longer than wide and rough to the touch.

HABITAT: Moist, open woods; roadsides; woodland edges

REGION: Statewide except Shawnee Hills and Jackson Purchase

FREQUENCY: Common

YELLOW JEWELWEED, PALE JEWELWEED

Impatiens pallida

BALSAMINACEAE

This annual, which can reach 5 ft. tall, has a slender, succulent or watery, smooth stem and oval, alternate, toothed leaves. The "windsock"-like flowers with a tail hang from delicate stems. These flowers have 3 sepals, one of which forms the "windsock tunnel," and 3 petals: 1 upper petal and 1 on each side; these 2 are joined and appear to be a single 2-lobed petal.

HABITAT: Stream banks, seeps, springs, wet soils, moist woods

REGION: Statewide

FREQUENCY: Common

PURPLE-HEADED SNEEZEWEED

Helenium flexuosum

ASTERACEAE

This 1- to 2-ft. plant has winged stems with leaves that are spoon shaped, toothed, and attached to the plant with a winged stalk. The 1- to 2-in.-wide flower heads have 10 to 18 drooping, wedge-shaped, 3-lobed rays with a dark brown to purplish center cone.

HABITAT: Moist fields, meadows, roadsides

REGION: Statewide

FREQUENCY: Common

SOUTHERN AGRIMONY
Agrimonia parviflora
ROSACEAE

This is the largest of this group of plants, attaining 4 to 6 ft. in height. It also has leaves with the largest number of segments, 9 to 17. The lance-shaped leaf segments are toothed and hairy underneath. The 1/4-in.-wide, 5-petaled flower occurs in a wandlike spike. The fruits at the top of the spike have hooked and curved bristles.

HABITAT: Wet meadows, open woods

REGION: Statewide

FREQUENCY: Common

The other two common agrimony species, the woodland agrimony, *A. rostellata*, and downy agrimony, *A. pubescens*, have only 5 to 7 leaflets and are much smaller woodland plants, growing to only 2 ft. Woodland agrimony has a smooth stem, whereas downy agrimony has a hairy stem.

PARTRIDGE PEA
Cassia fasciculata
FABACEAE

This is an open, multibranched, 1- to 2-ft. annual that has 1- to 2-in. leaves with 10 to 15 narrow or oblong segments per leaf. The 5-petaled, 1- to 1 1/2-in.-wide flowers arise at the base of the leaf, and the petals are unequal in size. The lower petals are usually larger, and some have a red blotch. Note that there are both yellow and purple anthers in the center of the flower.

HABITAT: Prairie patches, grasslands, fields, roadsides

REGION: Statewide

FREQUENCY: Abundant

WILD SENNA
Cassia marilandica
FABACEAE

This large, coarse plant reaches a height of
5 ft. or more. The alternate leaves have 6 to
10 lance-shaped to pointed oblong segments.
The flowers occur in a loose cluster at the base
of a leaf. Each 3/4-in.-wide flower has 5 petals
that are about equal in size. The stamens are
unequal in length, and the lower ones curve
downward and then back up. The leaves are
sensitive to the touch.

HABITAT: Open, moist woods; fields;
meadows; roadsides

REGION: Statewide

FREQUENCY: Common

Another wild senna, *C. hebecarpa,* is a similar species that is uncommon and has more
flowers and a dome-shaped gland on the leaf stem.

SENSITIVE PLANT
Cassia nictitans
FABACEAE

The leaves of this
annual look similar to
those of the partridge
pea, but the
individual leaf
segments usually do
not exceed 1/2 in. in
length. The small,
1/4-in.-wide flowers have 5 petals, and the lower petal is about twice as large as the
others. The leaves are sensitive to the touch.

HABITAT: Prairie patches, grasslands, meadows, disturbed soil

REGION: Statewide

FREQUENCY: Common

AMERICAN LOTUS
Nelumbo lutea
NELUMBONACEAE

Note the large, round to saucer-shaped leaves that may reach up to 3 ft. in diameter. Some leaves may float, while others are held 1 to 2 ft. above the water. The pale yellow flowers may reach up to 12 in. in diameter and are held above the water on stems.

HABITAT: Shallow wetlands and ponds

REGION: Mississippian Plateau, Shawnee Hills, Jackson Purchase

FREQUENCY: Uncommon but locally abundant

WILD GOLDENGLOW
Rudbeckia laciniata
ASTERACEAE

There are numerous branches on this tall (up to 10 ft.), smooth plant. Most leaves have 3 to 7 sharp, finely haired segments that attach to the plant with a stalk. The 2- to 4-in.-wide flower heads have 6 to 10 drooping rays with a greenish or grayish yellow center that gets longer as the flower head ages.

HABITAT: Moist woods, woodland edges

REGION: Statewide

FREQUENCY: Common

WHORLED ROSINWEED
Silphium trifoliatum
ASTERACEAE

The long, narrow, pointed leaves on this plant, which may reach 7 ft. tall, are attached to the smooth stem in whorls of 3 or 4 with short stalks. The leaves are usually rough to the touch. The 2-in. flower heads have 15 to 20 rays.

HABITAT: Prairie patches, roadsides, open woods

REGION: Statewide

FREQUENCY: Common

The rosinweed, *S. integrifolium,* has similar flower heads, but the plant is hairy with opposite leaves.

MULLEIN FOXGLOVE
Dasistoma macrophylla
SCROPHULARIACEAE

This is a large, 3- to 5-ft., slightly hairy, multiple-branched plant with numerous large, deeply cut, and irregularly lobed lower leaves. The upper leaves are broadly lance-shaped and get smaller as they go up the stem. The 1/2- to 3/4-in.-long flowers have 5 lobes with a hairy center.

HABITAT: Dry, open woods

REGION: Bluegrass, Mississippian Plateau, Jackson Purchase

FREQUENCY: Common

NARROW-LEAVED CATTAIL
Typha angustifolia
Typhaceae

This aquatic species is similar to the common cattail but smaller. The stem is about 3 ft. tall with 1/2-in.-wide leaves. The male and female parts of the flower spike are not connected and are separated by 1 to 3 inches of bare stem.

HABITAT: Shallow ponds, marshes

REGION: Statewide in scattered locations

FREQUENCY: Uncommon

COMMON CATTAIL
Typha latifolia
Typhaceae

This is a stiff, tall aquatic plant with leaves that are 3 ft. or longer leaves and form a sheath at the base of the stalk. The 1-in.-wide leaves are flat and linear. The 3- to 6-ft. stem is topped by a cluster of tiny flowers forming a dense, brown spike. The lower, thicker portion of the spike contains the female flowers; the male flowers form a smaller cluster that tops the spike in early summer. The male and female parts of the flower spike are connected in this species.

HABITAT: Wet ditches, shallow ponds

REGION: Statewide

FREQUENCY: Abundant

INFLATED BLADDERWORT
Utricularia inflata
LENTIBULARIACEAE

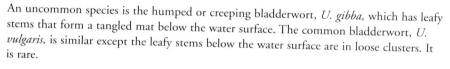

This delicate water plant has inflated stalks that serve as a float. The leaves are arranged in a whorl with the flowering stem arising from the center. The 2/3-in.-wide flowers rise 1 to 3 in. above the water.

HABITAT: Shallow-water wetlands, ponds

REGION: Statewide

FREQUENCY: Rare

An uncommon species is the humped or creeping bladderwort, *U. gibba,* which has leafy stems that form a tangled mat below the water surface. The common bladderwort, *U. vulgaris,* is similar except the leafy stems below the water surface are in loose clusters. It is rare.

EVENING PRIMROSE
Oenothera biennis
ONAGRACEAE

This usually unbranched plant with a reddish-tinted stem, except at the top, reaches 6 ft. tall. It has many alternate, lance-shaped, curvy- or wavy-edged leaves without a stalk. The 1-in.-wide flower has 4 somewhat notched lobes and a cross-shaped stigma. The flowers open at twilight and close during the heat of the day.

HABITAT: Roadsides, fields, disturbed sites

REGION: Statewide

FREQUENCY: Abundant

TALL TICKSEED
Coreopsis tripteris
ASTERACEAE

This is a large yet delicate plant reaching a height of 6 to 9 ft. This plant has many smooth branches and stems and 1 1/4- to 1 3/4-in.-wide flower heads with 6 to 10 rays. The lower leaves are smooth and have a short stalk. The leaves typically have 3 linear segments that roughly resemble a turkey's foot.

HABITAT: Prairie patches, open woods, woodland edges, roadsides, stream banks

REGION: Statewide except Bluegrass

FREQUENCY: Common

HAIRY HAWKWEED
Hieracium gronovii
ASTERACEAE

Most of the leaves of this 1- to 3-ft. plant are at the base and lower stem. They are elongated, spoon-shaped, and quite hairy. The lower leaves do not have stalks, while the leaves at the base of the plant have stalks. The 1/2-in.-wide flower heads are supported on a long stem with an open, elongated cluster of flowers, typically less than 40 per plant.

HABITAT: Fields, road-sides, open woods

REGION: Statewide

FREQUENCY: Common

YELLOW PASSIONFLOWER
Passiflora lutea
PASSIFLORACEAE

This trailing vine reaches 9 ft. in length but is easy to overlook because the 1-in.-wide flowers are somewhat inconspicuous and often hide near or under the 1- to 3-in.-long leaves. Each leaf has 3 lobes that are wider than long and roughly triangular in shape. They stand apart from each other at right angles.

HABITAT: Moist woodland edges, thickets

REGION: Statewide

FREQUENCY: Common

YELLOW LEAFCUP, BEAR'S FOOT
Polymnia uvedalia
ASTERACEAE

This large, coarse plant may reach up to 5 to 7 ft. tall. It has large, 12-in.-wide, lobed, triangular leaves with sharp points. They attach to the plant with a winged stalk and are usually hairy. The 1 1/2-in.-wide flower heads are often found in a small cluster. They have 8 to 11 notched rays with a yellow center.

HABITAT: Moist woods, woodland edges, roadsides

REGION: Statewide

FREQUENCY: Common

ORANGE CONEFLOWER
Rudbeckia fulgida
ASTERACEAE

This is a highly variable species with many varieties. The plant grows from 1 to 3 ft. tall and usually is sparingly branched. The flower heads are 1 to 1 1/2 in. wide with 8 to 15 short, notched rays. The leaves are only slightly hairy and elongated oval in shape and attach to the plant with long stalks.

HABITAT: Prairie patches, fields, roadsides

REGION: Mississippian Plateau, Knobs, Appalachian Plateaus

FREQUENCY: Common

This plant is similar to the black-eyed Susan, but look at the Y-shaped styles of the disk flowers. They are short and blunt in the orange coneflower and slender and pointed in the black-eyed Susan.

EARLY GOLDENROD
Solidago juncea
ASTERACEAE

The leaves at the base of the plant are large, ranging from 7 to 14 in. in length. The leaves taper to a thin stalk. The stem and leaves of this 2- to 4-ft. plant are smooth. The individual flowers have 7 to 13 rays.

HABITAT: Roadsides, open woods, prairie patches

REGION: Statewide

FREQUENCY: Uncommon to locally common

YELLOW WINGSTEM, YELLOW IRONWEED

Verbesina alternifolia

ASTERACEAE

This large, coarse plant reaches 8 ft. or more in height. The leaves are longer than

wide and taper at the base to a stalk, proceeding down the stem to form a wing along each side of the stem. The individual flower heads have 2 to 8 unequal-length rays in an open cluster.

HABITAT: Moist, open woods; meadows; roadsides; fields

REGION: Statewide

FREQUENCY: Abundant

NORTHERN HORSE BALM

Collinsonia canadensis

LAMIACEAE

Note the open, somewhat pyramid-shaped cluster of 1/2-in.-long, tubular flowers with 2 stamens and a fringed lower lip. This is a large, 2- to 3-ft.-tall plant with 6- to 8-in., toothed, oval leaves with a stalk.

HABITAT: Rich woods

REGION: Statewide

FREQUENCY: Common except in Jackson Purchase and Shawnee Hills where it is rare

SHOWY PRIMROSE
Oenothera speciosa
ONAGRACEAE

This is the easiest evening primrose to identify because it has 2- to 3-in.-wide, 4-petaled pink flowers with a yellow center. The 1- to 3-in.-long, narrow oval to linear leaves are gently toothed or lobed and often tinted with pink. The flower buds nod.

HABITAT: Roadsides, prairie patches

REGION: Jackson Purchase, Mississippian Plateau, Bluegrass

FREQUENCY: Uncommon

This species has been widely planted as a horticultural species across the state and can be found along roadsides in great abundance in some locations across the state.

INDIAN PINK
Spigelia marilandica
LOGANIACEAE

This 12- to 28-in.-tall plant with alternate, 2- to 4-in.-long, lance-shaped leaves has an unmistakable flower. The 1 1/2- to 2-in. tubular flowers have deep red petals on the outer surface that become green to yellow on the inner side with widely spreading yellowish to greenish tips that look like a star.

HABITAT: Moist woods and thickets

REGION: Mississippian Plateau, Shawnee Hills, Jackson Purchase

FREQUENCY: Uncommon

LEATHER VASE VINE
Clematis viorna
RANUNCULACEAE

This semiwoody vine has 2 to 4 leaflets that are green underneath. The red to purplish sepals form an interesting flower that resembles a leathery, upside-down urn. The feathery style in the center of the flower is a useful identification characteristic.

HABITAT: Rich woods, thickets, woodland borders

REGION: Statewide except Jackson Purchase and Shawnee Hills

FREQUENCY: Common

The leaves of the leather flower, *C. glaucophylla,* are somewhat powdery and whitish underneath. It is rare and found in southern Kentucky in river cobblebar habitats. The leaves of the pale leather flower, *C. versicolor,* are similar to the *C. glaucophylla,* and each leaf has 4 leaflets. It is uncommon and found on limestone rocky woods and woodland edges in the Mississippian Plateau. Bluebill leather flower, *C. pitcheri,* is similar to the other species except it has 3 to 5 leaflets and the style is hairy except at the end, where it is smooth. It is uncommon and found in the Jackson Purchase, Shawnee Hills, and Mississippian Plateau.

ROUNDLEAF CATCHFLY
Silene rotundifolia
CARYOPHYLLACEAE

This plant has quite showy flowers. It is often seen creeping along the ground at the base of sandstone cliffs and natural arches where it can reach heights of up to 3 ft. The 3- to 4-in., oval to nearly round, opposite leaves are attached directly to the slightly hairy stems, which are sticky to the touch and branch often. The 1 1/2- to 2-in.-wide flowers have deeply notched petals.

HABITAT: Sandstone cliffs but occasionally in limestone rockhouses

REGION: Appalachian Plateaus, Cumberland Mountains

FREQUENCY: Common but rare in Shawnee Hills and Mississippian Plateau

WIDOW'S CROSS, PINK STONECROP
Sedum pulchellum
CRASSULACEAE

This 4- to 12-in.-tall annual has fleshy, needlelike leaves that are up to 1 in. long. The flowers occur in flat-topped clusters on 4 to 7 forked branches. The 3/8-in.-wide, star-shaped flowers have 5 petals and conspicuous dark anthers. This plant is usually found in large colonies.

HABITAT: Limestone glades, cliff edges, exposed limestone rock, roadsides

REGION: Bluegrass, Mississippian Plateau

FREQUENCY: Locally abundant

CAROLINA THISTLE
Cirsium carolinianum
ASTERACEAE

This 1- to 3-ft.-tall biennial is mostly smooth; its leaves are longer than wide with a prickly edge and a whitish color underneath. The modified leaves under the 3/4-in.-wide flower heads are spiny. This is a more delicate plant than the exotic musk thistle, *C. nutans.*

HABITAT: Sandy forest openings, woodland edges, roadsides

REGION: Appalachian Plateaus, Mississippian Plateau, Shawnee Hills

FREQUENCY: Uncommon to rare

BUTTERFLY PEA
Clitoria mariana
FABACEAE

This is a short, 1- to 3-ft. twining vine with 3 oval leaflets. A showy, open, pealike flower, up to 2 in. long, on a short stem arises at the base of the leaf.

HABITAT: Open, dry oak and pine woods

REGION: Statewide except Bluegrass

FREQUENCY: Uncommon

COMMON MILKWEED
Asclepias syriaca
ASCLEPIADACEAE

This tall, coarse plant has a thick, finely haired stem that can reach up to 5 ft. tall and exudes a milky sap when broken. It has elongated oval, alternate leaves that are up to 6 in. long. The 1/2-in.-wide flowers occur in a globe- or ball-shaped cluster and may be found at the end of the stem and in the axils of the upper leaves. The flower clusters are quite fragrant.

HABITAT: Fields and roadsides

REGION: Statewide

FREQUENCY: Abundant

The purple milkweed, *A. purpurascens,* looks similar except it is a smaller, less coarse plant with flowers that are deeper pink to reddish purple. It is an uncommon species that occurs statewide in grasslands and along woodland edges.

BUTTERFLY WEED
Asclepias tuberosa
ASCLEPIADACEAE

This is an easy species to identify because it has clusters of showy, 1/2-in.-wide, bright orange flowers that occur in dense clusters from the bases of stem branches. It has a rough, hairy, and leafy stem that can reach up to 28 in. tall. The leaves range to 4 in. in length and are narrow, lance or elongated oval in shape.

HABITAT: Fields, grasslands, roadsides

REGION: Statewide

FREQUENCY: Abundant

SMOOTH PHLOX
Phlox glaberrima
POLEMONIACEAE

This showy plant has a spectacular, dome-shaped, dense cluster of 5/8- to 3/4-in.-wide flowers on a smooth-stemmed plant that is less than 2 ft. tall. It has smooth-edged, linear to lance-shaped leaves.

HABITAT: Wet roadsides, open woods, stream banks

REGION: Statewide

FREQUENCY: Common

GLADE CONEFLOWER
Echinacea simulata
ASTERACEAE

This, our most common coneflower, is 2 to 3 ft. tall at flowering; the leaves are found primarily at the base of the plant. The leaves and stem are rough and hairy to the touch. The leaves look like elongated spoons with veins running the length of the leaf. The large, showy flower heads have drooping, 1- to 3-in.-long rays with a rust-colored center disk. The yellow pollen is the diagnostic field characteristic for this species.

HABITAT: Prairie patches, glades, roadsides

REGION: Knobs, Bluegrass, Mississippian Plateau, Shawnee Hills

FREQUENCY: Common

Narrow-leaved coneflower, *E. pallida,* looks essentially the same and grows in the same habitat, but it is not as common as the glade coneflower. The primary difference between these two species is pollen color. Narrow-leaf coneflower has white pollen.

SPREADING POGONIA
Cleistes divaricata
ORCHIDACEAE

The single, 12- to 24-in.-tall, smooth flowering stem bears a single, linear, 2- to 3-in.-long, clasping leaf. A smaller, erect bract covers the base of the single flower stem. All the petals are joined to form a 2-in.-long tubular flower. The 2 linear, widely spread purplish brown sepals are even longer.

HABITAT: Dry, open woods; prairie patches

REGION: Cumberland Mountains, Appalachian Plateaus

FREQUENCY: Uncommon to rare

WOOD LILY

Lilium
philadelphicum

LILIACEAE

This might very well be
our rarest native lily and
one of the showiest. It has
a 30-in.-tall flowering
stem with 4-in.-long,
lance-shaped leaves. The

upper leaves occur in whorls. The large flowers, up to 4 in. wide, occur at the top
of the stem, usually singly. The 6 purple-spotted segments are widely separated at
the base and are upright, not drooping.

HABITAT: Woodland edges and openings

REGION: Appalachian Plateaus

FREQUENCY: Rare

GRASS PINK

Calopogon tuberosus

ORCHIDACEAE

This 12- to 24-in.-tall plant has a single
grasslike leaf that clasps the stem near the base.
The 1-in.-wide, roughly triangular-shaped
flowers occur in loose, open clusters at the top
of the stem. Individual flowers are unique in
that the yellow-bearded lip is held upright
instead of hanging down as in our other native
orchids.

HABITAT: Wet soil on open, sunny ridge tops

REGION: Cumberland Mountains, Appalachian
Plateaus

FREQUENCY: Rare

Although rare and known from very few locations,
colonies of this plant infrequently appear and
disappear as conditions permit.

ROSE PINK, MEADOW PINK
Sabatia angularis
GENTIANACEAE

Note the 4-angled stem with wings on this 12- to 24-in.-tall annual with opposite branches. It has smooth-edged, opposite, pointed-oval leaves. The 5-lobed, 1-in.-wide flowers smell good and have a star-shaped center with a yellowish or greenish border.

HABITAT: Prairie patches, meadows, roadsides

REGION: Statewide

FREQUENCY: Common

WINGED LOOSESTRIFE
Lythrum alatum
LYTHRACEAE

This is a 1 1/2- to 3-ft.-tall, multibranched plant with a 4-angled stem. The lower, lance-shaped leaves are opposite, whereas, the upper leaves are alternate. The 1/2-in.-wide flowers have 4 to 6 petals, and each flower arises at the base of a leaf.

HABITAT: Wet grasslands, meadows, stream banks

REGION: Western Knobs, Mississippian Plateau, Shawnee Hills, Jackson Purchase

FREQUENCY: Uncommon

This native species should not be confused with the exotic invasive purple loosestrife, *L. salicaria*, which is a taller, more robust species that has linear or lance-shaped leaves that occur in whorls of 3.

WILD BEAN
Phaseolus polystachios
FABACEAE

This twining vine can range from 4 to 15 ft. long. Each leaf has 3 large, pointed-oval segments; the side segments are unequal, and the terminal segment is broader. The flowers occur in an open-spike arrangement on a stem that arises at the base of the leaf. The 3/8-in.-wide flowers have a central, linelike ridge.

HABITAT: Moist woods

REGION: Statewide but more common in the east

FREQUENCY: Uncommon

The milk pea, *Galactia volubilis,* is a similar twining and climbing plant. It has 1 to 3, 1/3-in. flowers at the base of each hairy leaf that attach to the plant with a stalk. Each leaf has 3 oblong and rounded-tip, 2-in.-long segments. It is common statewide except in the Bluegrass and Jackson Purchase.

Galactia volubilis

ORANGE JEWELWEED
Impatiens capensis
BALSAMINACEAE

This annual can reach 5 ft. tall and has a slender, succulent or watery and smooth stem with oval, toothed, alternate leaves. The "windsock"-like flowers with a tail hang from delicate stems. These flowers have 3 sepals, one of which forms the "windsock tunnel," and 3 petals: 1 upper petal and 1 on each side; these 2 are joined and appear to be a single 2-lobed petal.

HABITAT: Stream banks, seeps, springs, wet or moist soils, roadsides, moist woods

REGION: Statewide

FREQUENCY: Abundant

This plant is also called the touch-me-not, because the seedpods burst with a startling suddenness when touched.

SENSITIVE BRIER
Schrankia microphylla
FABACEAE

This 3- to 7-ft. vine trails close to the ground and has hooked or cat-claw-like prickles on the stem. The alternate leaves have numerous small segments that close when touched. A short stalk attaches the globe-shaped, 1/2- to 5/8-in.-wide flower heads, which look like Koosh balls, on this spiny plant.

HABITAT: Dry, open fields; woodland edges; gravel bars

REGION: Southern Cumberland Plateau, Mississippian Plateau

FREQUENCY: Uncommon

SWAMP MILKWEED
Asclepias incarnata
ASCLEPIADACEAE

This 5-ft.-tall plant has 3- to 6-in.-long, narrow, lance-shaped leaves with rounded or nearly heart-shaped bases. The numerous 1/2-in.-wide, blunt-nosed, rocketlike flowers have 5, 1/4-in.-long petals that occur in a domelike cluster. Flower color can vary from almost pure white to deep rose or red.

HABITAT: Wet meadows, ditches, pond and stream edges

REGION: Statewide except Appalachian Plateaus and Cumberland Mountains

FREQUENCY: Common

Another purple-flowered milkweed that occurs in Kentucky is the clasping milkweed, *A. amplexicaulis.* It has alternate, wavy-edged, 4-in.-long, oval leaves that clasp the stem. It flowers in early summer. It is uncommon in the Mississippian Plateau and Jackson Purchase.

MEADOW PHLOX
Phlox maculata
POLEMONIACEAE

This 2- to 3-ft. plant usually has a purple-spotted or -streaked stem with opposite, lance-shaped leaves. The 1/2- to 5/8-in.-wide, 5-lobed flowers occur in a dense cluster that is somewhat cylindrical in shape and taller than it is wide.

HABITAT: Wet meadows, stream banks, fields

REGION: Statewide except Jackson Purchase

FREQUENCY: Common

Fall phlox, *P. paniculata,* is a similar species that is common statewide and occurs along stream banks and forests associated with streams. This species does not have a spotted stem, and the leaves are narrower and have numerous veins. This is the common garden phlox that occurs in a multitude of colors. The broadleaf phlox, *P. amplifolia,* is similar and grows in similar habitats, but the leaves are wider and hairier. It is uncommon in the Appalachian Plateaus, Knobs, Bluegrass, and Mississippian Plateau.

P. maculata

P. paniculata

P. amplifolia

PURPLE CONEFLOWER
Echinacea purpurea
ASTERACEAE

Note the large, showy, 3- to 4-in.-diameter flower heads with drooping rays that are 1 to 3 in. long. The 1-in.-wide center dome is a bright rust color. The plant has large oval, hairy, coarsely toothed, alternate leaves and can grow to 4 ft. tall.

HABITAT: Prairie patches, woods openings, roadsides with limestone soils

REGION: Appalachian Plateaus, Knobs, Bluegrass, Mississippian Plateau, Eastern Shawnee Hills

FREQUENCY: Uncommon to rare

NAKED-FLOWERED TICK-TREFOIL
Desmodium nudiflorum
FABACEAE

This plant has large, crowded leaves with 3 pointed oval segments that appear whorled at the base of the plant. The flowers occur on a 1- to 3-ft., leafless stalk that arises separately from the plant.

HABITAT: Woods

REGION: Statewide

FREQUENCY: Common

The pointed-leaved tick-trefoil, *D. glutinosum,* is similar but has sharply pointed leaf segments, and the leaves and flowers are on the same stem.

VIRGINIA LESPEDEZA
Lespedeza virginica
FABACEAE

This medium-sized, linear-looking plant may
have a few arching branches. The 1/4-in.-
wide by 1-in.-long linear leaves have long
stalks and are crowded around the stem. The
flowers occur in dense clusters at the top of
the plant.

HABITAT: Prairie patches, roadsides

REGION: Statewide

FREQUENCY: Common

Wandlike lespedeza, *L. intermedia,* is a similar
species with purple flowers that can be found in
dry, open, upland woods and fields statewide
except the Bluegrass. The leaves of this species are more oblong. A similar species with white
flowers is the round-headed bush clover, *L. capitata,* which is found primarily in the
Mississippian Plateau; it is uncommon to rare.

TRAILING BUSH CLOVER
Lespedeza procumbens
FABACEAE

This creeping plant has a
hairy stem with flowering
branches that stick up
from the base of the leaves.
Each leaf has 3, 1/2-in.-
long, oval segments. The
small cluster of flowers has
from 3 to 12, 1/3-in.-long,
pealike flowers.

HABITAT: Dry, open woods; fields

REGION: Statewide

FREQUENCY: Common

Creeping bush clover, *L. repens,* looks similar except it has smooth stems.

CANADA LILY
Lilium canadense
LILIACEAE

This is our most common native lily. It has a 2- to 5-ft.-tall flowering stem with 6-in.-long, lance-shaped leaves. The lower leaves are alternate, whereas the upper leaves are in whorls of 4 or more. The large, 3-in.-wide, gracefully arching flowers have 6 purple-spotted segments that recurve at the end; the flowers occur singly or in clusters.

HABITAT: Open woods, woodland edges

REGION: Cumberland Mountains, Appalachian Plateaus

FREQUENCY: Uncommon

MICHIGAN LILY
Lilium michiganense
LILIACEAE

The flowers look similar to both the Turk's cap lily and the Canada lily, but the segments are more recurved than in the Canada lily and not as recurved as in the Turk's cap. The 5 to 20 lance-shaped, whorled leaves of this species are rough along the margins. This is considered by some authors to be a variety of the Turk's cap lily.

HABITAT: Prairie patches, open woods

REGION: Bluegrass, Mississippian Plateau

FREQUENCY: Rare

TURK'S CAP LILY
Lilium superbum
LILIACEAE

The largest of our native lilies, this species can reach 7 ft. tall. It has 6-in.-long, smooth, lance-shaped leaves. The lower leaves occur in whorls whereas the upper leaves are alternate. The 3-in.-wide flowers occur in a loose cluster with individual flowers nodding from long stems. The segments are strongly recurved and have purple spots with blotches of green near the base. The flower has a distinctive green throat in the center.

HABITAT: Rich woods

REGION: Cumberland Mountains, Appalachian Plateaus

FREQUENCY: Rare

PURPLE FRINGELESS ORCHID
Platanthera peramoena
ORCHIDACEAE

This is a large, showy plant with 2 to 4, 6- to 8-in.-long, lance-shaped leaves that get smaller toward the top of the stem. The individual 1-in.-long flowers occur in a loose and open cylindrical structure with a large lip that has 3 fan-shaped lobes with irregular jagged tips and a small amount of fringe on the lower lobe.

HABITAT: Damp, open woods; roadside ditches; wet meadows

REGION: Appalachian Plateaus, Bluegrass, Mississippian Plateau, Shawnee Hills, Jackson Purchase

FREQUENCY: Uncommon to locally common

The purple fringed orchid, *P. psycodes,* is rare in the Cumberland Mountains. Even though the lip of the purple fringeless orchid is finely fringed on the margin, the purple fringed orchid is readily distinguished by the degree of fringing.

VIRGINIA MEADOW BEAUTY
Rhexia virginica
MELASTOMATACEAE

Note the square stem with short wings on this 12- to 18-in.-tall plant. The pointed oval leaves attach directly to the plant and have short, stiff hairs on the edge. The 1-in.-wide, 4-petaled flowers have 8 showy, drooping anthers.

HABITAT: Wet meadows, pond margins, stream banks

REGION: Statewide except Bluegrass

FREQUENCY: Common

MARYLAND MEADOW BEAUTY
Rhexia mariana
MELASTOMATACEAE

The flowers of this species are similar to those of Virginia meadow beauty except they are light pink to white. The leaves of this species are narrower and more lanceshaped.

HABITAT: Wet meadows, pond margins

REGION: Statewide except Bluegrass

FREQUENCY: Common

FIELD MILKWORT
Polygala sanguinea
POLYGALACEAE

This 6- to 12-in.-tall annual has narrow, linear, alternate leaves. The 1/2- to 1-in.-long and 1/2-in.-wide cylindrical or oblong flower head with a flat top is a dense overlapping cluster of 3-petaled flowers.

HABITAT: Moist or dry fields, meadows

REGION: Statewide

FREQUENCY: Common

OBEDIENT PLANT
Physostegia virginiana
LAMIACEAE

Like other mints, this 2- to 3-ft.-tall plant has a 4-angled or square stem. The 1-in.-long, tubular flowers with a 3-lobed, spotted lower lip occur in a dense spike at the top of the plant. The opposite, toothed leaves are narrow lance to linear in shape.

HABITAT: Prairie patches, moist openings, thickets

REGION: Statewide except Inner Bluegrass

FREQUENCY: Uncommon

This plant gets its common name because it has the curious habit of the flowers being "obedient," or remaining in whatever position they have been bent.

FIELD THISTLE
Cirsium discolor
ASTERACEAE

This large biennial reaches up to 7 ft. tall. Note that the stem is smooth and does not have wings and the leaves are whitish underneath. The leaves are somewhat soft to the touch. The flower heads range in size from 1 to 2 in. wide. Also note that the modified leaves under the flower heads are colorless bristles.

HABITAT: Prairie patches, fields, roadsides

REGION: Statewide

FREQUENCY: Common

Do not confuse this native species with the invasive exotic nodding or musk thistle, *C. nutans.* The musk thistle usually flowers earlier, the leaves are not soft to the touch, and they are not silver or whitish underneath. Also notice the sharp, stout modified leaves under the flower head. Another native species, the tall thistle, *C. altissimum,* is similar to field thistle except the stem leaves are generally unlobed.

CARDINAL FLOWER
Lobelia cardinalis
CAMPANULACEAE

It is hard to mistake the brilliant scarlet, 1 1/2-in.-long flowers in a large spike cluster at the top of this plant. The individual flowers have 3 lower lobes and 2 upper lobes that form a tubular flower. The white stamens project up and through the flower. The leaves of this 1- to 4-ft.-tall plant are toothed, alternate, and lance shaped.

HABITAT: Wet or moist soil, meadows, roadsides, pond or stream banks

REGION: Statewide

FREQUENCY: Common except in the Bluegrass, where it is uncommon

This may be the best hummingbird-attracting plant in the state.

BLUE JASMINE
Clematis crispa
RANUNCULACEAE

Unlike the other species in this genus, the flower color is often blue and the sepals are more recurved and often wavy or crisped. It is a typical leather-flower vine with 3 oval leaflets.

HABITAT: Wet woods, marshes

REGION: Jackson Purchase

FREQUENCY: Rare

SCURF-PEA
Psoralea psoralioides
FABACEAE

This slender and smooth-stemmed, 1- to 2-ft.-tall, delicate plant has a spikelike cluster of 1/4-in.-wide flowers on top of a long stem. The leaves have 3, 1- to 3-in.-long linear segments.

HABITAT: Dry, open woods; woodland edges; prairie patches

REGION: Statewide except Bluegrass and Cumberland Mountains

FREQUENCY: Common but more abundant in the west

The ground roots of this plant, also known as Sampson's snakeroot, were sometimes used to make a tea to treat colic.

NARROW-LEAVED VERVAIN
Verbena simplex
VERBENACEAE

This 6- to 18-in.-tall plant has narrow, lance-shaped leaves that taper toward the plant stem. The spikelike flower cluster has multiple 1/8-in.-wide, tubular, 5-lobed flowers.

HABITAT: Open, rocky ground; roadsides; glades; disturbed soil

REGION: Statewide

FREQUENCY: Common and locally abundant

DOWNY WOOD MINT
Blephilia ciliata
LAMIACEAE

This 12- to 18-in., square-stemmed plant is somewhat hairy and has runners at its base. The leaves on these runners are oval and have stalks. The leaves on the stem are more lance shaped with rounded tips and are hairy underneath. One of the key field identification characteristics is that the leaves of this species attach directly to the plant stem. The circular flower head is a tight cluster of 1/2-in.-long flowers that have 2 stamens and 2 lips instead of 5 lobes.

HABITAT: Open woods, fields, meadows

REGION: Bluegrass, Knobs, Mississippian Plateau, Jackson Purchase

FREQUENCY: Common and locally abundant in the Bluegrass

The hairy wood mint, *B. hirsuta,* is an uncommon species that flowers a few weeks earlier on rocky, open, and exposed ground. It has similar flowers and is hairy; the primary difference is that the leaves on the stem have stalks.

BERGAMOT, BEE BALM
Monarda fistulosa
LAMIACEAE

Look for the tuft of white hairs at the end of the upper lip on each individual flower. The 1-in.-long, 2-lipped, tubular flowers are arranged in a circular cluster at the top of this multibranched plant. The upper part of the stem may be hairy. The leaves are hairy and oval and have stalks.

HABITAT: Fields, meadows, roadsides

REGION: Statewide

FREQUENCY: Abundant

Scarlet bee balm, *M. didyma,* has red, tubular flowers. It is rare and only occurs in a few locations in the northern Bluegrass and along the western edge of the Appalachian Plateaus.

HEAL-ALL
Prunella vulgaris
LAMIACEAE

Note that the upper lip of the 1/2- to 5/8-in., short, tubular flower is hoodlike and arches over the 4 stamens. The lower lip is somewhat fringed. The flowers occur in a dense, short spike- or cylinder-like arrangement. The stem of this 6- to 18-in. plant is hairy, and it has pointed oval leaves.

HABITAT: Fields, meadows, open lands

REGION: Statewide

FREQUENCY: Common

ERECT SKULLCAP
Scutellaria elliptica
LAMIACEAE

This 1- to 2-ft.-tall, usually unbranched plant is covered with short, curvy hairs. There are 2 to 5 pairs of oval leaves with blunt, rounded edges. The 2/3-in.-long, helmet-shaped, tubular flowers occur in a small, 1- to 2-in., open cluster at the top of the stem.

HABITAT: Dry, open woods; woodland edges

REGION: Statewide

FREQUENCY: Common

The heart-leaved skullcap, *S. ovata,* is a similar species that is less common and has heart-shaped leaves. This species is not hairy.

S. ovata

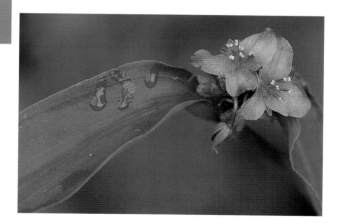

ZIGZAG SPIDERWORT
Tradescantia subaspera
COMMELINACEAE

This is a thick-stemmed, smooth, 16- to 36-in.-tall plant with 4- to 6-in.-long, lance-shaped, dark green leaves with bases that wrap around the stem. The 3-petaled flowers occur in clusters at the top of the plant and at the bases of upper leaves.

HABITAT: Moist woods

REGION: Statewide

FREQUENCY: Common

PICKEREL WEED
Pontederia cordata
PONTEDERIACEAE

This showy aquatic plant can reach up to 36 in. tall and is often seen in a large colony. The leaves at the base may reach 7 in. long, and on the lower stem the leaves are narrowly heart-shaped with long stalks. Each plant produces a flowering stalk that may reach up to 5 in. long with numerous 3/8- to 1/2-in.-long, trumpet-shaped flowers; the upper lobes of the flowers are marked with yellow spots.

HABITAT: Stream banks, shallow ponds

REGION: Jackson Purchase, Shawnee Hills, Mississippian Plateau

FREQUENCY: Uncommon

SOUTHERN BLUE-FLAG IRIS
Iris virginica
IRIDACEAE

This is a tall iris with arching, 2- to 3-ft.-long, sword-shaped leaves. The showy, 3-in.-wide flowers occur at the tip of a 2-ft. flowering stalk. The flowers can vary in color from very light blue to dark blue and have 6 segments: 3 small erect petals, and 3 spreading sepals with dark veins and a yellow patch at the base.

HABITAT: Wet woods, swamps, marshes

REGION: Statewide

FREQUENCY: Uncommon

SCALY BLAZING STAR
Liatris squarrosa
ASTERACEAE

This small, 1- to 2-ft.-tall plant may be either hairy or smooth depending on the variety. The narrow or linear leaves are quite stiff and range in size from 1/4 to 1/2 in. wide and are up to 10 in. long. The clusters of flower heads at the top of the plant attach to the plant with a very short stalk. Each flower head may have 20 to 45 individual flowers. The modified leaves under the flower heads are thick, pointed, turned outward, and spreading.

HABITAT: Prairie patches, roadsides, fields

REGION: Statewide except Cumberland Mountains

FREQUENCY: Common to locally abundant

CAROLINA WILD PETUNIA
Ruellia caroliniensis
ACANTHACEAE

This 1- to 3-ft.-tall plant is quite hairy with opposite, lance-shaped leaves. The leaves have a short stalk. The 2-in.-long, 5-lobed, tubular flowers arise at the base of the leaf.

HABITAT: Roadsides, open woods edges, grasslands, fields

REGION: Statewide

FREQUENCY: Common

R. caroliniensis

The glade wild petunia, *R. humilis,* is a less common species that occurs in glades, prairie patches, and dry, rocky soil. It is also hairy but the leaves are sessile. The least common species in Kentucky is the limestone wild petunia, *R. strepens,* which has smooth leaves with stalks.

R. strepens

VENUS'S LOOKING GLASS
Triodanis perfoliata
CAMPANULACEAE

This 6- to 18-in., unbranched winter annual has a finely haired, angled stem. The 1-in.-long roundish leaves with heart-shaped bases clasp around the stem. The 5-lobed, 1/2-in.-wide flower arises at the base of the leaf.

HABITAT: Open woods, roadsides, fields

REGION: Statewide

FREQUENCY: Common

LARGE BLUETS, SUMMER BLUETS
Houstonia purpurea
RUBIACEAE

The smooth-edged, opposite, pointed oval leaves on this 10- to 18-in.-tall plant have 3 veins. The 4-lobed, tubular, 3/8-in.-wide flowers occur in small clusters at the end of the branches.

HABITAT: Dry, open woods; fields; meadows

REGION: Statewide

FREQUENCY: Common

BLUEHEARTS
Buchnera americana
SCROPHULARIACEAE

This is an erect, 1- to 3-ft.-tall, rough, hairy, nonbranching plant. It has 2- to 4-in.-long, somewhat toothed, opposite, lance-shaped leaves without stalks. The upper leaves get smaller and narrower as they go up the stem. The 1/2-in.-long, tubular flowers have 5 lobes and occur in a spike at the top of the plant.

HABITAT: Prairie patches

REGION: Mississippian Plateau, Shawnee Hills, Jackson Purchase

FREQUENCY: Rare

HORSE NETTLE
Solanum carolinense
SOLANACEAE

This 10- to 20-in., spiny-stemmed plant has wavy-edged, 3- to 5-in.-long, oblong leaves that are both spiny and hairy. The 5-lobed flowers with prominent yellow anthers occur in small clusters at the end of the branches.

HABITAT: Fields, roadsides, disturbed soil

REGION: Statewide

FREQUENCY: Abundant

The yellow berries are deadly poisonous.

HYSSOP-LEAVED SKULLCAP, LARGE-FLOWERED SKULLCAP
Scutellaria integrifolia
LAMIACEAE

This is the only skullcap with spoon-shaped, smooth-edged, opposite leaves without stalks. This 12- to 18-in. tall plant has 1-in.-long, helmet-shaped flowers in an open cluster at the top of the plant.

HABITAT: Moist or wet meadows, usually acidic

REGION: Statewide except Bluegrass and Cumberland Mountains

FREQUENCY: Uncommon

VIRGINIA DAYFLOWER
Commelina virginica
COMMELINACEAE

This 12- to 24-in.-tall plant has smooth, 4- to 7-in.-long, lance-shaped leaves with bases that wrap around the stem. The 1/4- to 1/2-in.-wide flowers occur near the top of the stem and have 3 petals. The flowers are said to last only 1 day.

HABITAT: Moist woods

REGION: Statewide

FREQUENCY: Uncommon

The most common species in this group is the Asiatic dayflower, *C. communis,* which has larger flowers and a lower petal that is usually clear. Erect dayflower, *C. erecta,* looks similar to the Asiatic dayflower except the petals are lighter blue and it has narrower leaves. Creeping dayflower, *C. diffusa,* is the other native species that looks similar to Virginia dayflower, but the leaves are more lance shaped and the lower petal is often quite small.

PASSIONFLOWER
Passiflora incarnata
PASSIFLORACEAE

The unique, unusual, and intricate 2-in.-wide flower makes this species easy to identify. It is a smooth-stemmed vine that can grow up to 24 in. long. It has 3-lobed leaves with slightly toothed, lance-shaped lobes.

HABITAT: Roadsides, meadows, fields

REGION: Statewide

FREQUENCY: Common

SPREADING ERYNGO, PROSTRATE ERYNGO
Eryngium prostratum
APIACEAE

This small, 6- to 20-in.-long plant is easy to overlook because it creeps along the ground in the mud. It has oval to linear leaves that are irregularly toothed or lobed. The tiny flowers occur in a 1/4-in.-long dome- or cylinder-shaped cluster.

HABITAT: Wet meadows, moist soil, seeps, springs

REGION: Mississippian Plateau, Shawnee Hills, Jackson Purchase

FREQUENCY: Uncommon

SHARP-WINGED MONKEY FLOWER

Mimulus alatus

SCROPHULARIACEAE

This 2- to 3-ft., erect plant has a 4-angled and winged stem. The toothed, lance-shaped leaves have short stalks. The 1-in.-long, tubular flowers have a flared, ruffled lower lip and a "closed" mouth.

HABITAT: Wet meadows, pond and stream banks

REGION: Statewide

FREQUENCY: Common

Square-stemmed monkey flower, *M. ringens,* looks similar and is found in the same habitat statewide except the Shawnee Hills and Jackson Purchase. The leaves of this species are attached directly to the plant and the stem does not have wings.

TALL BELLFLOWER

Campanula americana

CAMPANULACEAE

This 2- to 6-ft.-tall annual or biennial has toothed, lance-shaped leaves. The 1-in.-wide, 5-pointed, lobed flowers have a style in the center of the flower that arches downward and then upward at the tip. The flowers occur in a spike at the top of the plant.

HABITAT: Moist, open woods; woodland edges; roadsides

REGION: Statewide

FREQUENCY: Common

DITTANY
Cunila origanoides
LAMIACEAE

A wiry, much-branched. 12- to 18-in. semiwoody plant that smells like diesel oil when crushed. It has smooth-edged, opposite, 1- to 1 1/2-in.-long oval leaves. The 3/8-in.-long, tubular flowers have 2 protruding stamens and occur in a short cluster at the top of the branch.

HABITAT: Dry, open or rocky woods with noncalcareous soil

REGION: Statewide except Bluegrass

FREQUENCY: Common

ROUGH BUTTONWEED
Diodia teres
RUBIACEAE

A short (1 to 2 ft.) annual, this plant has linear, lance-shaped, opposite, rough leaves tipped with a bristle. Note the stiff hairs at the base of the leaves. The 4-lobed, short (3/8 in.), tubular flowers arise at the base of the leaves.

HABITAT: Dry, exposed, rocky soil

REGION: Statewide except Bluegrass

FREQUENCY: Common

ELEPHANT FOOT
Elephantopus carolinianus
ASTERACEAE

The lower leaves on this 1- to 2-ft. plant are oval and taper at the back into a winged stalk. The upper leaves are alternate on this multibranched, hairy-stemmed species. At the end of the branches small blue flowers, without rays, are found in clusters. There are usually 3, 1/2-in.-wide flowers per cluster. Note the large modified leaves under the flowers.

HABITAT: Dry or moist open woods, meadows, roadsides

REGION: Statewide

FREQUENCY: Common except Jackson Purchase

BLUE LETTUCE
Latuca floridana
ASTERACEAE

This is a tall (up to 7 ft.) annual or biennial. The 1/2-in.-wide, dandelion-like flower heads are not abundant (usually 11 to 17 heads) in the open cluster. There are hairs behind the modified leaves near each flower head. The stems are smooth and sometimes have a reddish tint. The leaves have winged stalks and are variable but often have deep lobes with the end of the leaf in a triangle shape.

HABITAT: Woodland edges, open woods

REGION: Statewide except Cumberland Mountains

FREQUENCY: Uncommon

DENSE BLAZING STAR
Liatris spicata
ASTERACEAE

This is our most common blazing star. It grows up to 5 ft. tall and has a a spike of flower heads at the top. The flowers begin blooming at the top of the spike. Each flower head attaches directly to the stem and has 8 flowers. However, the flower heads are quite dense on the spike. The leaves are up to 12 in. long and 1/4 to 1/2 in. wide and occur mostly on the lower portion of the plant.

HABITAT: Prairie patches, woodland openings, roadsides

REGION: Statewide except Cumberland Mountains

FREQUENCY: Common

BLUE VERVAIN
Verbena hastata
VERBENACEAE

This is a tall, coarse plant reaching a height of 5 ft. or more. It has lance-shaped leaves with stalks. The lower leaves are sometimes lobed. There are multiple flower heads or pencil-like spikes of 1/8-in.-wide, 5-lobed, tubular flowers.

HABITAT: Wet fields, meadows

REGION: Statewide

FREQUENCY: Common

DOWNY SKULLCAP
Scutellaria incana
LAMIACEAE

This is a 2- to 3-ft.-tall species that has fine hairs on the stem, giving it a whitish appearance. There are multiple branches with flowering stalks. The 1-in.-long, helmet-shaped flowers are in an open cluster at the top of each flowering branch. The toothed, pointed oval leaves have a long stalk.

HABITAT: Moist woods, streamside forests

REGION: Statewide

FREQUENCY: Common

MAD-DOG SKULLCAP
Scutellaria lateriflora
LAMIACEAE

Note the 1-sided, small spike cluster of 1/4-in., tubular flowers that arise at the base of the leaves and appear to be closed. This 1- to 2-ft.-tall, leafy plant has somewhat toothed, pointed oval, opposite leaves.

HABITAT: Wet, open woods, wetlands

REGION: Statewide

FREQUENCY: Common

This species was of particular interest to herbalists because of its reputation as a cure for rabies.

OZARK MILKWEED
Asclepias viridis
ASCLEPIADACEAE

This is one of the smaller milkweeds; it reaches a height of 24 in. It has 5-in.-long, lance-shaped to oblong leaves that are narrowed at the base. The 1/2- to 3/4-in.-wide flowers occur in a dense, dome-shaped cluster at the top of the plant.

HABITAT: Meadows, roadsides, prairie patches

REGION: Bluegrass, Mississippian Plateau, eastern Shawnee Hills, western Appalachian Plateaus

FREQUENCY: Uncommon except in the Outer Bluegrass, where it is common

Another greenish purple milkweed in our state is the poke milkweed, *A. exaltata.* It has a smooth, 5-ft.-tall stem with 10-in.-long, thin, oval, alternate leaves that taper to the tip. Poke milkweed is uncommon but widely scattered statewide. Another green milkweed is the prairie milkweed, *A. hirtella.* It has a rough, hairy, 36-in.-tall stem with narrow linear leaves ranging in size up to 8 in. It is rare in the Mississippian Plateau and Jackson Purchase.

GREEN ORCHID
Platanthera flava
ORCHIDACEAE

The leaves may be the most interesting aspect of this species as there are 2 to 5 lance-shaped leaves that clasp around the stem. The leaves get progressively smaller as they ascend the stem of this 6- to 18-in.-tall species. The flowers are not showy and occur in a compact spike arrangement. Each individual flower has a 1/4-in. or shorter spur and a slightly longer spur projecting from the rear.

HABITAT: Wet woods, ditches

REGION: Cumberland Mountains, Appalachian Plateaus

FREQUENCY: Uncommon

There is another variety of this species that flowers in late summer and looks similar except the bracts do not extend past the flowers.

HAIRY ALUMROOT
Heuchera villosa
SAXIFRAGACEAE

Note that both the stems and flowers are hairy in this species. The heart-shaped, usually 5-blunt-lobed leaves with long stalks occur at the base of this 1- to 3-ft.-tall plant. The flowering stalk is 1 to 2 ft. tall and supports a loose, cone-shaped flower cluster with numerous 1/8-in.-long, widely spaced, 3-petaled, bell-shaped flowers that droop.

HABITAT: Moist woods, cliffs

REGION: Statewide except Jackson Purchase

FREQUENCY: Common

AMERICAN COLUMBO
Frasera caroliniensis
GENTIANACEAE

Note the large (12- to 15-in.), shiny, lance-shaped leaves that occur in whorls of 4 at the base of the plant. The leaves get progressively smaller up the stem toward the large cluster of flowers. The 1- to 1 1/2-in.-wide, 4-petaled flowers are usually bicolored with brownish or purplish spots. There is a noticeable gland on each petal.

HABITAT: Dry, open woods; meadows; roadsides on limestone

REGION: Bluegrass, Mississippian Plateau

FREQUENCY: Common

This plant is a triennial. The first year it produces a set of basal leaves. The second year the basal leaves get larger, and the plant flowers in the third year.

GREEN MILKWEED
Asclepias viridiflora
ASCLEPIADACEAE

This is another short milkweed, reaching a height of up to 24 in. The hairy stem is sticky to the touch and may be either erect or slightly twining. It has alternate, elongated-oval leaves that are up to 4 in. long. The rounded cluster of individual flowers arises in the axils of the upper leaves.

HABITAT: Prairie patches, glades

REGION: Mississippian Plateau, Knobs, Jackson Purchase

FREQUENCY: Common

ANGLE-POD
Matelea obliqua
ASCLEPIADACEAE

This is a twining vine with opposite, very round, heart-shaped leaves that are up to 5 in. wide. The 5 wavy, linear-petaled, hairy flowers occur in open clusters at the base of the leaf. The broken stem produces a milky sap.

HABITAT: Woodland edges, glades

REGION: Knobs, Bluegrass, Mississippian Plateau, Shawnee Hills

FREQUENCY: Uncommon

Three other species of angle-pod occur in Kentucky. Milkvine, *M. carolinensis,* has heart-shaped leaves with long, tapering tips. It is uncommon in the Mississippian Plateau and Jackson Purchase. Another angle-pod, *M. decipiens,* is very similar to spiny-pod and can be distinguished only by its longer petals. It is uncommon but widely scattered in the Mississippian Plateau and Jackson Purchase. Common angle-pod, *M. gonocarpa,* also has heart-shaped leaves with tapered tips but can be distinguished by its smooth petals. It is uncommon in a variety of habitats in the Bluegrass, Mississippian Plateau, and Shawnee Hills.

GREEN ADDER'S MOUTH
Malaxis unifolia
ORCHIDACEAE

This is a small, delicate, 12-in.-tall plant with a single, 2-in.-long, oval leaf that clasps around the middle of the stem. The flowers occur in a loose cylindrical spike. Individual flowers are about 1/8 in. long and have a whitish lip with 2 pointed lobes and 1 minute tooth.

HABITAT: Dry to moist woods

REGION: Cumberland Mountains, Appalachian Plateaus, Mississippian Plateau

FREQUENCY: Rare

FALSE ALOE
Manfreda virginica
AGAVACEAE

The stiff, succulent, lance-shaped leaves near the ground may reach up to 16 in. long. The leaves have spines along the edges and at the tips. The flowering stalk may reach 6 ft. tall, terminating with a spike of 6-segmented, tubular flowers with protruding stamens.

HABITAT: Woodland edges, glades, cliff edges, dry openings

REGION: Statewide except Cumberland Mountains

FREQUENCY: Common

CRESTED CORALROOT
Hexalectris spicata
ORCHIDACEAE

Even though this is a relatively large species reaching heights of 24 in. or more, it is difficult to find because this saprophytic species with straw-colored or brown stems blends into its surroundings. It has an open, loose spike of 1-in.-wide, showy flowers. The widespread sepals and petals of the individual flowers are yellowish with purple veins. The lip is pale yellow to white with purple veins.

HABITAT: Dry woods, usually limestone

REGION: Statewide except Jackson Purchase

FREQUENCY: Uncommon to rare

CRANE-FLY ORCHID
Tipularia discolor
ORCHIDACEAE

This plant produces a single, papery, 2- to 4-in.-long, light green leaf with prominent veins above and dark purple below in late summer. In late spring, this single leaf withers, and a dark brown flowering stem appears in midsummer. The individual 3/4-in.-long flowers occur in a loose cluster that may be 12 to 18 in. tall. Individual flowers have widely separated petals and sepals with long, slender spurs.

HABITAT: Rich woods

REGION: Statewide

FREQUENCY: Common but rare in the Bluegrass

FALL
FLOWERS

August–October

CREEPING BURHEAD

Echinodorus cordifolius

ALISMATACEAE

This aquatic plant is often found growing in large colonies because it has a creeping stem that sends down roots at various places. The large, 4- to 6-in.-long, heart-shaped leaves arise from this creeping stem. The 3/4- to 1-in.-wide, 3-petaled flowers occur in clusters of 5 or more at the base of a leafless flowering stalk.

HABITAT: Swamps, ditches

REGION: Mississippian Plateau, Shawnee Hills, Jackson Purchase

FREQUENCY: Uncommon

COMMON ARROWHEAD, DUCK POTATO

Sagittaria latifolia

ALISMATACEAE

This 18- to 36-in.-tall aquatic plant has arrow- or triangular-shaped leaves, up to 12 in. long, with deep lobes at the base of the plant. The 1/2- to 3/4-in.-long flowers occur in whorls along a leafless flowering stalk. On larger plants the upper flowers tend to be male and the lower ones female.

HABITAT: Swamps, ditches, shallow ponds

REGION: Statewide

FREQUENCY: Common

Three other species of arrowhead occur in Kentucky. The Appalachian arrowhead, *S. australis,* is common throughout the state. Midwestern arrowhead, *S. brevirostra,* is found occasionally throughout the state, and the Mississippi arrowhead, *S. montevidensis,* is common in Kentucky west of the Appalachians. These species are distinguished from common arrowhead by minute differences in the structures of their flowers and fruit.

VIRGIN'S BOWER, OLD MAN'S BEARD

Clematis virginiana

RANUNCULACEAE

This somewhat woody vine has 3 slightly toothed leaflets. The flowers are quite fragrant and usually found in abundance on the plant. The 3/4- to 1-in.-wide flowers have 4 to 9 sepals and no petals.

HABITAT: Moist woods, stream banks, roadsides, urban areas

REGION: Statewide

FREQUENCY: Abundant

After the plant flowers, the fruit has the appearance of long, silver-gray plumes resembling an old man's beard, giving rise to one of the plant's common names.

THREE-BIRDS ORCHID

Triphora trianthophora

ORCHIDACEAE

This species has a delicate, 3- to 6-in.-tall flowering stem with a few 1/2- to 3/4-in.-long, oval leaves that clasp the stem. A single 3/4-in.-long flower can be observed nodding at the end of each stem. The sepals and petals are white, sometimes tinged with pink, and have a crystalline appearance. The lip is white with green veins.

HABITAT: Moist woods

REGION: Statewide

FREQUENCY: Rare

Flower buds sometimes wait for days to open and appear to be triggered into flowering by a relatively cool night. Individual flowers close as soon as they are pollinated, so catching this plant in flower is a matter of careful timing or good luck.

THE ASTERS

The asters can be a challenging group of plants to identify because of the large number of species in this group. You can make this task easier by identifying distinct groups that have similar characteristics, particularly leaf shape. Four groupings will help with identification:

1. *The lower leaves are heart shaped and have stalks.*

2. *No leaves are heart shaped or have stalks, but the stem leaves clasp around the plant stem.*

3. *No leaves are heart shaped or clasping; the plant has colored rays.*

4. *No leaves are heart shaped or clasping; the plant has white rays.*

More than 29 species of asters are found in Kentucky, and the majority have blue or lavender rays. These species occasionally produce plants with white flowers, so if you find a species with white flowers that doesn't fit the leaf characteristics, check the descriptions of those that have predominantly blue flowers.

LARGE-LEAF ASTER
Aster macrophyllus
ASTERACEAE

The distinctive feature of this species is the 4- to 8-in., heart-shaped leaves on a short to medium-sized flowering stem that reaches 1 1/2 to 2 1/2 ft. tall. It has a creeping underground stem that forms large colonies, which often have few flower heads. Each flower head has approximately 15 widely spaced rays with yellow centers. The flowering stems have small, toothed leaves that generally attach directly to the plant but have a stalk toward the base of the plant.

HABITAT: Woodland slopes

REGION: Appalachian Plateaus, Knobs, Bluegrass, Mississippian Plateau

FREQUENCY: Locally common

Schreber's aster, *A. schreberi,* has very similar leaves, except the basal leaves are thinner and have a much broader space between the lobes. The flower heads typically have fewer rays. It is also locally common.

WHITE WOOD ASTER

Aster divaricatus

ASTERACEAE

This medium-sized plant reaches 2 ft. tall and has 3/4- to 1-in. flower heads in a somewhat flat-topped cluster. The heads have a yellowish to brownish center with 5 to 10 rays per head. The stem has a slight zigzag appearance, and the leaves are heart shaped, toothed, and attach to the plant with a stalk.

HABITAT: Rich woods

REGION: Cumberland Mountains, Appalachian Plateaus, Bluegrass

FREQUENCY: Abundant but rare in the Bluegrass

CALICO ASTER

Aster lateriflorus

ASTERACEAE

This is a highly variable species; the typical form grows from 1 to 3 ft. tall with somewhat smallish, 1/4- to 1/2-in.-wide flower heads. The center of the flower heads turns from yellow to reddish purple as the heads age. The plant has widely spreading branches, and the 10 to 15 rays often have a slight lavender color.

HABITAT: Moist, open woods; streamside forests

REGION: Statewide

FREQUENCY: Common

A similar species, the small white aster, *A. vimineus,* has smaller flower heads but more flower heads that have 15 to 30 rays. The leaves are usually narrower and longer.

A. lateriflorus   *A. vimineus*

PANICLED ASTER

Aster lanceolatus

ASTERACEAE

This upright plant reaches up to 5 ft. tall and has 1/2- to 3/4-in.-wide flower heads that have a yellow and brown center with 20 to 40 rays

in a dense cluster; the rays do not spread outward. The toothed leaves are wider than long and taper to a point.

HABITAT: Wet woods, streamside forests

REGION: Statewide except Shawnee Hills and Jackson Purchase

FREQUENCY: Common

FROSTWEED ASTER

Aster pilosus

ASTERACEAE

This is a weedy, bushy, 2- to 5-ft. plant with dense clusters of 1/2-in. flower heads on many branched, hairy stems. The leaves are mostly small and narrow, so that the plant appears to be mostly white when in full flower.

HABITAT: Roadsides, fields, meadows, disturbed sites

REGION: Statewide

FREQUENCY: Abundant

BONESET
Eupatorium perfoliatum
ASTERACEAE

This is a large, coarse plant reaching a height of 5 ft. or more. Note the long, tapering, wrinkled leaves that appear to be fused at the stem. There are 9 or more 1/8-in.-wide flowers in each flat-topped cluster.

HABITAT: Wet meadows, streamside forests, wet soils

REGION: Statewide

FREQUENCY: Common

Two species with similar flower heads are upland boneset, *E. sessilifolium,* which has a smooth stem and lance-shaped leaves that attach directly to the plant, and round-leaf thoroughwort, *E. rotundifolium,* which has a hairy stem and somewhat heart-shaped or broad oval leaves that clasp around the stem.

WHITE SNAKEROOT
Ageratina rugosum
ASTERACEAE

The 15 to 30, 1/8- to 1/4-in.-wide flowers in the flat-topped cluster are quite showy. This smooth-stemmed, 1- to 5-ft.-tall plant has opposite, toothed, oval leaves with a stalk.

HABITAT: Moist woods

REGION: Statewide

FREQUENCY: Abundant

The leaves and stems are poisonous to livestock and toxic to humans through the milk of cows that have eaten the plant.

HYSSOP-LEAVED THOROUGHWORT

Eupatorium hyssopifolium

ASTERACEAE

This is our only white-blooming Eupatorium species with grasslike or linear leaves, which occur in whorls of 4 around the stem. The 2- to 4-ft.-tall plant is rough to the touch and has a hairy stem. The open, flat-topped flower heads have 5, 1/8- to 1/4-in.-wide flowers per cluster.

HABITAT: Prairie patches, fields, meadows

REGION: Appalachian Plateaus, Mississippian Plateau, Shawnee Hills

FREQUENCY: Common

LATE THOROUGHWORT

Eupatorium serotinum

ASTERACEAE

A 4- to 6-ft.-tall, finely haired, coarse plant with sharp, toothed, opposite leaves with a long stalk. The flower heads are open, flat-topped clusters; each cluster contains 7 to 15, 1/8- to 1/4-in.-wide flowers.

HABITAT: Fields, roadsides, streamsides

REGION: Statewide

FREQUENCY: Common

This is the weediest of all the *Eupatorium* spp.

NODDING LADIES' TRESSES
Spiranthes cernua
ORCHIDACEAE

This is our most common ladies' tresses orchid and may
have the most fragrant flowers. It has narrow, lance-shaped
leaves, up to 12 in. long, which are close to the ground,
and a flowering stalk that can reach up to 16 in. tall. The
individual, 1/4- to 1/2-in.-long, tubular flowers occur along
a spike in 3 spirals. The lip of each individual flower is
white with a cream-colored center.

HABITAT: Meadows, open woods

REGION: Statewide

FREQUENCY: Uncommon

Great Plains ladies' tresses, *S. magnicamporum,* is rare on the Mississippian Plateau and in
the Bluegrass. The plant is similar, but the leaves wither before the plant comes into flower.
In addition, the lateral sepals are more widely spread and the lip has a yellowish color. The
flower has the odor of almonds.

SLENDER LADIES' TRESSES
Spiranthes lacera
ORCHIDACEAE

This is a slender, delicate species that has up to 2-in.-long,
oblong leaves on the ground. The leaves wither before the
plant flowers. The flowering stalk, up to 24 in. tall,
supports small, 1/4- to 1/2-in.-long, tubular flowers in a
single tight spiral. One diagnostic characteristic is the
white lip with a green center.

HABITAT: Moist prairie patches, meadows, fields

REGION: Statewide

FREQUENCY: Uncommon but rare in the Bluegrass

OVAL LADIES' TRESSES
Spiranthes ovalis
ORCHIDACEAE

This delicate species has 6-in.-long, lance-shaped leaves that are broadest near the blunt tip. The flowering stalk may reach 16 in. tall and supports numerous small (less than 1/4 in. long), tubular flowers in spiraling rows.

HABITAT: Moist woods

REGION: Cumberland Mountains, Appalachian Plateaus, Mississippian Plateau, Jackson Purchase, Bluegrass

FREQUENCY: Uncommon to rare

LITTLE LADIES' TRESSES
Spiranthes tuberosa
ORCHIDACEAE

This is a small and easily overlooked species that reaches 8 in. tall. The 1 1/2-in.-long, oval leaves on the ground disappear prior to flowering, leaving only the slender flowering stem with a single loose spiral of tiny tubular flowers.

HABITAT: Moist to dry woods, meadows

REGION: Cumberland Mountains, Appalachian Plateaus, Mississippian Plateau, Jackson Purchase

FREQUENCY: Uncommon

STRIPED GENTIAN

Gentiana villosa

GENTIANACEAE

This smooth-stemmed, 10- to 20-in.-tall plant has numerous opposite, lance-shaped, smooth-edged, 2- to 4-in. leaves. The flowers are in a tight cluster at the top of the plant. The 1- to 2-in.-long flower is often closed at the top but opens to reveal purple stripes on the inside.

HABITAT: Wet meadows, woods, woodland edges, open woods

REGION: Statewide except Bluegrass and Jackson Purchase

FREQUENCY: Uncommon

This plant is sometimes called Sampson's snakeroot. A similar species, the pale gentian, *G. flavida,* differs in that the flowers do not open, it flowers a good month earlier, and the leaves are more broadly triangular. It is only known from a handful of locations in central Kentucky.

TICKSEED SUNFLOWER
Bidens aristosa
ASTERACEAE

This medium-size plant reaches 2 to 3 ft. tall. It has 1 3/4- to 2-in.-wide flower heads with a yellowish to brownish or greenish center and 6 to 9 rays. The upper, toothed leaves are divided into 3 segments. and the lower leaves are divided into 5 to 7 segments.

HABITAT: Wet meadows, roadsides, fields, stream banks

REGION: Statewide

FREQUENCY: Abundant

SPANISH NEEDLES
Bidens bipinnata
ASTERACEAE

The leaves of this 1- to 3-ft. plant appear almost fernlike, with 2 to 3 deeply lobed segments. The flower heads are not showy and may have no rays at all. If rays are present, there are few. The fruits look like needles with 4 sharp, barbed spines at the tip.

HABITAT: Disturbed sites, roadsides, fields

REGION: Statewide

FREQUENCY: Common

STICKTIGHT
Bidens frondosa
ASTERACEAE

The stems of this 1- to 3-ft.-tall plant are smooth with many branches and often have a purplish tint. The toothed leaves have 3 to 5 sharply pointed segments and are attached to the plant with a long stalk. The flower heads are not showy, as the rays may be absent or quite small.

HABITAT: Moist fields, meadows, roadsides, stream and pond banks

REGION: Statewide

FREQUENCY: Common

BROWN-EYED SUSAN
Rudbeckia triloba
ASTERACEAE

This often bushy, 1- to 4-ft.-tall plant has multiple branches and flower heads. It has hairy stems and lower leaves that are usually divided into at least 3 segments. The 1 1/2- to 2-in.-wide flower heads have 8 to 12 notched rays and a dark brownish purplish center.

HABITAT: Roadsides, fields, open woods

REGION: Statewide

FREQUENCY: Common

PRAIRIE DOCK
Silphium terebinthinaceum
ASTERACEAE

The leaves at the base of the plant can be enormous, growing to 2 1/2 ft. long and 1 ft. wide. They feel like sandpaper and have sharp teeth. The flowering stalk can reach 7 ft. or more. The flower heads are found at the end of the flowering stalks, and each head has 12 to 20 notched rays.

HABITAT: Prairie patches, glades

REGION: Northern Appalachian Plateaus, Knobs, northern Bluegrass, Mississippian Plateau, Jackson Purchase

FREQUENCY: Uncommon to locally common

CUT-LEAF PRAIRIE DOCK
Silphium pinnatifidum
ASTERACEAE

The leaves at the base of the plant are large, reaching 2 1/2 ft. long and 1 ft. wide. The leaves have numerous lobes and feel like sandpaper. The flowering stalk can reach 7 ft. or more. The flower heads look similar to those of the preceding species.

HABITAT: Prairie patches, glades

REGION: Mississippian Plateau, Shawnee Hills, Jackson Purchase

FREQUENCY: Uncommon

The compass plant, *S. laciniatum,* is uncommon in the Jackson Purchase, Mississippian Plateau, and western Knobs. It has similar leaves, but they extend up the stem. The flower heads are larger, have dark (not yellow) centers, and do not have as many rays.

S. pinnatifidum   *S. laciniata*

CUP PLANT
Silphium
perfoliatum
ASTERACEAE

This large, tall, coarse plant grows to 8 ft. and has smooth, 4-angled stems. The two upper leaves under the flower head join around the stalk to form a

cup. The 6-in. or larger opposite leaves are sharply toothed. The flower heads are 2 to 3 in. across and have 20 to 30 rays.

HABITAT: Moist meadows, streamside habitats

REGION: Statewide

FREQUENCY: Common

GUMWEED
Grindelia
squarrosa
ASTERACEAE

Note the whitish resin that is visible in the center of the 1/2- to 1-in.-wide flower heads, which have 15 to 30 rays. The blunt, rounded, toothed

leaves clasp around the stem. The numerous glands make this plant sticky to the touch.

HABITAT: Dry, exposed soil

REGION: Outer Bluegrass, Knobs, Shawnee Hills

FREQUENCY: Uncommon to rare

AUTUMN SNEEZEWEED
Helenium autumnale
ASTERACEAE

Note the numerous 1- to 2-in.-wide, globe- or sphere-shaped flower heads with 10 to 18 wedge-shaped, somewhat drooping rays that have 3 lobes. The stem on this 1- to 3-ft. plant is winged, and the toothed leaves are lance shaped and attach directly to the plant.

HABITAT: Moist fields, meadows, prairie patches, roadsides

REGION: Statewide

FREQUENCY: Abundant

The sneezeweeds do not cause hay fever, because they have heavy pollen that is carried by insects, not the wind. However, the dried and crushed foliage can cause sneezing.

WATER STARGRASS
Heteranthera dubia
PONTEDERIACEAE

This is a creeping aquatic plant that forms mats in the mud or shallow water. It can reach up to 18 in. tall and has narrow, grasslike leaves that grow up to 1/8 in. wide and 4 in. long. The 3/4- to 1-in.-wide flowers have 6 linear segments.

HABITAT: Riverbanks, ponds

REGION: Bluegrass, Mississippian Plateau

FREQUENCY: Uncommon

YELLOW FRINGED ORCHID
Platanthera ciliaris
ORCHIDACEAE

Note the large, 2-in.-diameter cluster of flowers atop a 12- to 32-in.-tall flowering stem that has 2 or 3 elliptical leaves. The lip of the 1/2-in.-long individual flower is long and narrow and noticeably fringed with a basal spur extending back that is longer than the reproductive parts.

HABITAT: Damp acid soil, open woods, meadows

REGION: Cumberland Mountains, Appalachian Plateaus, Shawnee Hills, Jackson Purchase

FREQUENCY: Uncommon, but occasionally found in large populations

The crested fringed orchid, *P. cristata,* is similar, but the lip is short and wide. It is a smaller plant overall and has a short spur that is equal to, or shorter than, the length of reproductive parts. It is rare and found in the Appalachian Plateaus.

MARYLAND GOLDEN ASTER
Chrysopsis mariana
ASTERACEAE

This is a short plant, growing to 12 to 24 in. The oblong, alternate, smooth-edged leaves are sticky to the touch.

Each plant has several 1-in.-wide flower heads, which have 12 to 40 rays with a yellow center.

HABITAT: Dry, sandy ridge tops, pine-oak woods

REGION: Cumberland Mountains, Appalachian Plateaus, eastern Mississippian Plateau

FREQUENCY: Common

GRASS-LEAVED GOLDEN ASTER
Chrysopsis graminifolia
ASTERACEAE

The alternate leaves of this 12- to 24-in. plant are quite distinctive. They are long and narrow with veins that run the length of the leaf. They also look silvery because they are covered with numerous soft, white hairs. The 1-in.-wide flower heads have 12 or more rays.

HABITAT: Dry, sandy ridge tops; pine-oak woods

REGION: Cumberland Mountains, Appalachian Plateaus

FREQUENCY: Common

OX-EYE SUNFLOWER
Heliopsis helianthoides
ASTERACEAE

This 3- to 5-ft., smooth-stemmed plant has opposite, elongated-oval, toothed leaves with stalks. The leaves are hairy and rough above but smooth underneath. The multiple 2-in.-wide flower heads have 8 to 15 rays with a yellow center.

HABITAT: Moist fields, roadsides, woodland edges

REGION: Statewide

FREQUENCY: Common and locally abundant in the Bluegrass

COMMON SUNFLOWER
Helianthus annuus
ASTERACEAE

This is a large plant reaching a height of 10 ft. or more. It has 3- to 4-in.-wide flower heads with 13 to 40 rays and a dark brown center. It is a widely branching, open plant with multiple flower heads. The leaves are hairy and rough to the touch. They are somewhat oval to triangular shaped with a heart-shaped base and a long stalk.

HABITAT: Roadsides, disturbed soil

REGION: Statewide

FREQUENCY: Common but locally abundant in the Bluegrass and Mississippian Plateau

This is the annual sunflower that is cultivated and available in a wide variety of colors.

ASHY SUNFLOWER, DOWNY SUNFLOWER
Helianthus mollis
ASTERACEAE

Note the whitish, hairy stem and leaves on this mostly unbranched, 2- to 3-ft.-tall plant. The large, 2- to 3-in.-wide flower heads have 15 to 25 rays and a yellow center. The short, oval, opposite leaves attach directly to the plant or sometimes clasp around the stem.

HABITAT: Prairie patches, fields

REGION: Jackson Purchase, Shawnee Hills, Mississippian Plateau

FREQUENCY: Uncommon but locally abundant

WOODLAND SUNFLOWER
Helianthus divaricatus
ASTERACEAE

This 2- to 5-ft. plant has smooth stems and rough, opposite, lance-shaped leaves with rounded bases that attach directly to the plant. The 2-in.-wide flower heads have 8 to 15 rays and a yellow center.

HABITAT: Open woods

REGION: Statewide

FREQUENCY: Common

NARROW-LEAVED SUNFLOWER
Helianthus angustifolius
ASTERACEAE

Note the long, narrow, and stiff alternate leaves on this 4- to 6-ft.-tall plant. The stem is rough to the touch. The plant has numerous 1-in.-wide flower heads, each with 10 to 15 rays and a dark purplish center.

HABITAT: Wet meadows, prairie patches, roadsides

REGION: Statewide except Cumberland Mountains and Bluegrass

FREQUENCY: Uncommon

THIN-LEAVED SUNFLOWER, FOREST SUNFLOWER

Helianthus decapetalus

ASTERACEAE

Note the winged stalks on the opposite leaves on this smooth-stemmed, 2- to 5-ft.-tall plant. The long, narrow, pointed, toothed leaves are green underneath. The 2 1/2-in.-wide flower heads have 8 to 15 rays with a small yellow center.

HABITAT: Open, moist woods; streamside forests

REGION: Statewide

FREQUENCY: Uncommon

SAWTOOTH SUNFLOWER

Helianthus grosseserratus

ASTERACEAE

This is a large, 4- to 6-ft.-tall plant with smooth stems. The upper part of the stem is often a reddish color. The plant has multiple 3- to 4-in.-wide flower heads with 10 to 20 rays and a yellow center. The slightly toothed leaves are long and narrow with short hairs on the underside and a short stalk.

HABITAT: Roadsides, moist fields

REGION: Appalachian Plateaus, Bluegrass, Knobs, Mississippian Plateau, Jackson Purchase

FREQUENCY: Uncommon

SMALL-HEADED SUNFLOWER
Helianthus microcephalus
ASTERACEAE

This much-branched, smooth-stemmed, 3- to 6-ft. plant has numerous 1- to 1 1/2-in.-wide flower heads with 5 to 10 rays and a small yellow center. The opposite, lance-shaped leaves are rough on the top and have short, soft hairs on the underside.

HABITAT: Open woods, woodland edges, roadsides

REGION: Statewide

FREQUENCY: Common

ROUGH-LEAVED SUNFLOWER
Helianthus strumosus
ASTERACEAE

Note the wings on the stalks of the thick, hairy, lance-shaped, opposite leaves, which are rough to the touch and whitish underneath. The upper leaves are alternate on the 2- to 5-ft., smooth-stemmed plant. The 2- to 3-in.-wide flower heads have 8 to 15 rays and a small yellow center.

HABITAT: Dry or moist woods

REGION: Statewide

FREQUENCY: Uncommon

JERUSALEM ARTICHOKE
Helianthus tuberosus
ASTERACEAE

This is a large, coarse plant growing as tall as 10 ft. It has multiple hairy stems with large, thick leaves that feel like sandpaper. There are numerous 2- to 3-in.-wide flower heads, which have 12 to 20 rays and a yellow center. The large, 4- to 8-in.-long, toothed leaves have 3 veins and are rough above and hairy beneath.

HABITAT: Roadsides, moist meadows, fields

REGION: Statewide

FREQUENCY: Abundant

THE GOLDENRODS

The goldenrod is Kentucky's state flower; more than 30 species are found in the state. Contrary to popular opinion, the goldenrods do not cause allergies or hay fever. Their pollen is heavy and sticky and transported primarily by insects, not the wind. This group of plants is very important to the insect world. There are a number of hybrids known to occur, and the flowers look very similar. The flower heads are small and the rays short. Thus it is important to pay particular attention to the vegetative portions of the plant when trying to identify individual species. The species we have highlighted are the ones you would most likely encounter. Eight rare species are found in the state, including the federally endangered Short's goldenrod, Solidago shortii, *named for Charles Wilkins Short, a botany professor at Transylvania University, which is found primarily in the Blue Licks State Park area; and the white-haired goldenrod,* Solidago albopilosa, *which is a federally threatened species that grows in rockshelters.*

TALL GOLDENROD
Solidago altissima
ASTERACEAE

This may be our most common and weediest goldenrod. It is a large, coarse plant reaching up to 7 ft. tall. There are many rough, 3-veined, linear leaves on the grayish stem with many fine hairs.

HABITAT: Roadsides, fields, pastures, woodland edges

REGION: Statewide

FREQUENCY: Abundant

S. altissima

Two similar species are the common goldenrod, *S. canadensis,* which has more leaves that are long and narrow with sharp teeth; and the great goldenrod, *S. gigantea,* which has smooth, purplish stems and leaves with 3 main veins.

S. canadensis   *S. gigantea*

FOREST GOLDENROD
Solidago arguta
ASTERACEAE

This 2- to 6-ft.-tall species has a smooth stem that is sometimes reddish brown with multiple flowering branches with clusters of flowers typically positioned on one side. Each individual flower head has 5 to 8 rays. The lower leaves are somewhat oval but taper at the base and at the point. The leaf edges are sharply toothed. The upper leaves are usually smaller and attach directly to the stem.

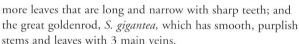

HABITAT: Moist woods

REGION: Cumberland Mountains, Appalachian Plateaus, Bluegrass, Shawnee Hills

FREQUENCY: Uncommon

WREATH GOLDENROD, BLUE-STEMMED GOLDENROD

Solidago caesia

ASTERACEAE

This 1- to 3-ft. tall species has a gently arching, smooth or waxy stem that often has a bluish cast. The small clusters of flower heads, each with 3 to 5 rays, are found at the base of the leaves. The alternate, toothed leaves are attached directly to the plant.

HABITAT: Dry or moist woods

REGION: Statewide

FREQUENCY: Common to locally abundant

ERECT GOLDENROD, SLENDER GOLDENROD

Solidago erecta

ASTERACEAE

This species has a cluster of flower heads, with 6 to 9 rays, in a spikelike arrangement on a smooth stem. The larger, toothed, lower leaves are spoon shaped and have a winged stalk. The upper leaves are smaller and narrower and usually attach directly to the plant.

HABITAT: Dry woods, prairie patches, roadsides

REGION: Statewide

FREQUENCY: Common

The hairy goldenrod, *S. hispida,* is similar except the stem is hairy. The white goldenrod or silverrod, *S. bicolor,* is similar to the hairy goldenrod except the flowers are both yellow and white.

ZIGZAG GOLDENROD
Solidago flexicaulis
ASTERACEAE

This is a highly variable species, but the typical form has a definite 1- to 3-ft.-tall zigzag stem with the clusters of flower heads in a spikelike arrangement. This species has large, oval, toothed leaves that are widely spaced. The leaves attach to the plant via a distinct winged stalk.

HABITAT: Moist woods

REGION: Statewide

FREQUENCY: Uncommon to locally common

GRAY GOLDENROD
Solidago nemoralis
ASTERACEAE

This is a smaller species of goldenrod that reaches heights of 2 to 4 ft. The stems are hairy and have a grayish tint. The lower leaves are toothed and spoon shaped and taper to the plant stem. The upper leaves are smaller and narrower, attach directly to the plant, and have 2 small leaflets at the base of the leaf. Individual flower heads have 5 to 9 rays.

HABITAT: Prairie patches; dry, exposed soil; meadows

REGION: Statewide

FREQUENCY: Common

GRASS-LEAVED GOLDENROD
Solidago graminifolia
ASTERACEAE

This is a somewhat unusual-looking goldenrod; the individual flower heads have 12 to 20 rays and occur in a flat-topped cluster with more than 20 flower

heads per cluster. This is a tall plant reaching 5 ft. The leaves are thin, have 3 to 5 veins, and taper at each end.

HABITAT: Moist meadows, fields, roadsides

REGION: Statewide

FREQUENCY: Uncommon to locally common

STIFF GOLDENROD, RIGID GOLDENROD
Solidago rigida
ASTERACEAE

The flat-topped clusters of flower heads are quite showy with numerous flower heads in a cluster. Each individual flower head has 7 to 14 rays. The blunt, toothed lower leaves are rough to the touch and somewhat oval; they taper to a point and attach to the plant with a stalk. The upper leaves generally attach directly to the plant and are much smaller and rounder. This is a large plant that can reach 4 ft. in height.

HABITAT: Limestone prairie patches, roadsides, fields

REGION: Appalachian Plateaus, Knobs, Bluegrass, Mississippian Plateau

FREQUENCY: Uncommon to locally common

ROUGH GOLDENROD
Solidago rugosa
ASTERACEAE

This species has a hairy stem that is rough to the touch and can reach 6 ft. in height. There are usually several branches with flower heads that have 6 to 10 rays. The toothed lower leaves are spoon shaped and taper into winged stalks. The upper leaves are more linear and less hairy and have very short stalks. The leaves have a wrinkled appearance.

HABITAT: Moist meadows, roadsides, streamsides

REGION: Statewide

FREQUENCY: Common

SHOWY GOLDENROD
Solidago speciosa
ASTERACEAE

This is a tall, stout species with a slender stem and smooth leaves; the plant can reach 6 ft. in height. The cluster of flower heads is somewhat cylindrical to cone shaped. Each flower head has 6 to 8 rays. The large, 4- to 10-in. lower leaves are broader than long and are not toothed.

HABITAT: Prairie patches, dry woods openings

REGION: Appalachian Plateaus, eastern Knobs, Mississippian Plateaus

FREQUENCY: Uncommon

FALSE GOLDENROD
Solidago sphacelata
ASTERACEAE

This is a leafier species with few flowering stalks. The leaves at the base of the plant are 3 to 5 in. long, broadly heart shaped, and attached to the plant with a long stalk. The leaves become progressively smaller up the stem. The uppermost leaves attach directly to the plant. Individual flower heads have 3 to 6 rays.

HABITAT: Dry, rocky, open woods; woodland edges

REGION: Cumberland Mountains, Appalachian Plateaus, Knobs, Bluegrass, Mississippian Plateau

FREQUENCY: Common

ELM-LEAVED GOLDENROD
Solidago ulmifolia
ASTERACEAE

The stem of this 2- to 4-ft.-tall species is not hairy, yet the flowering stalks have very fine hairs. Each plant has a few flowering branches that have 3- to 5-rayed flower heads on one side. The toothed lower leaves are spoon shaped and taper at the back to a stalk that attaches the leaf to the plant. The upper leaves are not toothed and attach directly to the stem.

HABITAT: Woods, woodland edges

REGION: Statewide

FREQUENCY: Common

TRAILING WILD BEAN

Strophostyles umbellata

FABACEAE

This trailing or twining plant, up to 3 ft. long, grows close to the ground. The leaves have 3 oblong to oval segments. The small cluster of 1/2-in.-wide flowers occurs on a very stiff or rigid stem. Note that the lower 2 petals are united and curved upward, resembling a beak.

S. helvola

HABITAT: Prairie patches, dry upland meadows, woodland edges

REGION: Mississippian Plateau, Shawnee Hills, Jackson Purchase

FREQUENCY: Common

The annual trailing wild bean, *S. helvola,* occurs in the same range, and the flower looks similar. The primary difference is there is a bulge on the back edge of the leaflet.

PERPLEXING TICK-TREFOIL, STICKTIGHTS

Desmodium perplexum

FABACEAE

This is a many-branched, bushlike species that grows 12 to 24 in. tall. It has 3 oval, hairy leaf segments that are twice as wide as they are long and lie flat next to the plant. It also has 2 lance-shaped, leaflike structures at the base of the leaves. The 1/2-in.-wide flowers occur in small clusters that arise from near the base of the upper leaves.

HABITAT: Fields, roadsides, woodland edges

REGION: Appalachian Plateaus, Bluegrass, Mississippian Plateau

FREQUENCY: Abundant

There are many species of sticktights in the state. All species have small purple, pealike flowers. A similar species to the perplexing tick-trefoil is the hoary tick-trefoil, *D. canescans,* which is hairy and quite sticky to the touch. Other easily identifiable species include the round-leaved tick-trefoil, *D. rotundifolium,* which has rounded leaf lobes and creeps along the ground in open oak woods. Panicled tick-trefoil, *D. paniculatum,* has long, slender leaves with a stalk. Sessile-leaved tick-trefoil, *D. sessilifolium,* is similar to the preceding species except the leaves are not stalked.

D. perplexum

D. rotundifolium

D. canescans

D. sessilifolium

JOE-PYE WEED
Eupatorium fistulosum
ASTERACEAE

This is a large plant reaching as much as 10 ft. tall. It has a smooth, hollow stem that is often tinted with purple. The 4 to 7 lance-shaped, toothed leaves occur in whorls around the stem. The flowers occur in a large, multibranched, open or dome-shaped cluster with 5 to 8 flowers in each head.

HABITAT: Moist meadows, streamside forests, wet soils

REGION: Statewide

FREQUENCY: Common

Green-stemmed joe-pye weed, *E. purpureum,* is similar except that the leaves occur in whorls of 3 or 4 and the stem is not hollow and has a greenish tint with purplish rings at the leaf junctions.

PURPLE GERARDIA
Agalinis purpurea
SCROPHULARIACEAE

This wiry, multibranched annual, up to 3 ft. tall, has 1 1/2-in.-long linear and pointed leaves. The 1 1/2-in.-long, tubular flowers have 5 lobes with yellow stripes on the inside of the throat. Note that the upper lobe does not appear to close the throat as in the slender gerardia.

HABITAT: Wet meadows, roadsides, fields

REGION: Statewide except Bluegrass

FREQUENCY: Uncommon

SLENDER GERARDIA
Agalinis tenuifolia
SCROPHULARIACEAE

This is a smooth, many-branched, thin-stemmed, wiry-looking annual with 1/2-in.-long, tubular flowers. The flower has 5 lobes, with the upper lip nearly closing the opening. The 1-in.-long leaves are linear and pointed.

HABITAT: Prairie patches, roadsides, fields

REGION: Statewide

FREQUENCY: Common

PINESAP
Monotropa hypopithys
MONOTROPACEAE

This is a 6- to 10-in.-tall, saprophytic plant that gets its nutrition from a soil fungus. It is similar to Indian pipe but has yellowish brown to reddish stems that are densely covered with scales. There are multiple flowers in a dense cluster at the top of the plant.

HABITAT: Dry to moist woods

REGION: Cumberland Mountains, Appalachian Plateaus, Mississippian Plateau

FREQUENCY: Uncommon

SOUTHERN HAREBELL

Campanula divaricata

CAMPANULACEAE

This is a delicate, open-branched, 1-
to 2-ft. plant with toothed, lance-
shaped leaves. The small, 1/4-in.-
long, bell-shaped flowers, which have
recurved lobes and a style that
protrudes from the center, hang from
the end of the slender branches.

HABITAT: Dry sandstone
ridge tops, rock outcrops

REGION: Cumberland
Mountains, Appalachian
Plateaus

FREQUENCY: Common

BLUE WAXWEED

*Cuphea
viscosissima*

LYTHRACEAE

This slightly
branched annual
grows up to 2 ft. tall
and is hairy and
sticky to the touch.
The lance-shaped,
smooth-edged,

opposite leaves have stalks. The 1-in.-long, tubular flowers have petals in a
spokelike arrangement with the upper 2 petals being the largest.

HABITAT: Moist woods, open woods

REGION: Statewide

FREQUENCY: Uncommon

DOWNY LOBELIA
Lobelia puberula
CAMPANULACEAE

This 1- to 3-ft. plant has a finely haired stem and toothed, oval, alternate leaves. The 3/4-in.-wide, 5-lobed, tubular flowers are arranged in an open spike where the flowers generally occur on one side of the stem.

HABITAT: Dry or wet open woods, fields, prairie patches

REGION: Statewide except Shawnee Hills

FREQUENCY: Common

GREAT BLUE LOBELIA
Lobelia siphilitica
CAMPANULACEAE

This is a smooth, stout, 1- to 3-ft.-tall plant with numerous alternate, lance-shaped leaves. The showy 1-in.-wide, 5-lobed, tubular flowers are arranged in a dense spike. The lower lobes bend downward; if you look carefully, it appears there are two dark lines in the flower, especially on the underside.

HABITAT: Wet meadows, stream banks, pond edges, wet soil

REGION: Statewide

FREQUENCY: Common

MIST FLOWER
Eupatorium
coelestinum
ASTERACEAE

This 1- to 3-ft.-tall plant
has triangular, toothed,
opposite leaves on a hairy
stem. The numerous
1/8- to 1/4-in.-wide
flowers occur in dense,
flat-topped clusters that
have a fuzzy appearance.

HABITAT: Moist mead-
ows, ditches, fields

REGION: Statewide

FREQUENCY: Abundant

This is sometimes called wild or hardy ageratum because it resembles the annual
horticultural species *Ageratum* spp.

FALSE
PENNYROYAL
Isanthus brachiatum
LAMIACEAE

This is a small, nondescript, 6- to
18-in., smooth or finely haired,
slender-stemmed annual with 1-
to 2-in.-long, lance-shaped leaves
that taper at each end. From 1 to
3 small, 5-lobed flowers arise at
the base of the upper leaves.

HABITAT: Glades; roadsides; dry,
rocky, exposed limestone soil

REGION: Statewide

FREQUENCY: Uncommon

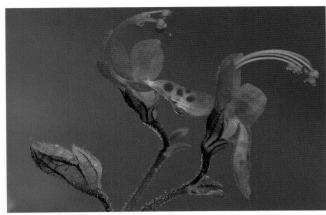

BLUE CURLS
Trichostema dichotomum
LAMIACEAE

This is a multibranched, hairy, 6- to 24-in.-tall annual with lance shaped, opposite lower leaves. The unique 1/4- to 1/2-in.-long flowers have a drooping lower lip and 4 long, curled stamens that arch up and over the rest of the flower.

HABITAT: Glades; roadsides; dry, rocky, exposed sandstone soil

REGION: Statewide except Bluegrass

FREQUENCY: Uncommon

ROUGH BLAZING STAR
Liatris aspera
ASTERACEAE

There are numerous 1/2- to 1 1/2-in.-wide by 2- to 12-in.-long, smooth, alternate leaves on a 1- to 4- ft. plant. Most of the leaves occur on the lower portion of the plant and become smaller and more inconspicuous near the top. The flower heads occur in individual clusters with 25 to 40 flowers in each head. Note that the modified leaves around the flower heads are rough, rounded, and whitish in the center with pinkish purple edges.

HABITAT: Prairie patches, fields, meadows, roadsides

REGION: Statewide

FREQUENCY: Uncommon

IRONWEED
Vernonia gigantea
ASTERACEAE

This is a large, coarse, and weedy plant that reaches up to 10 ft. in height. The flat-topped flower clusters at the top of the plant support up to 30 flowers per head. The alternate, toothed leaves are longer than wide and taper to a point attaching directly to the plant.

HABITAT: Fields, pastures, roadsides

REGION: Statewide

FREQUENCY: Abundant

SMOOTH ASTER
Aster laevis
ASTERACEAE

The upper leaves of this 1- to 3-ft.-tall plant are bluish green and have rounded bases that curl around the plant stem. The lower leaves have a short, winged stalk. The leaves are smooth to the touch and are not toothed. This plant has a very open appearance with numerous 3/4-in.-wide heads that have a yellow center and 15 to 20 rays.

HABITAT: Limestone prairie patches, open woods

REGION: Statewide except Jackson Purchase

FREQUENCY: Common in the Knobs, Outer Bluegrass, and Mississippian Plateau and rare in remainder of its range

SPREADING ASTER
Aster patens
ASTERACEAE

This is a very open and airy, 1- to 3-ft.-tall plant with single 1-in.-wide flower heads at the end of each stem. The flower heads have a reddish or yellow center and approximately 15 rays. The toothless, oblong leaves are unique in that they form rounded, almost earlike lobes at the base of the stem, which they almost encircle.

HABITAT: Prairie patches, fields, meadows, roadsides

REGION: Statewide

FREQUENCY: Common

SHORT'S ASTER
Aster shortii
ASTERACEAE

The 1-in.-wide flower heads of this 1- to 3-ft.-tall plant have 10 to 15 rays; the flower heads have yellow centers and are arranged in a loose, open cluster at the top. The edge of the leaves is mostly smooth, and the lower, somewhat heart-shaped leaves have short stalks. The upper leaves attach directly to the stem.

HABITAT: Dry or moist woods

REGION: Bluegrass, Knobs, Mississippian Plateau, Jackson Purchase

FREQUENCY: Common

This plant was named for the noted Transylvania University botanist Charles Wilkins Short in 1834.

STIFF-LEAF ASTER, STIFF ASTER
Aster linariifolius
ASTERACEAE

This is a medium-sized plant reaching 1 to 2 ft. tall with 1-in.-wide flower heads that have 10 to 20 rays and a yellow center. Note the 1- to and 1 1/2-in.-long, linear, almost needlelike, clumped and stiff leaves that attach directly to the plant.

HABITAT: Prairie patches, oak-pine forests, river cobble bars

REGION: Cumberland Mountains, Appalachian Plateaus, Mississippian Plateau, Jackson Purchase

FREQUENCY: Common

NEW ENGLAND ASTER
Aster novae-angliae
ASTERACEAE

This is one of our largest and showiest asters, reaching 5 or 6 ft. tall. It has large, 1- to 2-in., purple, rose, or occasionally white flower heads with 50 or more rays on stout, hairy stems. The 2- to 5-in.-long, rough leaves form a heart-like shape at the base of the leaf around the stem.

HABITAT: Grasslands, fields, meadows, roadsides

REGION: Statewide

FREQUENCY: Common to locally abundant in the Bluegrass, uncommon in the rest of the state

CROOKED-STEM ASTER

Aster prenanthoides

ASTERACEAE

The stem on this 1 1/2- to 2-ft.-tall, smooth-stemmed plant is often zigzag. The leaves are oblong and taper into a winged stalk that clasps around the plant. The 1-in.-wide flower heads have 20 to 30 rays.

HABITAT: Wet woods, stream banks, pond edges

REGION: Statewide except Shawnee Hills and Jackson Purchase

FREQUENCY: Common

WAVY-LEAF ASTER

Aster undulatus

ASTERACEAE

The rough and slightly hairy, 1- to 3-ft. plant has lower leaves that have toothed, wavy edges with a winged stalk that clasps around the plant. The upper leaves are shorter and wider and often attach directly to the plant, although they do not clasp around the plant. The 3/4- to 1-in.-wide flower heads have 8 to 15 rays.

HABITAT: Dry, open woods; roadsides; woodland edges

REGION: Statewide except Bluegrass and Jackson Purchase

FREQUENCY: Common

CREEPING ASTER

Aster surculosus

ASTERACEAE

This low-growing plant is 8 to 24 in. tall. The leaves are narrow at each end and rough to the touch, and the primary leaves attach to the plant with a stalk. The modified leaves under the flower heads are quite stiff and spreading or turned outward. The 1-in.-wide flower heads have 15 to 30 rays in a small cluster.

HABITAT: Dry, sandy ridge tops

REGION: Cumberland Mountains, Appalachian Plateaus

FREQUENCY: Common

HEART-LEAVED ASTER, BLUE WOOD ASTER

Aster cordifolius

ASTERACEAE

This large, 3-ft.-tall plant has 1/2- to 3/4-in.-wide flower heads with 10 to 20 rays. The large leaves are heart shaped and sharply toothed and have a stalk.

HABITAT: Moist woods

REGION: Statewide except Shawnee Hills and Jackson Purchase

FREQUENCY: Common

The arrow-leaved aster, *A. sagittifolius,* is similar but has larger, 3/4- to 1-in.-wide flower heads. The lower leaf stalks are winged and more oval, whereas the upper leaves are narrower and attach directly to the plant. Lowrie's aster, *A. lowrieanus,* is a similar species with 1/2-in. flower heads, but it is easily distinguished by smooth leaves that have a greasy feel.

A. cordifolius   *A. sagittifolius*   *A. lowrieanus*

AROMATIC ASTER

Aster oblongifolius

ASTERACEAE

This medium-sized, 2-ft.-tall plant often forms a large colony. The 1-in.-wide flower heads have 15 to 40 rays, and each one grows at the end of a short stalk. The brittle stems support oblong and toothless leaves that slightly clasp around the stem.

HABITAT: Cliff ledges, limestone prairie patches, glades

REGION: Appalachian Plateaus, Bluegrass, Knobs, Mississippian Plateau

FREQUENCY: Common to locally abundant in the Bluegrass and eastern Knobs

SOAPWORT GENTIAN

Gentiana saponaria

GENTIANACEAE

A smooth-stemmed plant that reaches 2 ft. in height. It has opposite, linear to pointed-oval leaves. The 1- to 2-in.-long, tubular flowers are closed at the top and occur in a cluster at the base of the leaves.

HABITAT: Wet meadows; wet, open woods

REGION: Statewide

FREQUENCY: Uncommon

STIFF GENTIAN
Gentiana quinquefolia
GENTIANACEAE

This 1- to 2-ft.-tall, branched annual or biennial has 1- to 2-in.-long, opposite, lance-shaped to oval leaves on the sharply angled stem. The 3/4- to 1-in.-long, tubular flowers occur in a dense cluster at the top or at the base of the leaves. They appear pointed and can vary in color from very light blue to dark blue or even lilac.

HABITAT: Barrens, woodland edges, prairie patches

REGION: Knobs, Bluegrass, Mississippian Plateau

FREQUENCY: Uncommon

A larger, showier blue gentian with deep blue tubular flowers that have a star-shaped opening is prairie or blue gentian, *G. puberulenta*. It is rare and found only in several prairie patches.

SOUTHERN BLAZING STAR
Liatris squarrulosa
ASTERACEAE

This showy plant has soft, hairy stems that can reach 2 to 4 ft. tall. The stiff leaves are 1/2 to 2 in. wide and 4 to 12 in. long and are reduced in number up the stem. There are multiple clusters of flower heads, often more than 20, in the flowering spike. Each cluster has 14 to 24 flowers.

HABITAT: Cedar glades; dry, open prairie patches; roadsides with exposed soil

REGION: Jackson Purchase, Mississippian Plateau, Knobs

FREQUENCY: Uncommon to locally common

RATTLESNAKE ROOT
Prenanthes altissima
ASTERACEAE

The flowers on this large, 4- to 6-ft. plant resemble small bells hanging in a group. This species can be identified by having only 5 or 6 flowers per cluster. The stem often has a purplish tint. The leaves are highly variable, but most have a toothed, stalked, and roughly triangular or arrow shape with lobes of some sort.

HABITAT: Open woods, woodland edges, roadsides

REGION: Statewide

FREQUENCY: Common

There are five other species of rattlesnake root in Kentucky, and all have more than 6 flowers per head and most are much smaller plants. With one exception, the lion's foot, *P. serpentaria,* all these other species are either uncommon or rare.

GROUNDNUT
Apios americana
FABACEAE

A climbing vine with a slender stem that has alternate leaves. Each leaf has 5 to 7 broad, lance-shaped segments on a long stem. The cluster of 1/2-in.-wide flowers arises from a short stalk.

HABITAT: Stream banks, wet soils, marshes, wetlands

REGION: Statewide

FREQUENCY: Common

FALL CORALROOT
Corallorhiza odontorhiza
ORCHIDACEAE

This is an easily overlooked, 4- to 8-in.-tall species that blends in with the brown leaf litter. The stem is leafless and supports an open flower spike with several small, 1/4-in.-long, tubular flowers. The individual flowers have greenish yellow sepals, lateral petals, and a white lip with purple spots that extends beyond the other petals and is not lobed.

HABITAT: Open woods

REGION: Statewide

FREQUENCY: Uncommon but found mostly in the Appalachian Plateaus

Like spring coralroot, this species is saprophytic.

BEECHDROPS
Epifagus virginica
OROBANCHACEAE

This parasite of beech trees is a multiple-branched, 6- to 18-in.-tall plant with 1/4-in.-wide, 2-lipped flowers. The upper flowers are male and the lower flowers are female. The tiny triangular leaf scales are sparse on the stem.

HABITAT: Rich woods under beech trees

REGION: Statewide

FREQUENCY: Common

ROCKHOUSE ALUMROOT

Heuchera parviflora

SAXIFRAGACEAE

This species has rounder leaves than the other alumroots; the leaves are softly haired. The flower clusters look similar to those of other alumroots.

HABITAT: Sandstone clifflines, rockshelters

REGION: Cumberland Mountains, Appalachian Plateaus, Shawnee Hills

FREQUENCY: Common

FAMILY
DESCRIPTIONS

A WORD ABOUT PLANT NAMES

The plates in the species descriptions are arbitrarily grouped by flower color and season for ease in identification. In this section we group the species by families and genera to show how the species are related. In classification systems, the species is the particular entity that is being described. Carolus Linnaeus (Carl von Linné), a Swedish botanist, devised the modern system of classification. Prior to the publication in 1753 of his *Species Plantarum*, plants were given long, Latin polynomial names—names that used many words to describe the species. Linnaeus developed the binomial classification system in which each individual organism is given just two names. The first name, a noun, is the genus; a group of closely related plants shares the same genus. This name is always capitalized. The second name is an adjective that describes the particular species. Standard practice is to italicize these Latin names. In technical scientific work, professional botanists often add a final component to give credit to the person or persons who first described the plant and proposed the scientific name. This personal name is often abbreviated. For example, southern red trillium's technical name is *Trillium erectum* L. The L is shorthand for Linnaeus. The dwarf larkspur's botanical name is *Delphinium tricorne* Michx. It was named by the famous French botanist André Michaux.

Similar species are grouped together into a genus (plural, genera) because they share common characteristics and a common lineage. At a coarser level, genera are placed into families, and related families are placed into an order. Orders are grouped into classes and classes into divisions, which are the major categories of any particular kind of organism. Plants are grouped into the kingdom Plantae; more than 350,000 plants are placed in an orderly arrangement that ideally shows the relationship between various kinds of plants. Unfortunately, taxonomists (scientists who study, describe, and name plants) are continually changing this arrangement (called phylogeny) as new information, especially at the molecular level, becomes available. Thus we have chosen here to organize the families alphabetically.

Why use these Latin names at all? you may ask. Why not just use the everyday English terms? Common names are often simple and easy to remember (bluebell), or they may be fanciful (jack-in-the-pulpit) or descriptive (old man's beard). Common names for the same plant, however, may vary from place to place and, of course, from language to language or culture to culture. For instance, old man's beard is also known as virgin's bower; and plants known as brown-eyed Susans in Kentucky are called black-eyed Susans in Texas.

Another common problem is that a vernacular plant name may be shared by two or more species. For example, the term black-eyed Susan is used in the horticultural trade to refer to the *Rudbeckia fulgida* varieties fulgida, goldstrum, and sullivantii. These in fact are not black-eyed Susans *(Rudbeckia hirta)* but are what is known in the botanical community as orange coneflowers. Furthermore, several additional *Rudbeckia* species are referred to as black-eyed Susans; these include sweet Susan *(R.*

subtomentosa), brown-eyed Susan *(R. triloba)*, and wild goldenglow or tall coneflower *(R. laciniata)*. Each of these species has different flowering periods and leaf and flower shapes. These few examples illustrate the advantage of using the Latin (botanical or technical) name. Don't let the difficult Latin or arcane language of botanical nomenclature deter you from enjoying wildflowers; the botanical or technical name is essential to properly identifying the plant you are looking at.

As noted earlier, however, scientific names are not static. Every six years the rules governing their use are revised during a special session of the International Botanical Congress. The agreed-upon changes are published in the International Code of Botanical Nomenclature. The last revisions were made in 1999 in St. Louis, Missouri.

Most regional wildflower guides historically based their classification on *Gray's Manual of Botany*, eighth edition, by M. L. Fernald. Unfortunately, the latest edition of *Gray's Manual* is more than 50 years old, and numerous name changes have been made since its publication. At present there are two widely recognized authoritative references for naming plants in the United States: *A Synonymized Checklist of the Vascular Flora of the United States, Canada, and Greenland* by John. T. Kartesz (1994) and the *Manual of the Vascular Plants of the Northeastern United States and Adjacent Canada* (1991) by H. A. Gleason and A. Cronquist, which was our main reference. If a species was not found in Gleason, we used the common and scientific name as listed by Kartesz.

FERNS AND FERN ALLIES: SEEDLESS VASCULAR PLANTS

Many botanical references have used the name Pteridophytes for all seedless vascular plants, and many botanists have called these plants "ferns and fern allies." Modern classification systems, however, tend to stress the differences among these plants since they represent more than one ancestral line. Therefore most references today apply the name Pteridophytes only to the true ferns and use Sphenophytes for the horsetails and Lycophytes for the clubmosses, spike mosses, and quillworts. In this book there is no need to call attention to the anatomical differences that distinguish these groups. We will instead concentrate on the key features that they share: these are vascular plants that reproduce by spores instead of bearing flowers and seeds.

REPRODUCTION IN SEEDLESS PLANTS

Spores are single cells that are capable of germinating and forming a new individual plant. A spore has a simple structure and is incredibly small. In fact, twenty average-sized fern spores lined up end to end would stretch out to about 1 millimeter (about

.039 in.). Being so small and simple makes spores relatively inexpensive for the plants, but it also means that the survival of a spore is dependent upon its landing by chance in a spot within a very narrow range of environmental conditions.

Spores are produced in special structures called **sporangia.** The sporangia are located in different places, often on the undersides of fertile leaves of ferns, but sometimes on separate fertile stems. The sporangia are tiny, but they usually occur in clusters, called **sori,** that are visible to the naked eye. Size, shape, color, and location of the spore-bearing structures are important keys to the identification of nonflowering plants.

All plants go through a reproductive life cycle called the **alternation of generations.** The familiar green plants we call ferns represent the **sporophyte** generation, which produces large numbers of wind-dispersed spores. If the spores land in a moist, shady environment, they may germinate and grow into a mature **gametophyte** stage, called a **prothallus.** Most people have never seen this generation of ferns because most gametophytes are less than 1/4 in. across and live for only a few days. On the underside of the prothallus two fertile regions will develop, one that produces sperm cells and another that produces eggs. If the prothallus is covered in a thin film of water from dew or a raindrop, the sperm can swim to an egg. The embryo thus formed inside the female gametophyte grows into a genetically unique sporophyte.

Most of the plants in this book produce only one kind of spore and are therefore called **homosporous** plants. The spores of these plants grow into bisexual gametophytes, producing eggs at one end and sperm near the other. A few of our plants are called **heterosporous** because they release spores that grow into either male or female gametophytes. When the male and female gametophytes are separate plants, the movement of sperm to the egg is more difficult, but the chance occurrence of two gametophytes of the correct sexual persuasion does happen, and the species lives on.

A few ferns reproduce by **apogamy,** that is, without gametes. These ferns—for example, several members of the genus *Asplenium* that live on dry cliffs—produce spores that grow into gametophytes, though no gametes are formed. A new sporophyte, essentially a clone of the parent plant, grows out of the gametophyte. Although apogamy does not result in new gene combinations, it does allow the species to survive and spread, and represents a survival advantage for ferns that live in extremely dry environments.

Alternation of generations is a significant process; by this method plants generate genetic variability. It occurs in all plants, but in the flowering plants the process is hidden, taking place deep inside a pollinated flower. In seedless vascular plants the gametophyte generation exists as a completely separate organism and requires a moist environment, partially explaining why flowering plants are so much more successful in our world. Ferns and fernlike plants have been around for a long time and continue to flourish under certain conditions. The flowering plants are relative newcomers but have colonized a much wider range of environments.

THE FAMILIES

Aspleniaceae (Spleenwort Family)

About 700 species in 1 genus make up the family. The complex of hybrid spleenwort ferns in Kentucky is particularly interesting. Three parental species—mountain spleenwort, ebony spleenwort, and walking fern—are capable of interbreeding and forming unique hybrid species. In some cases a parental species can interbreed with its own hybrid offspring, forming another unique hybrid species. The result is a fascinating variety of small, cliff-dwelling ferns that include parents, fertile hybrids, and sterile hybrids.

Asplenium bradleyi	Bradley's spleenwort
A. x ebenoides	Scott's spleenwort
A. montanum	Mountain spleenwort
A. pinnatifidum	Lobed spleenwort
A. platyneuron	Ebony spleenwort
A. resiliens	Blackstem spleenwort
A. rhizophyllum	Walking fern
A. ruta-muraria	Wall rue
A. trichomanes	Maidenhair spleenwort

Azollaceae (Mosquito Fern Family)

The family is made up of 1 genus and 6 species of aquatic ferns found in stagnant water. Azolla is in a sense a commercially valuable plant, since it forms a symbiotic relationship with the nitrogen-fixing cyanobacterium (blue-green alga) Anabaena. Azolla has long been introduced into Asian rice fields to supply nitrogen to rice crops. Kentucky has 1 species.

Azolla caroliniana	Mosquito fern

Blechnaceae (Deer Fern Family)

This is a largely tropical family of 10 genera and over 250 species. The deer fern Blechnum is an important component of the Pacific Northwest rain forests. In Kentucky we have 1 species.

Woodwardia areolata	Netted chain fern

Dennstaedtiaceae (Hay-Scented Fern Family)

Most of the 20 genera and approximately 400 species in this family are tropical plants; in Kentucky we have 2 species in 2 genera. Bracken is an Old English word used for many different kinds of ferns, but over the years the name has become fixed on one in particular. The bracken fern that is so common in Europe and Asia is the very same species as our native bracken fern, making it one of the most widely distributed species of plants on Earth.

Dennstaedtia punctiloba	Hay-scented fern
Pteridium aquilinum	Bracken fern

Dryopteridaceae (Wood Fern Family)

This is a diverse family of about 3,000 species in 60 genera found around the world. As the family name implies, these are typical ferns of woodland areas. The group includes so many of the large, showy ferns we are likely to notice in Kentucky forests that many older reference works referred to this as the Polypodiaceae or fern family. Spores are produced on the undersides of fertile leaves in most, but not all, of the genera. The gametophytes are fairly large and grow above ground, being able to sustain themselves by photosynthesis for several weeks.

Athyrium felix-femina	Lady fern
Cystopteris bulbifera	Bulblet fern
C. protrusa	Fragile fern
C. tennesseensis	Tennessee bladder fern
Deparia acrostichoides	Silvery glade fern
Diplazium pycnocarpon	Glade fern
Dryopteris goldiana	Goldie's wood fern
D. intermedia	Wood fern
D. marginalis	Leather wood fern
Onoclea sensibilis	Sensitive fern
Polystichum acrostichoides	Christmas fern
Woodsia obtusa	Blunt-lobed woodsia

Equisetaceae (Horsetail Family)

This is a small family of 15 species in 1 genus, *Equisetum*. The majority of species occur in the Northern Hemisphere in wet or damp habitats. Modern horsetails in our region are small, herbaceous plants, but in other areas there are horsetails that grow several feet tall. Horsetails are worthy of appreciation: during the Paleozoic era Kentucky had horsetails as large as trees, and our modern horsetails may have existed virtually unchanged for hundreds of millions of years. *Equisetum* could well be the oldest surviving genus of vascular plants on Earth.

At first glance they appear to consist of leafless stems, which are jointed into nodes and internodes, noticeably ribbed, and hollow at maturity. The stems contain deposits of silica called opal that give the plant a rough texture. Most people overlook the leaves: tiny megaphylls arranged in rings at the nodes. (Megaphyll literally means "large leaf"; a megaphyll is larger than a microphyll [see below] and has a more complex anatomy.) Deep underground is a rhizome from which the stems arise, and vegetative propagation from the rhizome forms dense colonies.

Sexual reproduction is accomplished by the formation of spore-bearing cones called strobili that are borne either at the tips of vegetative stems or on separate fertile stems. Each strobilus is made up of spirals of umbrella-shaped structures that produce spores and forcefully sling them from the mother plant. Horsetails are homosporous, although individual gametophytes may be bisexual or male only. Spores that fall on moist soil germinate readily, and mound-shaped green gametophytes a few millimeters in diameter mature in a few weeks.

Equisetum arvense	Common horsetail
E. hyemale	Scouring rush

Hymenophyllaceae (Filmy Fern Family)

There are 6 genera and about 650 species in the filmy fern family. Although filmy ferns are common in wet tropical regions around the world, only 2 species, both in the genus *Trichomanes,* have been found in Kentucky. They seem to be restricted to habitats where they are protected from drying out; in fact, they are known only from sheltered areas in the backs of sandstone rockshelters. The occurrence of filmy ferns in Kentucky suggests that they could be relicts from a time before the Pleistocene ice age when Kentucky's climate was considerably warmer and wetter than it is today.

One of our species of *Trichomanes* has apparently lost the ability to form the typical fernlike sporophyte generation and is known only as a gametophyte that resembles a finely branched, green thread. The continued existence of the gametophyte generation is made possible by the production of vegetative buds called gemmae that break off and grow into new gametophytes.

Trichomanes boschianum	Filmy fern
T. intricatum	Appalachian bristle fern

Isoetaceae (Quillwort Family)

The family consists of over 60 members contained within a single genus, *Isoetes.* Quillworts are interesting to botanists because they have secondary growth: within the stem a layer of actively growing cells called a cambium causes the stem to increase in diameter in yearly increments. Unlike the cambial layer of trees, however, which produces water-conducting xylem tissue to the inner side of the cambium and sugar-conducting phloem to the outer side, the cambial layer of quillworts produces a strange combination of xylem and phloem on the inner side.

Quillworts are also interesting because they utilize a photosynthetic pathway called CAM, or crassulacean acid metabolism, characteristic of succulent plants that live in arid environments.

The leaves of *Isoetes* are microphylls, or tiny leaves with a single, unbranched vein and a very simple connection to the vascular system of the plant's stem. The leaves contain four long air chambers, an adaptation for surviving periodic flooding. Most leaves can become sporophylls, although the outermost leaves may be sterile. Quillworts are heterosporous: male sporangia form on the bases of the innermost leaves, female spores develop to the outside. The unisexual gametophytes are extremely small, consisting of only a few cells.

Isoetes butlerii   Quillwort
I. engelmanii
I. melanopoda

Lycopodiaceae (Clubmoss Family)

Lycopods in our region are called clubmosses, fir-mosses, or ground pines. About 400 species are recognized worldwide, mostly in the tropics, where they tend to be epiphytic. Our temperate species, on the other hand, are terrestrial, and therefore much easier to observe. All of our modern lycopods are small plants without woody tissue, but in Paleozoic times much of Kentucky was covered by forests of tree-sized woody lycopods that dominated swamplands and left behind many of the fossils we call "petrified wood."

The lycopod plant consists of erect stems growing from a horizontal rhizome. Tiny leaves (microphylls) are borne in a spiral around the stem.

Lycopods reproduce both vegetatively and sexually. Many species produce vegetative reproductive structures called gemmae that can break away from the mother plant and grow into a new, albeit genetically identical, sporophyte plant. Sexual reproduction takes place by the production of spores, and the nature of the spore-forming leaves, or sporophylls, is an important characteristic used to distinguish members of the family. Some species produce spores on the upper sides or in the axils of fertile leaves that are similar to and intermingled with the vegetative leaves. Other species bear sporophylls in a cone-shaped strobilus at the tip of a special branch.

Lycopods are homosporous, producing only one kind of spore, which grows into a bisexual gametophyte. Lycopod spores require several years to develop into mature gametophytes, which are in turn capable of living for several years and producing more than one sporophyte. The gametophytes of members of the genus *Lycopodiella* are partially subterranean with some photosynthetic tissue protruding above ground. Gametophytes in *Huperzia, Lycopodium,* and *Diphasiastrum* are completely subterranean structures, nutritionally dependent on associations with mycorrhizal fungi (underground fungi that grow into the roots of the plant and help it absorb water and nutrients).

Lycopods have little commercial or horticultural value, although some have been gathered for Christmas greenery and the spores of certain species were once collected and sold as lycopodium powder, a highly flammable material used in fireworks and magic shows.

For many years botanists have considered all Kentucky lycopods to be members of the genus *Lycopodium,* but modern treatments divide them into 4 genera based on differences in the structure of their sporophylls and gametophytes, as well as the number and size of their chromosomes.

Diphasiastrum digitatum	Southern ground cedar
D. tristachyum	Wiry ground cedar
Huperzia lucidula	Shining clubmoss
H. porophila	Rock clubmoss
Lycopodium clavatum	Running pine
L. obscurum	Ground pine

Lygodiaceae (Climbing Fern Family)

This family contains a single genus, *Lygodium,* and about 40 species. Climbing ferns are found around the world, mostly in the tropics, but only 1 species is native to Kentucky. Two Asian species of *Lygodium* have escaped from cultivation in the southeastern United States and are now considered to be invasive pests.

Lygodium palmatum	Climbing fern

Ophioglossaceae (Adder's-Tongue Fern Family)

Plants in this family usually produce one leaf per year; each leaf consists of two segments, one vegetative, the other fertile. The structure of this fertile leaf and its spore-bearing tissue is unique, and the family is considered to be distinct from all other living ferns. The spores germinate and grow very slowly, taking several years to form mature bisexual gametophytes. The gametophytes are found entirely underground and rely on mycorrhizal fungi for their nutrition.

The name *Botrychium* comes from the Greek word *botrys,* which refers to a cluster of grapes. Ferns in the genus *Botrychium,* called grape ferns, are primarily found in the temperate regions of the Northern Hemisphere and are unique among all living ferns because their stem contains a vascular cambium.

Members of the genus *Ophioglossum,* which means "snake tongue" in Greek, are most common in the tropics. One species of *Ophioglossum* has 1,260 chromosomes, the highest diploid number known of any living organism. About 60 species of this family have been described worldwide.

Botrychium dissectum	Cut-leaf grape fern
B. virginianum	Rattlesnake fern
Ophioglossum engelmannii	Adder's-tongue fern
O. pycnostichum	Adder's-tongue fern

Osmundaceae (Royal Fern Family)

Three genera and 18 species of this family have been described around the world. There are 10 species in the genus *Osmunda*, including 3 that are found in Kentucky. Members of this family bear two kinds of fronds: green vegetative fronds, which feed the plant; and brown fertile fronds, which produce spores. Several species are grown as ornamentals, and the roots of tropical *Osmunda* are ground up and used as a potting medium by orchid growers.

Osmunda cinnamomea	Cinnamon fern
O. claytonii	Interrupted fern
O. regalis	Royal fern

Polypodiaceae (Polypody Family)

Polypody is Greek for "many feet," referring to the branched rhizome that forms the base of the plant. This is a complex family of 45 genera and about 500 species of mostly tropical ferns. Several are cultivated as ornamentals, including *Platycerium*, the staghorn fern, a popular greenhouse plant. Two species in the genus *Polypody* occur in Kentucky.

Polypodium polypodioides	Resurrection fern
P. virginianum	Rockcap fern

Pteridaceae (Maidenhair Fern Family)

This is a large and complex group, consisting of about 40 genera and close to 1,000 species. Some authors prefer the name Adiantaceae for the family, which apparently contains several distinct evolutionary lines. Changes in classification of the group are likely.

Adiantum capillus-veneris	Southern maidenhair fern
A. pedatum	Maidenhair fern
Cheilanthes lanosa	Woolly lip fern

| *Pellaea atropurpurea* | Purple cliffbrake |
| *P. glabella* | Smooth cliffbrake |

Selaginellaceae (Spikemoss Family)

Selaginella is a particularly interesting genus because it is heterosporous: unlike ferns, the plants produce two kinds of spores, male and female. Both kinds of spores are produced within the same strobilus, or cone made up of fertile leaves. Spores are released from the mother plants, and spores from many different individuals can intermingle in an appropriate environment. Spikemoss spores germinate very quickly, and the unisexual gametophytes that develop are extremely small and short-lived.

Over 700 species of *Selaginella* have been identified, mostly in the tropics, but spikemosses are found in temperate areas as well. Some species of spikemosses are showy enough to be cultivated as ornamentals for use in small indoor pot gardens.

| *Selaginella apoda* | Spikemoss |

Thelypteridaceae (Marsh Fern Family)

Depending upon which reference one checks, this family has been considered to include from 1 to as many as 30 genera and 900 species worldwide. Historically, authors have included these ferns in the Dryopteridaceae or Aspleniaceae, but the most modern treatments have set them apart in their own family. In Kentucky the group is represented by 3 species in 2 genera.

Phegopteris hexagonoptera	Beech fern
Thelypteris novaboracensis	New York fern
T. palustris	Marsh fern

Vittariaceae (Shoestring Fern Family)

This is a fairly common tropical family, consisting of 10 genera and about 100 species. In Florida there is a shoestring fern that grows on the trunks and branches of palm trees, with long, narrow fronds hanging in clumps. Our native *Vittaria* doesn't look much like a shoestring—in fact, it doesn't look much like a fern. The *Vittaria* found in Kentucky is one of those species of ferns that exists only in the gametophyte stage, reproducing vegetatively through the production of gemmae. Like the filmy ferns, these plants are able to survive Kentucky's climate only in the moist twilight of overhanging sandstone rockshelters.

| *Vittaria appalachiana* | Appalachian gametophyte |

FLOWERING PLANTS: THE SEED PRODUCERS

The production of seeds is obviously a very successful strategy for plant reproduction, since seed plants are by far the dominant group of plants, and arguably the dominant life form on the planet. A seed is much more complex and much larger than a spore. The outer surface of a seed is covered by a seed coat that protects the contents from harsh environmental conditions. Inside, a seed contains the embryo of a new plant, which inside the seed already consists of a tiny leaf or two, a little shoot, and a tiny little root. Along with the embryo there is usually a packet of stored food to nourish the developing plant during the critical stages of germination. Seed plants invest a large portion of their resources in the production of their seeds, but each individual seed stands a fair chance of surviving and successfully germinating.

All seed plants are vascular plants, but not all vascular plants are seed plants. Seed plants make up most of the familiar plants in our world, including trees, shrubs, herbs, and grasses. We divide the seed plants into two divisions based on the manner in which their seeds are borne. Gymnosperms, such as coniferous trees, produce cones instead of flowers and bear naked seeds on the surface of ripened cone scales. Our attention in this book focuses on angiosperms, those seed plants that produce flowers and bear seeds inside a protective vessel called a carpel.

THE FUNCTION OF FLOWERS

Although the flower may seem to wildflower enthusiasts to be the most important part of a plant, it is certainly not the most important to the plant itself. The flower is merely a means to an end. The most important part of a flowering plant has to be the next crop of seeds. The function of the flower is to facilitate the exchange of genetic information and bring about the formation of new plants. The mechanics of this process are called pollination, the transfer of pollen from one plant to another. Actually, some plants can pollinate themselves, but this does not promote the kind of genetic exchange that results in new combinations of genes and improves a population of plants.

The transfer of pollen from one flower part to another is accomplished in one of several ways. Some plants merely release their pollen into the wind; some of that pollen, by random chance, will fall on the appropriate parts of flowers of other individuals of the same species. The odds of any particular grain of wind-carried pollen landing in just the right place are astronomically small, but it only takes one to do the job. Wind pollination seems to work best when large numbers of individuals of a species are living close together. A more precise mechanism would be specific carriers that visited one individual after another of the same species, literally carrying pollen from one flower to the next. The potential carriers are out there, but there has to be a reason for them to perform this work.

The first animal pollinators might have been beetles. Beetles have a fairly well developed sense of smell, so if a plant has even a hint of an attractive odor, it stands a good chance of attracting beetles. Individuals with a fruity, spicy, or fermented scent would certainly draw beetles, but even beetles would eventually learn that they need more than just a whiff of pleasant perfume. Plants are loaded with sugars, and if even a tiny drop of sugar could be gleaned from inside a flower, those beetles would not only be attracted to the scent of the flowers, they would also be rewarded for their efforts. When one of those beetles emerged from a flower, refreshed after a brief snort of perfume and a shot of nectar, and, by the way, dusted with pollen, it would be likely to crawl inside the next similar flower it smelled, and some of that pollen it was carrying might fall off in just the right spot.

Many animals act as pollinators for flowering plants. There are about 20,000 different kinds of bees, and most of them eat nectar and feed pollen to their young. Bees have a keen sense of sight and are attracted to flowers that are brightly colored, especially yellow. Flies, butterflies, moths, birds, and even bats can act as pollinators. The woods are full of fascinating combinations of attractive flowers and pollinators that have become specialized for particular groups of plants. Over countless generations the plants have refined their features to make the most of whatever pollinators are out there. After all, those with the most attractive features are more likely to get their pollen spread around.

Wildflower enthusiasts should think about what these plants are up to. They are organisms trying to survive and reproduce so more generations of these plants can exist. The plants are not capable of smelling their own fragrance. They cannot taste their own nectar, nor does the production of nectar serve any direct purpose for the plants themselves. Plants cannot be aware that they have beautiful, colorful, or wonderfully scented flowers and that humans find them attractive. Nevertheless, the fragrance, the nectar, and the bright colors do benefit the plants by attracting pollinators. It stands to reason that plants with these characteristics should be more successful at being pollinated than plants with drab, dull flowers or flowers with scents that repel potential pollinators. Now we are approaching the true function of beautiful flowers. It has everything to do with bees, beetles, and flies, and very little to do with humans.

THE STRUCTURE OF FLOWERS

Knowing the structure of a flower is very useful in the identification of flowering plants. The first thing to determine when trying to identify an unknown flowering plant is whether it is a monocot or a dicot. **Monocots** usually have parallel veins running the length of the leaf from base to tip and will almost always have flower parts such as petals and sepals in threes or multiples of three. The "cot" in monocot is short for cotyledon or seed leaf. Monocots have one seed leaf, which emerges from the soil as the seeds germinate. Only about 28 percent of all known species of flowering plants are monocots, but there are many outstanding and important plants in this group, including lilies, orchids, grasses, and even palm trees.

Dicots usually have leaf veins that fork in various ways and typically have flower parts in fours or fives. As the name implies, when dicotyledons (such as peas and sunflowers) germinate, they have two seed leaves.

It is also useful to note the overall appearance of an unknown flower when you are looking at it head-on. Flowers are said to have **radial symmetry** when there are several ways in which the flower could be divided into two mirror images. Flowers with radial symmetry are made up of parts that are all about the same size and appearance. Often some parts of the flower are larger or perhaps shaped differently than the others. This means there is only one plane along which the flower can be divided to form two mirror images, and the flower is said to have **bilateral symmetry**.

All of the different kinds of flowers on all of the many plants you will ever see are different only because of the modification or loss of just four fundamental parts. Learning to recognize these four parts will greatly enhance your ability to identify and distinguish wildflowers.

The **petals** are sterile segments that are often brightly colored to attract pollinators. As a group, all of the petals of a single flower are called the **corolla. Sepals**, typically green, are modified leaves that protect the flower while it is in the bud stage. After the flower bud opens, the sepals usually surround the bases of the petals. All together the sepals of a single flower are called the **calyx**. In some cases the sepals and petals are so similar that we use the term **segment** or **tepal** instead of trying to distinguish between them. The term **perianth** is used for the corolla and calyx taken as a whole.

The fertile parts of a flower are found in the center. The part we often think of as the female structure is the **pistil**, also called a **carpel**, often shaped something like a bud vase with a swollen bottom. The very top of the pistil is the **stigma**, the sticky surface upon which pollen grains land and germinate. The **style** forms the tube of the pistil and holds the stigma up above surrounding flower parts where it is most likely to catch pollen. The lower portion of the pistil is the **ovary**, and inside a fertile ovary are one or more chambers in which egg cells are produced.

Surrounding the pistil in most flowers are those fertile structures we often think of as the male parts, the **stamens,** which produce pollen. Stamens are made up of two parts: the **anthers** are the swollen tips of the stamens where pollen is actually produced; the **filaments** are the stalks that hold the anther up to better disperse the pollen. A flower that has both stamens and a pistil is said to be a **perfect flower**. Many flowers lack either stamens or pistils, or occasionally both, and are called **imperfect flowers**. A species with imperfect flowers may bear male and female flowers separately on the same plant, in which case we say the species is **monoecious**. In

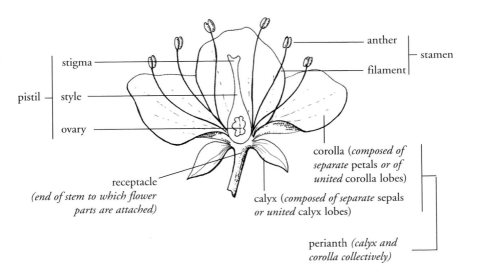

Generalized Flower Structure

dioecious species there are male plants, which have only staminate flowers, and female plants, which have only pistillate flowers.

Most flowers are produced at the tip of a short stalk called a **pedicel**. There is a structure at the end of the pedicel called a **receptacle** that holds the principal parts of the flower. Flowers may be borne singly or they may occur clustered in a group we call an **inflorescence**. The main stem of an inflorescence is called the **peduncle**. Each flower within an inflorescence may have its own pedicel, or it may be attached to the peduncle without any stalk, in which case we say the flowers are **sessile**. The simplest kind of inflorescence is a **spike**, an elongated peduncle with sessile flowers. A **raceme** is similar to a spike, but each flower is borne on a pedicel. A raceme with a branching peduncle is called a **panicle**. Two kinds of inflorescences have flat tops: **Corymbs** have pedicels attached along a vertical axis, but the lower pedicels are longer and hold their flowers at the same height as the shorter, uppermost pedicels. An inflorescence with all pedicels arising at the same point is called an **umbel**. Umbels can be simple or, if the flower stalks are branched, compound. Finally, flowers in the aster family are arranged in a **head**. The head is composed of a receptacle with many small modified leaves called bracts. The bracts are collectively called the **involucre**. Attached to the receptacle above the involucre are usually two kinds of flowers: short, tubular flowers in the center, called disk flowers; and longer, flat flowers around the margin of the disk, called ray flowers.

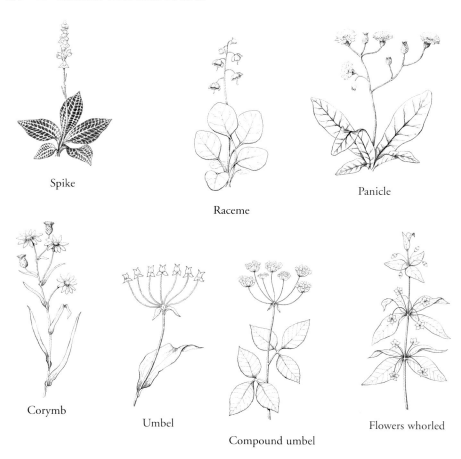

Spike

Raceme

Panicle

Corymb

Umbel

Compound umbel

Flowers whorled

Arrangement of Flowers

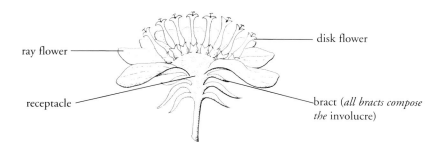

ray flower

disk flower

receptacle

bract (*all bracts compose the* involucre)

Section through a Composite Head

VEGETATIVE PARTS OF A FLOWERING PLANT

It is often possible, and sometimes necessary, to identify plants using only their leaves, stems, and roots. Leaves are organs for feeding the plant. Plants have the remarkable ability to use carbon dioxide from the atmosphere and water from the soil to make sugars. They not only feed themselves, but they also make such a huge surplus of sugars that animals are able to live on it. All animal life on the planet is totally dependent upon green plants for existence.

As photosynthetic organs, leaves are usually green, flat, and wide. Many plants have narrow leaves, however, because a narrow leaf is an advantage in some environments, such as very sunny or extremely dry habitats. Regardless of the shape, a typical leaf is made up of the **blade**, the broad part that harvests light for photosynthesis, and the stalk that holds the blade, the **petiole**. A leaf that has no petiole and is attached directly to the plant stem is said to be **sessile.** Near the base of the petiole there are sometimes small appendages that resemble tiny leaves and are called **stipules**.

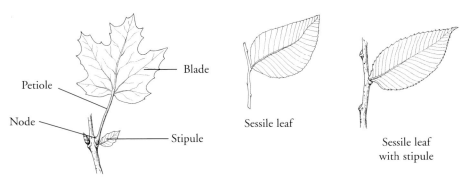

Parts of a Leaf

Types of Leaves

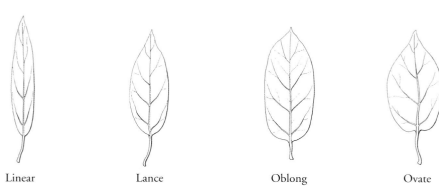

| Linear | Lance | Oblong | Ovate |

Leaf Shapes

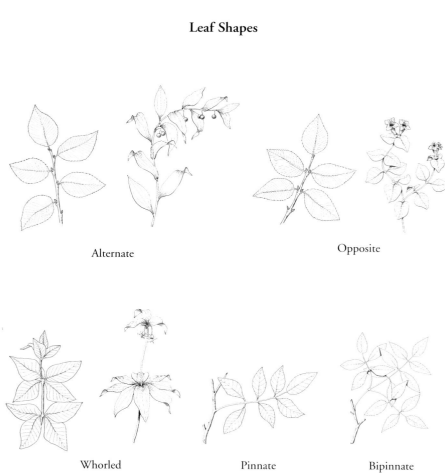

Alternate   Opposite

Whorled   Pinnate   Bipinnate

Arrangements of Leaves

The overall shape and appearance of the leaf blade are often important clues in plant identification. Botanists use an amazing number of terms to precisely describe the shape and texture of leaves, but we use lay terms as much as possible in this book. It will be helpful to review the line drawings of leaf shapes. Pay particular attention to the difference between **alternate** and **opposite** leaves. Note that alternate leaves are not necessarily arranged just left and right, as it might appear in a drawing. Alternate leaves usually, but not always, spiral around the stem when viewed from directly above. Opposite leaves arise from the same point along the stem and point in opposite directions. Opposite leaves are often staggered so the first pair may point north and south, the next pair might point east and west, and so on. This arrangement minimizes shading by overlapping leaves. Leaves can also be **simple** (made up of a single leaf blade) or **compound** (made up of several leaflets combined into one leaf). It is important not to mistake a single leaflet for an entire leaf.

Although the underground portions of the plant are hidden to us, in many cases we have included descriptions of the roots. The roots anchor the plant in the soil, absorb water and mineral nutrients, and store nutrient reserves over winter. Most dicots have a highly branched root system with a few large roots, maybe even a central taproot, and a network of smaller lateral roots. Most monocots have a cluster of similar-sized roots we call a **fibrous** root system. In addition to roots, many plants have extensive underground shoots. **Bulbs** are technically underground stems with thick overlapping leaves, like onions. **Corms** are underground stems growing vertically with thin, papery leaves; **rhizomes** are underground stems that grow horizontally. **Tubers** are underground stems that function as storage organs with numerous eyes, or buds, like potatoes.

LIFE CYCLES OF FLOWERING PLANTS

One key to understanding the lives of plants is to recognize that some plants flower and produce seed only once in their lifetime, while others flower and produce seed many times. **Annuals** are plants that complete their life cycle in less than one year. Summer annuals germinate in the spring, then grow to maturity, flower, produce seed, and die by the end of summer. Winter annuals germinate in the fall and overwinter as a basal rosette of leaves, ready to take off and bolt to maturity and death in the spring. Some plants have such short life cycles that they can germinate, mature, flower, and die within a few weeks. We call these plants **ephemerals. Biennials** are plants that require more than one year to grow to maturity but only flower once and then die when maturity is achieved. A biennial plant germinates from seed and grows into a basal rosette in the first year of its life, then overwinters that first year as a rosette. The plant will continue to grow as a rosette until it reaches a certain critical size that can be stimulated to flower. Biennials do not always flower in the second year of life; in fact it may take five or more years for the plant to be ready. There are very few woodland biennials in our region. Depending upon the specific environmental conditions, it is possible for a species to be an annual in some regions and a biennial in others. Plants that live, flower, and produce seed year after year are called **perennials.** Perennials do not live forever; they have life expectancies just like people, but many of our woodland perennials seem to live as long as, or longer than, most people. The flowers described in this book are perennials except where noted.

THE FAMILIES: DICOTS

Acanthaceae (Acanthus Family)

The acanthus family includes about 250 genera and 2,500 species of herbs and shrubs, mostly from tropical regions, and with centers of distribution in Africa and Southeast Asia. Included are several important ornamentals, such as bear's-breech, *Acanthus mollis,* and clockvines, *Thunbergia* spp. In Kentucky this family is represented by 4 species in 2 genera.

Justicia americana	American water willow
Ruellia caroliniensis	Carolina wild petunia
R. humilis	Glade wild petunia
R. strepens	Limestone wild petunia

Apiaceae (Carrot Family)

Older botanical books called this family Umbelliferae because the flowers are arranged in umbels. The modern name comes from *Apium,* the genus that includes *A. graveolens*, our garden celery plant. The carrot family consists of 300 genera and about 2,500 species of herbs, most found in temperate regions of the Northern Hemisphere. The family includes many poisonous species such as poison hemlock, as well as edible species like carrots, parsnips, celery, parsley, and dill and the spices anise and caraway.

Angelica venenosa	Hairy angelica
Cicuta maculata	Water hemlock
Erigenia bulbosa	Harbinger of spring
Eryngium prostratum	Spreading eryngo, prostrate eryngo
E. yuccifolium	Rattlesnake master
Osmorhiza claytonii	Bland sweet cicely
O. longistylis	Sweet cicely
Sanicula gregaria	Clustered snakeroot
Taenidia integerrima	Yellow pimpernel
Thaspium barbinode	Meadow parsnip
T. pinnatifidum	Narrow-leaved meadow parsnip

T. trifoliatum	Smooth meadow parsnip
Zizia aptera	Golden alexanders
Z. aurea	Twice-compound golden alexanders
Z. trifoliata	Mountain golden alexanders

Apocynaceae (Dogbane Family)

The dogbane family is a group of 200 genera and about 2,000 species of herbs, shrubs, trees, and woody vines found mostly in tropical regions. The family is named for *Apocynum cannabinum,* dogbane, a perennial herb with toxic sap, which is widespread in the United States. The family includes one member that is both a popular ornamental and an invasive, exotic plant: *Vinca minor,* periwinkle.

Amsonia tabernaemontana	Bluestar
Apocynum cannabinum	Indian hemp

Araliaceae (Ginseng Family)

The ginseng family includes about 55 genera and 700 species of herbs, shrubs, and trees, some of which are commercially important. Ginseng is cultivated and collected from natural populations for its reputed medicinal effects. The family also includes *Hedera helix,* English ivy, an invasive exotic; and *Schefflera,* a tropical shrub that is a popular houseplant in our country.

Aralia racemosa	Spikenard
Panax quinquefolius	Ginseng
P. trifolius	Dwarf ginseng

Aristolochiacea (Birthwort Family)

A family of 7 genera and about 625 species, mostly woody vines in the genus *Aristolochia.* Members are found around the world, principally in the tropics, with only a few species in temperate regions. The flowers have no petals, but the sepals are large and may be fused into unusual shapes. Unlike most dicots, the flower parts are found in threes or multiples of threes.

Asarum canadense	Wild ginger
Hexastylis arifolia	Little brown jug

Asclepiadaceae (Milkweed Family)

The milkweed family is a diverse group of 250 genera and roughly 2,000 species of herbs, shrubs, trees, and woody vines, usually with milky juice. This is primarily a tropical family, but there are many temperate members. The flowers commonly have 5 reflexed petals with extensions that form a projecting corona or crown.

Asclepias amplexicaulis	Clasping milkweed
A. exaltata	Poke milkweed
A. hirtella	Prairie milkweed
A. incarnata	Swamp milkweed
A. perennis	Smoothseed milkweed
A. purpurascens	Purple milkweed
A. quadrifolia	Four-leaved milkweed
A. syriaca	Common milkweed
A. tuberosa	Butterfly weed
A. variegata	White milkweed
A. verticillata	Whorled milkweed
A. viridiflora	Green milkweed
A. viridis	Ozark milkweed
Matelea carolinensis	Milkvine
M. decipiens	Angle-pod
M. gonocarpa	Common angle-pod
M. obliqua	Angle-pod

Asteraceae (Aster Family)

The aster family consists of nearly 1,100 genera and 20,000 species, mostly herbs, but there are some shrubs, woody vines, and even a few trees. The small flowers are arranged into large discoid heads, usually with tube-shaped disk flowers in the center and strap-shaped ray flowers around the margin. Because the flower heads are actually a composite of many little flowers of two different kinds, botanists historically called this family *Compositae,* the composite family. Within the family there are several subgroups, including some with only disk flowers, such as the ironweeds, joe-pye weed, and elephant's foot. There are also groups with only ray flowers, such as chicory, dandelions, and the lettuces. This is a huge family, with about 1,500 species of *Senecio,* 900 species of *Vernonia,* 800 species of *Hieracium,* and 600 species of *Eupatorium.* In Kentucky there are about 40 known species of *Aster* and 33 species of *Solidago,* the goldenrods, 1 of which is Kentucky's state flower, although officially the state has not decided which.

Genetic studies have shown that the genus *Aster* is not a monophyletic group and deserves to be split into several genera that reflect common ancestry. Future references are likely to show that there are no true species of the genus *Aster* in North America. Although the common names will probably not change, most of our species with flowers in panicles will be placed in *Symphyotrichum,* those with flat-topped flower clusters in *Eurybia,* the flat-topped white asters in *Doellingeria,* the stiff-leaved asters in *Ionactis,* those with cylindrical involucres in *Sericocarpus,* and so on. At least 8 genera will replace the old genus *Aster* on our continent, and the true members of *Aster* will be restricted to Europe and Asia.

The family is of some economic importance, featuring food plants such as lettuce, *Lactuca sativa*; the artichoke, *Cynara scolymus*; and endive, *Cichorium endivia.* The group also includes ornamentals like asters, *Aster* spp.; dahlias, *Dahlia pinnata*; daisies, *Chrysanthemum* spp.; zinnias, *Zinnia* spp.; and sunflowers, *Helianthus* spp. Finally, there are some troublesome agricultural weeds, such as ragweeds, *Ambrosia* spp.; thistles, *Cirsium* spp.; and dandelions, *Taraxacum officinale.*

Ageratina rugosum	White snakeroot
Antennaria plantaginifolia	Pussytoes
A. solitaria	One-flowered pussytoes
Aster cordifolius	Heart-leaved aster, blue wood aster
A. divaricatus	White wood aster
A. infirmus	Cornel-leaf aster
A. laevis	Smooth aster
A. lanceolatus	Panicled aster
A. lateriflorus	Calico aster
A. linariifolius	Stiff-leaf aster, stiff aster
A. lowrieanus	Lowrie's aster
A. macrophyllus	Large-leaf aster
A. novae-angliae	New England aster
A. oblongifolius	Aromatic aster
A. patens	Spreading aster
A. paternus	White-top aster
A. pilosus	Frostweed aster
A. prenanthoides	Crooked-stem aster
A. sagittifolius	Arrow-leaved aster
A. schreberi	Schreber's aster
A. shortii	Short's aster
A. solidagineus	Narrow-leaved white-topped aster
A. surculosus	Creeping aster
A. umbellatus	Flat-topped aster
A. undulatus	Wavy-leaf aster
A. vimineus	Small white aster
Astranthium integrifolium	Western daisy
Bidens aristosa	Tickseed sunflower
B. bipinnata	Spanish needles
B. frondosa	Sticktight

Cacalia atriplicifolia	Pale Indian plantain
C. muhlenbergii	Great Indian plantain
Chrysopsis mariana	Maryland golden aster
C. graminifolia	Grass-leaved golden aster
Cirsium altissimum	Tall thistle
C. carolinianum	Carolina thistle
C. discolor	Field thistle
Coreopsis auriculata	Eared tickseed
C. lanceolata	Lance-leaf coreopsis
C. major	Tickseed
C. tripteris	Tall tickseed
Echinacea pallida	Narrow-leaved coneflower
E. purpurea	Purple coneflower
E. simulata	Glade coneflower
Elephantopus carolinianus	Elephant foot
Erigeron annuus	Annual fleabane
E. philadelphicus	Philadelphia fleabane
E. pulchellus	Robin's plantain
E. strigosus	Daisy fleabane
Eupatorium coelestinum	Mist flower
E. fistulosum	Joe-pye weed
E. hyssopifolium	Hyssop-leaved thoroughwort
E. perfoliatum	Boneset
E. purpureum	Green-stemmed joe-pye weed
E. rotundifolium	Round-leaf thoroughwort
E. serotinum	Late thoroughwort
E. sessilifolium	Upland boneset
Gnaphalium obtusifolium	Sweet everlasting, pearly everlasting
G. purpureum	Purple cudweed
Grindelia squarrosa	Gumweed
Helenium autumnale	Autumn sneezeweed
H. flexuosum	Purple-headed sneezeweed
Helianthus annuus	Common sunflower
H. angustifolius	Narrow-leaved sunflower
H. decapetalus	Forest sunflower, thin-leaved sunflower
H. divaricatus	Woodland sunflower
H. grosseserratus	Sawtooth sunflower
H. microcephalus	Small-headed sunflower
H. mollis	Ashy sunflower, downy sunflower
H. strumosus	Rough-leaved sunflower

H. tuberosus	Jerusalem artichoke
Heliopsis helianthoides	Ox-eye sunflower
Hieracium gronovii	Hairy hawkweed
H. venosum	Hawkweed
Krigia biflora	Dwarf dandelion
Lactuca floridana	Blue lettuce
Liatris aspera	Rough blazing star
L. spicata	Dense blazing star
L. squarrosa	Scaly blazing star
L. squarrulosa	Southern blazing star
Parthenium integrifolium	Wild quinine
Polymnia canadensis	Pale-flowered leafcup
P. uvedalia	Yellow leafcup, bear's foot
Prenanthes altissima	Rattlesnake root
P. serpentaria	Lion's foot
Ratibida pinnata	Gray-headed coneflower
Rudbeckia fulgida	Orange coneflower
R. hirta	Black-eyed Susan
R. laciniata	Wild goldenglow
R. triloba	Brown-eyed Susan
Senecio anonymus	Appalachian ragwort
S. aureus	Golden ragwort
S. glabellus	Butterweed
S. obovatus	Round-leaved ragwort
Silphium integrifolium	Rosinweed
S. laciniatum	Compass plant
S. perfoliatum	Cup plant
S. pinnatifidum	Cut-leaf prairie dock
S. terebinthinaceum	Prairie dock
S. trifoliatum	Whorled rosinweed
Solidago altissima	Tall goldenrod
S. arguta	Forest goldenrod
S. bicolor	Silverrod, white goldenrod
S. caesia	Wreath goldenrod, blue-stemmed goldenrod
S. canadensis	Common goldenrod
S. erecta	Slender goldenrod, erect goldenrod
S. flexicaulis	Zigzag goldenrod
S. gigantea	Great goldenrod
S. graminifolia	Grass-leaved goldenrod
S. hispida	Hairy goldenrod

S. juncea	Early goldenrod
S. nemoralis	Gray goldenrod
S. rigida	Stiff goldenrod, rigid goldenrod
S. rugosa	Rough goldenrod
S. speciosa	Showy goldenrod
S. sphacelata	False goldenrod
S. ulmifolia	Elm-leaved goldenrod
Verbesina alternifolia	Yellow wingstem, yellow ironweed
V. occidentalis	Yellow crownbeard
V. virginica	Frostweed, white crownbeard
Vernonia gigantea	Ironweed

Balsaminaceae (Touch-Me-Not Family)

The touch-me-not family consists of 4 genera and 500 species of herbs, occurring mostly in tropical and subtropical Africa and Asia. There are over 450 species of *Impatiens,* mostly native to Southeast Asia, including many horticulturally important ornamental plants.

Impatiens capensis	Orange jewelweed
I. pallida	Yellow jewelweed, pale jewelweed

Berberidaceae (Barberry Family)

The barberry family is a group of close to 600 species in about 15 genera, mostly shrubs and perennial herbs of the temperate Northern Hemisphere. Most members of the family, in fact nearly 500 species, are barberries—thorny shrubs that are popular ornamentals because of their flowers, attractive fruit, and fall color.

Caulophyllum thalictroides	Blue cohosh
Jeffersonia diphylla	Twinleaf
Podophyllum peltatum	Mayapple

Boraginaceae (Borage Family)

The borage family is made up of about 100 genera and 2,000 species, mostly herbs found in the Mediterranean region. The name comes from borage, *Borago officinalis,* a common weed in Europe that has been used since the Middle Ages to impart a fresh cucumber-like flavor to food and water.

Cynoglossum virginianum	Wild comfrey
Lithospermum canescens	Hoary puccoon
Mertensia virginica	Virginia bluebells
Myosotis verna	White forget-me-not

Brassicaceae (Mustard Family)

Named for *Brassica,* the generic name for several plants whose seeds are ground to make prepared mustard, this family includes about 3,000 species in 350 genera, mostly herbs found in temperate regions. Because the basic flower plan is 4 petals in the shape of a cross, older botanical references called this family Cruciferae. Flowers typically have 6 stamens, 4 long and 2 short. The fruit is a long capsule called a siliqua or silicula. This is an important horticultural family, including ornamentals such as *Alyssum, Hesperis, Mathiola,* and garden vegetables such as broccoli, brussels sprouts, cabbage, cauliflower, radish, kohlrabi, and turnips.

Arabis laevigata	Smooth rock cress
A. hirsuta	Hairy rock cress
A. lyrata	Lyre-leaved rock cress
A. missouriensis	Missouri rock cress
A. perstellata	Rock cress
Cardamine bulbosa	Spring cress
C. douglassii	Purple cress
C. parviflora	Small-flowered bitter cress
C. pensylvanica	Bitter cress
C. rotundifolia	Mountain cress, round-leaved bitter cress
Dentaria diphylla	Two-leaved toothwort, crinkleroot, broad-leaved toothwort
D. heterophylla	Slender toothwort
D. laciniata	Cut-leaf toothwort
Iodanthus pinnatifidus	Purple rocket
Leavenworthia exigua	Pasture glade cress
L. torulosa	Beaded glade cress
L. uniflora	Small glade cress

Buxaceae (Boxwood Family)

This is a small family of about 100 species in 4 genera. The family is almost entirely made up of evergreen shrubs and small trees, but 1 genus, *Pachysandra,* consisting of 4 species found in eastern Asia and 1 in the southeastern United States, is herbaceous. Several members are of economic interest. The Japanese pachysandra, *Pachysandra terminalis,* is sold commercially in this country as an evergreen ground cover. Two species of boxwood, the Asian *Buxus microphylla* and the European *B. sempervirens,* are popular ornamental shrubs used as evergreen hedges. The wood of *B. sempervirens* was once in demand for use in wood engravings used to illustrate books and newspapers and is still prized for use in carving and the manufacture of rulers and small instruments.

Pachysandra procumbens	Allegheny spurge

Cactaceae (Cactus Family)

The cactus family is made up of about 2,000 species in 100 genera of herbs and shrubs found in the Western Hemisphere. Cacti are generally shallow-rooted plants adapted to dry climates, with spines that are considered to be reduced leaves and stems that carry out photosynthesis in place of leaves. Because their native habitats are very fragile and cactus gardens have become quite popular, the family is well represented on endangered- and threatened-species lists.

Opuntia humifusa	Prickly pear

Campanulaceae (Bellflower Family)

This is a family of about 70 genera and 2,000 species of herbs and a few shrubs that are most common in temperate regions of the Northern Hemisphere. The family includes nearly 300 species of *Campanula* and 300 more of *Lobelia;* many species are cultivated as ornamentals.

Campanula americana	Tall bellflower
C. divaricata	Southern harebell
Lobelia cardinalis	Cardinal flower
L. inflata	Indian tobacco
L. puberula	Downy lobelia
L. siphilitica	Great blue lobelia
L. spicata	Pale spiked lobelia
Triodanis perfoliata	Venus's looking-glass

Caprifoliaceae (Honeysuckle Family)

The honeysuckle family consists of about 18 genera and 450 species of small trees and shrubs, with only a few herbaceous members. The centers of diversity for the family are in eastern North America and eastern Asia. There are about 200 species of *Viburnum* and 150 species of *Lonicera,* the honeysuckles. Ornamentals include elderberries, *Sambucus* spp.; snowberry, *Symphoricarpos albus;* and weigelas, *Weigela florida.*

Triosteum angustifolium	Yellow horse gentian
T. aurantiacum	Red horse gentian
T. perfoliatum	Wild coffee

Caryophyllaceae (Pink Family)

The pink family contains about 2,000 species of herbs in 80 genera. These plants typically have opposite, simple leaves, and the flowers usually have 5 petals. The petals are often notched at the tips so that they appear to have 10 petals. The family includes many popular garden ornamentals as well as *Dianthus caryophyllus,* the carnation grown in greenhouses by florists.

Minuartia patula	Sandwort
Silene caroliniana	Carolina pink, wild pink
S. rotundifolia	Roundleaf catchfly
S. stellata	Starry campion
S. virginica	Fire pink
Stellaria pubera	Star chickweed

Clusiaceae (Mangosteen Family)

Old botanical reference books refer to this group as the Guttiferae, or Garcinia family, named for *Garcinia mangostana,* the mangosteen, a small tree cultivated in India and Southeast Asia for its edible fruits. The modern practice of ending botanical family names in the suffix *-aceae* has led to our current name of Clusiaceae for this group of about 1,000 species in 40 genera. The family is named for *Clusia,* a genus of small trees native to the American tropics, including *Clusia rosea,* the autograph tree found in Florida. Most members of this family are tropical, including several genera harvested for timber in tropical regions. There are over 350 species of *Hypericum,* and several are grown for ornamental value because of their bright yellow flowers.

Hypericum dolabriforme	Straggling St. John's wort
H. hypericoides	St. Andrew's cross
H. perforatum	St. John's wort
H. sphaerocarpum	Rough-fruited St. John's wort
H. stans	St. Peter's wort

Convolvulaceae (Morning Glory Family)

This family consists of about 1,500 species of herbs and vines in 50 genera, found mainly in subtropical and tropical regions around the world. There are over 400 species of *Ipomoea,* the morning glory, and 250 species of *Convolvulus,* the bindweeds. There are several plants of economic importance in this family, including the sweet potato, *Ipomoea batatas,* the ornamental morning glory, *I. purpurea,* and many species of *Convolvulus* that are troublesome weeds in North American grain fields.

Calystegia sepium	Hedge bindweed
Ipomoea pandurata	Wild potato vine

Crassulaceae (Stonecrop Family)

The stonecrop family consists of over 1,000 species in 30 genera, including about 300 species of *Sedum*. Most members are succulent plants found growing in poor soils in hot dry regions, and the greatest concentration of species is in South Africa. The group includes a number of ornamental species popular in rock gardens.

Sedum pulchellum	Widow's cross or pink stonecrop
S. ternatum	Stonecrop

Diapensiaceae (Diapensia Family)

The diapensia family consists of 20 species in 6 genera of herbs and small shrubs, most with evergreen leaves. The family is named for *Diapensia,* a creeping dwarf shrub native to the Himalayas.

Galax aphylla	Galax, beetleweed

Ericaceae (Heath Family)

The heath family comprises about 3,500 species in 125 genera, mostly shrubs and small trees growing in acid soils in temperate regions. There are over 1,000 species of *Rhododendron,* including more than 700 that occur in the Himalayan region and 300 on the island of New Guinea. The flowers typically have 5 petals and are often urn or bell shaped. The family includes many ornamental rhododendrons, azaleas, and mountain laurels as well as blueberries.

Epigaea repens	Trailing arbutus
Gaultheria procumbens	Wintergreen, teaberry, mountain tea

Euphorbiaceae (Spurge Family)

This family consists of about 7,500 species in 300 genera, including herbs, shrubs, and trees, often with fleshy stems and milky sap. They are found mainly in warm regions of the world and many species vegetatively resemble cacti. This is an economically and chemically important family, including plants such as *Hevea brasiliensis,* the source of most of the world's rubber; *Ricinus communis,* from which castor oil and the toxin ricin are made; *Vernicia,* the tung oil tree; *Poinsettia pulcherrima,* a popular holiday ornamental; *Sebastiana pavoniana,* the source of Mexican jumping beans; and *Manihot esculenta,* the source of manioc, a staple food in many tropical countries.

Euphorbia commutata	Wood spurge
E. corollata	Flowering spurge

Fabaceae (Pea Family)

The pea family consists of over 12,000 species of herbs, shrubs, and trees in 440 genera. Once known as Leguminosae, after the name of their characteristic fruit, the family is now named after faba, another name for bean. Most members have alternate, pinnately compound leaves. The flowers have 5 petals: the uppermost is called the standard; 2 lateral petals are called wings; and the 2 lower petals are fused together and called the keel. This is an important family of agricultural plants owing to their associations with nitrogen-fixing bacteria in nodules on the roots of many members. The plants are of tremendous economic importance, including food crops such as beans, peas, soybeans, and peanuts; and forage crops, including clover and alfalfa.

Amphicarpaea bracteata	Hog peanut
Apios americana	Groundnut
Baptisia australis	Blue false indigo
B. bracteata	Cream false indigo
B. leucantha	White false indigo
B. tinctoria	Yellow false indigo
Cassia fasciculata	Partridge pea
C. hebecarpa	Wild senna
C. marilandica	Wild senna
C. nictitans	Sensitive plant
Clitoria mariana	Butterfly pea
Dalea candidum	White prairie clover
D. purpurea	Purple prairie clover
Desmanthus illinoensis	Illinois bundleflower
Desmodium canescens	Hoary tick-trefoil
D. glutinosum	Pointed-leaved tick-trefoil
D. nudiflorum	Naked-flowered tick-trefoil
D. paniculatum	Panicled tick-trefoil
D. perplexum	Perplexing tick-trefoil, sticktights
D. rotundifolium	Round-leaved tick-trefoil
D. sessilifolium	Sessile-leaved tick-trefoil
Galactia volubilis	Milk pea
Lespedeza capitata	Round-headed bush clover
L. intermedia	Wandlike lespedeza
L. procumbens	Trailing bush clover
L. repens	Creeping bush clover
L. virginica	Virginia lespedeza
Phaseolus polystachios	Wild bean

Psoralea psoralioides	Scurf-pea
Schrankia microphylla	Sensitive brier
Strophostyles helvola	Annual trailing wild bean
S. umbellata	Trailing wild bean
Stylosanthes biflora	Pencil flower
Tephrosia virginiana	Goat's rue, rabbit's pea
Vicia caroliniana	Carolina vetch, wood vetch

Fumariaceae (Fumitory Family)

Named for fumitory, a common European agricultural weed, this is a family of 16 genera and about 450 species of herbs found mainly in the Northern Hemisphere. Several species of *Corydalis* are cultivated as ornamentals.

Corydalis flavula	Yellow corydalis, scrambled eggs
C. sempervirens	Pale corydalis
Dicentra canadensis	Squirrel corn
D. cucullaria	Dutchman's-breeches

Gentianaceae (Gentian Family)

There are 75 genera and nearly 1,000 species of herbs found around the world in the gentian family. The group includes about 400 species of *Gentiana*. Many species of *Gentiana* and *Sabatia* are cultivated as ornamentals.

Frasera caroliniensis	American columbo
Gentiana decora	Appalachian gentian
G. flavida	Pale gentian
G. puberulenta	Blue gentian, prairie gentian
G. quinquefolia	Stiff gentian
G. saponaria	Soapwort gentian
G. villosa	Striped gentian
Obolaria virginica	Pennywort
Sabatia angularis	Rose pink, meadow pink

Geraniaceae (Geranium Family)

There are about 700 species in 11 genera in this family, widely distributed around the world from tropical to boreal regions. About 300 of the species are in the genus *Geranium,* and there are close to 250 species of *Pelargonium,* our cultivated geraniums, which are native to South Africa.

Geranium carolinianum	Carolina crane's bill
G. maculatum	Wild geranium

Hydrophyllaceae (Waterleaf Family)

This is a small family of 20 genera and about 250 species of herbs and shrubs and is especially prominent in the western United States. About 150 of the species are in the genus *Phacelia*, and several are grown as ornamentals.

Hydrophyllum appendiculatum	Lavender waterleaf
H. canadense	Broadleaf waterleaf
H. macrophyllum	Hairy waterleaf
Phacelia bipinnatifida	Purple phacelia
P. purshii	Miami mist
P. ranunculacea	Blue scorpion weed

Lamiaceae (Mint Family)

The mint family consists of about 200 genera and 3,000 species of herbs, shrubs, and a few trees. Members are found in almost every region of the world, with a center of diversity near the Mediterranean Sea. Most herbaceous members have square stems and opposite leaves, and the plants are often covered with glands that release a characteristic pleasant fragrance. The mint family includes several horticulturally significant members, including *Mentha*, the mints; *Salvia*, sage; *Ocimum*, basil; *Origanum*, oregano; and *Thymus*, thyme. The group features a variety of highly specialized pollination mechanisms and is considered to be one of the most highly evolved dicot families.

Agastache nepetoides	Giant hyssop
Blephilia ciliata	Downy wood mint
B. hirsuta	Hairy wood mint
Collinsonia canadensis	Northern horse balm
Cunila origanoides	Dittany
Isanthus brachiatum	False pennyroyal
Meehania cordata	Meehania
Monarda bradburiana	Eastern bergamot
M. clinopodia	Basil bee balm
M. didyma	Scarlet bee balm
M. fistulosa	Bergamot, bee balm
M. russeliana	White bergamot
Physostegia virginiana	Obedient plant
Prunella vulgaris	Heal-all
Pycnanthemum incanum	Hoary mountain mint
P. flexuosum	Slender mountain mint
P. pycnanthemoides	Hoary mountain mint
P. tenuifolium	Slender-leaved hoary mountain mint

Salvia lyrata	Lyre-leaved sage
Scutellaria elliptica	Erect skullcap
S. incana	Downy skullcap
S. integrifolia	Large-flowered skullcap, hyssop-leaved skullcap
S. lateriflora	Mad-dog skullcap
S. nervosa	Veiny skullcap
S. ovata	Heart-leaved skullcap
S. parvula	Small skullcap
Stachys nuttallii	Hedge nettle
S. tenuifolia	Narrow-leaved hedge nettle
Synandra hispidula	Synandra
Teucrium canadense	Germander
Trichostema dichotomum	Blue curls

Lentibulariaceae (Bladderwort Family)

The bladderwort family is a small group of carnivorous plants, usually found in water, or at least very moist habitats. There are about 180 species in 4 genera found around the world in tropical and temperate regions. Bladderworts are small plants with delicate stems and stemlike leaves. Attached to the stems are small, inflated bladders with open mouths that can be tripped to snap shut when a tiny insect crawls inside. Enzymes released inside the closed bladders digest the insect, providing a source of nitrogen for the plant.

Utricularia gibba	Creeping bladderwort, humped bladderwort
U. inflata	Inflated bladderwort
U. vulgaris	Common bladderwort

Linaceae (Flax Family)

There are about 300 species in 13 genera in the flax family, mostly herbs and a few shrubs. The most famous member is the flax plant, *Linum usitatissimum,* whose stem fibers are used to make linen cloth, fine writing paper, and cigarette paper. The seeds are pressed to make linseed oil, used in the manufacture of paints and varnishes for wood.

Linum medium	Common yellow flax
L. virginianum	Virginia yellow flax

Loganiaceae (Logania Family)

The logania family is a group of 20 genera and nearly 500 species of herbs, shrubs, and trees. The family is mostly tropical and includes several species that are harvested for timber. It also includes *Strychnos nux-vomica,* an Indonesian shrub from which strychnine is extracted; and *Strychnos toxifera,* the source of curare, a generic term for a variety of poisonous concoctions made from the bark of South American trees.

Spigelia marilandica	Indian pink

Lythraceae (Loosestrife Family)

There are about 25 genera and 500 species of herbs, shrubs, and trees in the loosestrife family. This is primarily a tropical group, but a few species occur in temperate regions. One famous member is *Lythrum salicaria,* Purple loosestrife, a native of Eurasia introduced into the eastern United States in the early 1800s and now considered a noxious weed in wet areas.

Cuphea viscosissima	Blue waxweed
Lythrum alatum	Winged loosestrife

Malvaceae (Mallow Family)

The mallow family is made up of about 50 genera and 1,200 species of herbs, shrubs, and trees that are scattered around the world in tropical and temperate regions. They are particularly abundant in tropical South America. About one-quarter of the species belong to the genus *Hibiscus.* The family is economically important, including fibrous plants like cotton, *Gossypium,* and jute, *Abutilon avicenae*; edible plants like okra, *Hibiscus esculentus;* and many ornamental plants such as *Hibiscus, Sida,* and *Althaea.*

Hibiscus laevis	Rose mallow
H. moscheutos	Wild cotton

Melastomataceae (Melastoma Family)

The melastoma family includes about 240 genera and nearly 3,000 species of tropical shrubs and small trees, with only a few temperate and herbaceous members. The group is particularly important in the tropical forests of South America. A few members of the family are harvested for timber, and there are other members with edible fruit in South America and Sumatra, but the principal economic value of the family is in the few species that are grown in gardens for their colorful flowers.

Rhexia mariana	Maryland meadow beauty
R. virginica	Virginia meadow beauty

Monotropaceae (Indian Pipe Family)

Considered to be closely related to the heath family, the Indian pipe family is made up of 12 species in 10 genera. Members of the family have no chlorophyll and therefore lack the ability to carry out photosynthesis, instead obtaining nutrients through interactions with mycorrhizal fungi. Their leaves are reduced to small scales, and the flowers usually lack petals. The family is distributed primarily in cool, temperate regions of the Northern Hemisphere.

Monotropa hypopithys	Pinesap
M. uniflora	Indian pipe
Monostropsis odorata	Sweet pinesap

Nelumbonaceae (Lotus-Lily Family)

The family consists of only 2 species in a single genus. These are perennial aquatic herbs with simple, alternate leaves and large, beautiful flowers held above water. Besides our native lotus, the other family member is the sacred lotus, *Nelumbo nucifera,* a Buddhist symbol of purity, found throughout Southeast Asia.

Nelumbo lutea	American lotus

Nymphaceae (Water Lily Family)

There are about 90 species of water-lilies in 7 genera found around the world. All are aquatic perennial herbs with more or less heart-shaped leaves and large flowers held above the water. Some members are grown as ornamentals in ponds and water gardens, while others are popular aquarium plants.

Nuphar advena	Spatterdock
Nymphaea odorata	Fragrant water-lily

Onagraceae (Evening Primrose Family)

A family of 17 genera and 675 species of herbs and shrubs with the highest diversity in western North America. They include the ornamentals clarkias, fuchsias, and evening primroses.

Circaea alpina	Small enchanter's nightshade
C. lutetiana	Enchanter's nightshade
Gaura biennis	Biennial gaura
G. filipes	Slender gaura
G. longiflora	Southern gaura
G. parviflora	Small-flowered gaura
Ludwigia alternifolia	Rattlebox

Oenothera biennis	Evening primrose
O. fruticosa	Southern sundrops
O. speciosa	Showy primrose
O. tetragona	Sundrops

Orobanchaceae (Broomrape Family)

The broomrape family is a group of 14 genera and about 180 species of fleshy herbs, including 140 species of *Orobanche,* the broomrapes. Although they superficially resemble saprophytic plants like Indian Pipes, these plants are parasitic on the roots of other plants. Most, but not all, members lack chlorophyll, and the leaves are reduced to scales. The root system is not well developed, because these plants merely tap into the roots of a neighboring green plant and absorb sugars from their host. The name broomrape was created by medieval botanists from the Latin *Rapum genistea,* which translates into something like "broom knob," and was originally applied to *Orobanche major.* The name *Orobanche* was created by Linnaeus in 1753 from the Greek words *orobos,* vetch, and *ancho,* to strangle, referring to the plant's parasitic life strategy. The family includes many species that are serious agricultural weeds.

Conopholis americana	Squawroot
Epifagus virginiana	Beechdrops
Orobanche uniflora	Cancerroot

Oxalidaceae (Wood Sorrel Family)

There are 7 genera and about 900 species in this family, including 800 species of *Oxalis.* Most are tropical herbs, but there are a few shrubs. The family includes some species of *Oxalis* that are grown as ornamentals and also includes *Averrhoa carambola,* the star fruit.

Oxalis grandis	Large wood sorrel
O. montana	Mountain wood sorrel
O. stricta	Yellow wood sorrel
O. violacea	Violet wood sorrel

Papaveraceae (Poppy Family)

There are about 200 species in 25 genera within the poppy family; most are herbaceous plants of the Northern Hemisphere. About one-half of the species are in the genus *Papaver,* including many species grown as ornamentals, as well as the opium poppy, a native of western Asia that is the source of the drugs opium, morphine, heroin, and codeine.

| *Sanguinaria canadensis* | Bloodroot |
| *Stylophorum diphyllum* | Celandine poppy, wood poppy |

Passifloraceae (Passionflower Family)

This is a family of about 20 genera and nearly 600 species of mostly tropical and subtropical vines, with some herbs, shrubs, and trees. The center of distribution for the family is South America, but members occur in tropical Africa, Southeast Asia, and New Zealand. About 400 of the species are in the genus *Passiflora,* and a few of these are cultivated for their edible fruits, such as granadilla and passion fruit, or for their attractive flowers.

| *Passiflora incarnata* | Passionflower |
| *P. lutea* | Yellow passionflower |

Phrymaceae (Phryma Family)

This is a strange little family of plants, made up of a single genus and 3 species. The group is restricted to eastern Asia and eastern North America—a very interesting pattern of distribution for those who study plant geography and historical climate change.

| *Phryma leptostachya* | Lopseed |

Phytolaccaceae (Pokeweed Family)

A family of about 125 species in 22 genera, consisting of trees, shrubs, and herbs mainly in the American tropics.

| *Phytolacca americana* | Pokeweed |

Polemoniaceae (Phlox Family)

The phlox family contains 18 genera and about 300 species of herbs and shrubs. This is primarily a North American family, with over half of the species occurring in California, but members are also found in South America and Eurasia. It includes many species of *Phlox, Polemonium,* and *Gilia* grown as ornamentals.

Phlox amoena	Hairy phlox
P. amplifolia	Broadleaf phlox
P. bifida	Lobed phlox
P. divaricata	Blue phlox
P. glaberrima	Smooth phlox
P. maculata	Meadow phlox
P. paniculata	Fall phlox

P. pilosa	Prairie phlox, downy phlox
P. stolonifera	Creeping phlox
P. subulata	Moss phlox
Polemonium reptans	Jacob's ladder

Polygalaceae (Milkwort Family)

The milkwort family consists of about 17 genera and 1,000 species of herbs, shrubs, and trees, including about 500 species of *Polygala*. The flowers closely resemble those of members of the pea family.

Polygala sanguinea	Field milkwort
P. senega	Seneca snakeroot
P. verticillata	Whorled milkwort

Polygonaceae (Smartweed Family)

There are about 1,000 species in 30 genera in this family, including close to 200 species of *Polygonum,* the smartweeds, and 200 more of *Rumex,* or dock. Many of these species are agricultural weeds, but the family also includes rhubarb, *Rheum rhaponticum,* and buckwheat, *Fagopyrum esculentum,* a widely cultivated cover crop.

Polygonum pennsylvanicum	Pennsylvania smartweed
P. scandens	Climbing false buckwheat
P. virginianum	Virginia knotweed
Rumex verticillatus	Dockweed

Portulacaceae (Purslane Family)

This is a group of about 500 species in 19 genera; members are mostly herbs found in open, sunny areas. Many species have what plant ecologists call the C_4 photosynthetic pathway, an adaptation for life in high-light-intensity habitats. The purslane family includes several species of poisonous plants as well as some important agricultural weeds.

Claytonia carolinianum	Carolina spring beauty
C. virginica	Spring beauty

Primulaceae (Primrose Family)

This is a family of about 30 genera and 1,000 species of herbs, found mostly in the Northern Hemisphere. About half of the species are in the genus *Primula,* the primroses. The family includes many ornamental plants, including cyclamens and primroses.

Dodecatheon meadia	Shooting star
Lysimachia ciliata	Fringed loosestrife
L. lanceolata	Lance-leaved loosestrife
L. quadrifolia	Whorled loosestrife

Pyrolaceae (Shinleaf Family)

This is a family of about 40 species of herbs and small shrubs in 4 genera. Members are found in the temperate regions of the Northern Hemisphere, especially in the higher latitudes, and are considered to be closely related to the heath family.

| *Chimaphila maculata* | Spotted wintergreen |

Ranunculaceae (Buttercup Family)

There are about 50 genera and nearly 2,000 species in the buttercup family, mostly herbs in the cool, temperate regions. Many genera lack true petals, instead having a perianth of tepals, or sepals that appear to be petals. Although it is not considered to be an economically important group, the family includes several familiar garden plants, such as clematis, globe flower, and monkshood.

Actaea pachypoda	Doll's eyes, baneberry
Anemone quinquefolia	Wood anemone
A. virginiana	Thimbleweed, tall anemone
Anemonella thalictroides	Rue anemone
Aquilegia canadensis	Columbine
Cimicifuga americana	American bugbane, summer cohosh
C. racemosa	Black snakeroot, black cohosh
Clematis crispa	Blue jasmine
C. glaucophylla	Leather flower
C. pitcheri	Bluebill
C. versicolor	Pale leather flower
C. viorna	Leather vase vine
C. virginiana	Virgin's bower, old man's beard
Delphinium tricorne	Dwarf larkspur
Enemion biternatum	False rue anemone
Hepatica acutiloba	Sharp-lobed hepatica
H. americana	Round-lobed hepatica
Hydrastis canadensis	Goldenseal
Ranunculus abortivus	Kidney-leaved buttercup
R. fascicularis	Early buttercup
R. hispidus	Hairy buttercup
R. micranthus	Small-flowered buttercup

R. recurvatus	Hooked crowfoot
Thalictrum dioicum	Early meadow rue
T. mirabile	Cliff rue
T. pubescens	Tall meadow rue
T. revolutum	Waxy meadow rue
Trautvetteria caroliniensis	False bugbane, tassel-rue

Rosaceae (Rose Family)

This is a complex family of over 100 genera and 3,000 species of herbs, shrubs, and trees. Members of the family occur worldwide but are most common in the temperate Northern Hemisphere. This is one of our most important horticultural families, with at least 300 species of *Crateagus,* the hawthorns; 200 species of *Rubus,* the blackberries and raspberries; about 200 species of *Prunus,* the cherries, peaches, and plums; and 100 species of *Rosa,* the roses. Other horticultural members include apples, crabapples, pears, and strawberries.

Agrimonia parviflora	Southern agrimony
A. pubescens	Downy agrimony
A. rostellata	Woodland agrimony
Aruncus dioicus	Goat's beard
Fragaria virginiana	Wild strawberry
Geum canadense	Avens
Porteranthus stipulatus	American ipecac
P. trifoliatus	Indian physic
Potentilla canadensis	Dwarf cinquefoil
P. simplex	Common cinquefoil
Waldsteinia fragarioides	Barren strawberry

Rubiaceae (Madder Family)

There are about 450 genera and 7,000 species in the madder family, mostly trees and shrubs growing in tropical and subtropical areas around the world. There are notable economically important members, such as coffee, *Coffea arabica* and *C. canephora,* and several species of South American shrubs in the genus *Cinchona* whose bark is the source of quinine. Ornamental members include gardenias, *Gardenia jasminoides,* and several genera of evergreen shrubs cultivated in the Deep South.

Diodia teres	Rough buttonweed
D. virginiana	Virginia buttonweed
Galium aparine	Bedstraw
Houstonia caerulea	Bluets, Quaker ladies
H. canadensis	Fringed bluets

H. crassifolia	Small bluets
H. longifolia	Long-leaf bluets
H. nigricans	Glade bluets
H. purpurea	Large bluets, summer bluets
H. serpyllifolia	Mountain bluets, creeping bluets
Mitchella repens	Partridgeberry

Saururaceae (Lizard's Tail Family)

There are only 7 species, but 5 genera, in the lizard's tail family. Three genera are restricted to Asia, including the monotypic *Houttuyania* that is cultivated in this country as an ornamental ground cover. Another monotypic genus, *Anemopsis,* is found in wet places in the American Southwest where it is called yerba mansa. There are 2 species of *Saururus,* both plants of shallow swamps and bogs. One species is found in eastern Asia, the other in eastern North America.

Saururus cernuus	Lizard's tail

Saxifragaceae (Saxifrage Family)

The saxifrage family is made up of about 40 genera and 700 species of herbs, including over 300 species of *Saxifraga.* They attain their greatest diversity in the higher latitudes of the Northern Hemisphere and are common members of arctic and alpine floras.

Astilbe biternata	False goat's beard
Heuchera americana	Alumroot
H. parviflora	Rockhouse alumroot
H. villosa	Hairy alumroot
Mitella diphylla	Bishop's cap, mitrewort
Saxifraga virginiensis	Early saxifrage
Tiarella cordifolia	Foam flower

Scrophulariaceae (Figwort Family)

The Scrophs or figworts include close to 220 genera and 3,000 species of herbs and shrubs, primarily found in temperate regions. The family name comes from scrofula, a disease that causes swelling of the nodes in the neck, and the ancient belief that figwort (*Scrophularia* spp.) would cure the condition. Economically important members of the family include *Digitalis purpurea,* the source of the heart medicine digitoxin, as well as ornamentals such as the snapdragon, *Antirrhinum majus*; beard-tongues, *Penstemon*; and Speedwells, *Veronica.*

Agalinis purpurea	Purple gerardia
A. tenuifolia	Slender gerardia
Aureolaria flava	Smooth false foxglove
A. laevigata	Appalachian false foxglove
A. pectinata	Fernleaf false foxglove
A. pedicularia	Annual false foxglove
A. virginica	Downy false foxglove
Buchnera americana	Bluehearts
Chelone glabra	White turtlehead
C. obliqua	Pink turtlehead
Collinsia verna	Blue-eyed Mary
Dasistoma macrophylla	Mullein foxglove
Mimulus alatus	Sharp-winged monkey flower
M. ringens	Square-stemmed monkey flower
Pedicularis canadensis	Wood betony
Penstemon canescens	Appalachian beardtongue
P. digitalis	Tall beardtongue, foxglove beardtongue
P. hirsutus	Hairy beardtongue
P. tenuiflorus	Kentucky beardtongue, slender-flowered beardtongue
Veronicastrum virginicum	Culver's root

Solanaceae (Nightshade Family)

This is a family of about 90 genera and nearly 3,000 species of herbs, shrubs, and a few trees. Members are found around the world in tropical and temperate regions, but there are centers of diversity in Central America and Australia. There are several well-known members of this group, including tobacco, *Nicotiana tabacum*; the potato, *Solanum tuberosum*; the tomato, *Lycopersicon esculentum*; peppers, *Capsicum* spp.; tomatillo, *Physalis ixocarpa*; belladonna, *Atropa belladonna*; and jimsonweed, *Datura stramonium*.

Solanum carolinense	Horse nettle

Valerianaceae (Valerian Family)

This is a group of about 13 genera and 400 species of herbs and shrubs, mostly found in the temperate Northern Hemisphere. The family includes nearly 250 species of *Valeriana* and 50 species of *Valerianella*.

Valeriana pauciflora	Valerian
Valerianella spp.	Corn salad

Verbenaceae (Vervain Family)

There are about 75 genera and nearly 3,000 species of herbs and a few shrubs and trees in this family. It is almost entirely tropical and includes a number of commercially valuable trees that are harvested for timber in tropical countries, such as the famous teak, *Tectona grandis,* found in Southeast Asia, and zither wood, *Citharexylum*, from Mexico and South America. Several members of the family are grown as ornamentals or for their pleasantly scented foliage.

Phyla lanceolata	Fogfruit
Verbena hastata	Blue vervain
V. simplex	Narrow-leaved vervain
V. urticifolia	White vervain

Violaceae (Violet Family)

There are about 900 species in 20 genera in the family, mostly perennial herbs, but also a few shrubs. Violet family members are found all over the world, mostly in temperate regions. There are about 400 species of *Viola* and nearly 150 species of *Hybanthus.* Many field guides call attention to the difference between "stemmed violets," those with leafy flower stems, and "stemless violets," those with basal leaves only and flowers on separate stems. Most field guides do not mention that many species of *Viola* produce two kinds of flowers, called chasmogamous and cleistogamous. The normal showy flowers are chasmogamous, which translates from Greek into something like "open flower." The chasmogamous flowers of violets are produced before the forest leaf canopy shades the plants, and are brightly colored with nectar-containing spurs to attract pollinators. Chasmogamous flowers seemed to be adapted to promoting outcrossing among individuals. Cleistogamous, or closed, flowers are inconspicuous, round, green flowers without petals produced in summer that do not open until they have self-pollinated and produced seed. This self-pollination may be a backup plan for seed production in years when pollinators are scarce. There are several plants of horticultural interest in the violet family, including over 100 species of *Viola* grown in this country as ornamentals, such as pansies, and *Viola odorata*, the English violet, which is grown in Europe for use in perfume and liqueur.

Hybanthus concolor	Green violet
Viola blanda	Sweet White violet
V. canadensis	Canada violet
V. conspersa	Dog violet
V. cucullata	Marsh blue violet
V. hastata	Halberd-leaved violet
V. lanceolata	Strap-leaf violet, lance-leaved violet
V. palmata	Wood violet

V. pedata	Bird's-foot violet
V. primulifolia	Primrose-leaved violet
V. pubescens	Yellow woodland violet, downy yellow violet
V. rafinesquii	Field pansy
V. rostrata	Long-spurred violet
V. rotundifolia	Round-leaved violet
V. sagittata	Arrow-leaved violet, arrowhead violet
V. sororia	Common blue violet, dooryard violet
V. striata	Cream violet
V. triloba	Three-lobed violet, wood violet

THE FAMILIES: MONOCOTS

Agavaceae (Agave Family)

The agave family consists of about 20 genera and 700 species of herbs, shrubs, and trees, including over 300 species of *Agave* and 40 species of *Yucca*. Members of the family are found around the world, mostly in warm, dry regions. They are considered by many authors to be part of the amaryllis family, and therefore others take them to be an extension of the lily family. Some members are prominent plants in the southwestern United States, including *Yucca brevifolia*, the Joshua tree; *Agave lecheguilla*, lecheguilla; and *A. potatorum*, the century plant. There are well-known horticutural plants, such as *Aloe vera* and *Yucca filamentosa*, Adam's needle. There are also economically important plants, including *Agave sisalana*, the source of fiber for sisal rope, and *Agave tequilana*, which is fermented and distilled into tequila.

Manfreda virginica	False aloe

Alismataceae (Water Plantain Family)

The water plantain family includes about 100 species in 12 genera of herbaceous plants that occur mainly in the Northern Hemisphere. They are aquatic, or in some cases semiaquatic, and most have leaves and flowering stems with long stalks. The flowers have 3 white petals and 3 green sepals. A few members of this family are cultivated as ornamentals for ponds and water gardens.

Alisma subcordatum	Southern water plantain
Echinodorus cordifolius	Creeping burhead
Sagittaria australis	Appalachian arrowhead
S. brevirostra	Midwestern arrowhead
S. latifolia	Common arrowhead, duck potato
S. montevidensis	Mississippi arrowhead

Amaryllidaceae (Amaryllis Family)

The amaryllis family is made up of about 1,100 species in 75 genera, mostly herbs found around the world in subtropical and warm temperate regions. The family is considered to be very close to the lilies, differing principally in the relative position of the ovary to the petals and sepals. In fact, many authors choose to include members of the amaryllis family within a more inclusive lily family. The amaryllis family includes several well-known ornamentals, including the daffodils and snowdrops.

Hymenocallis caroliniana	Spider lily
Hypoxis hirsuta	Yellow stargrass

Araceae (Arum Family)

The arum family consists of about 2,000 species in 110 genera, mostly herbs that grow in moist, tropical regions, but the group also includes some shrubs and woody vines. Aroid flowers are tiny, have no petals or sepals, and are rarely seen by most observers because they are positioned on a stalk, or spadix, that is hidden behind a sheathing bract called the spathe. It is the spathe that many wildflower observers think of when they recall a jack-in-the-pulpit, since few have ever seen the true flowers. A few aroids are grown in tropical countries for their starchy, edible roots. Many gardeners will recognize aroids that are cultivated as indoor foliage plants, such as *Caladium, Dieffenbachia, Anthurium,* and *Philodendron,* as well as those grown for their striking flowers, such as *Calla* and *Zantedeschia.*

Acorus calamus	Sweet flag
Arisaema dracontium	Green dragon
A. triphyllum	Jack-in-the-pulpit

Commelinaceae (Spiderwort Family)

The spiderwort family includes approximately 600 species in 50 genera, all herbaceous and mostly tropical. The largest genus is *Commelina,* the dayflowers, including nearly 200 species. A typical member of the family has flowers with 3 sepals and 3 petals, and jointed stems with swollen nodes at the leaf axils. Several members of the family are grown as foliage plants, including *Zebrina,* the wandering Jew.

Commelina diffusa	Creeping dayflower
C. erecta	Erect dayflower
C. virginica	Virginia dayflower
Tradescantia ohiensis	Ohio spiderwort, glaucous spiderwort
T. subaspera	Zigzag spiderwort
T. virginiana	Early spiderwort, Virginia spiderwort

Dioscoreaceae (Yam Family)

The yam family, consisting of about 6 genera and 630 species, consists mostly of tropical perennial herbs, but there are also a few shrubs and vines. There are over 600 species of *Dioscorea,* including about 60 species of yams that are cultivated as staple food crops in tropical regions of South America, Asia, and Africa.

Dioscorea quaternata	Wild yam

Iridaceae (Iris Family)

The iris family includes about 80 genera and 1,800 species of herbs and shrubs with a center of diversity in Africa. Like the lilies, irises have 3 petals and 3 sepals colored alike. Like members of the amaryllis family, irises bear their petals and sepals above the ovary. Unlike both the lily and amaryllis families, there are 3 stamens in the flower instead of 6. The group contains about 200 species of *Iris* and includes other plants of horticultural interest such as *Gladiolus* and *Crocus.*

Iris cristata	Crested dwarf iris
I. verna	Dwarf iris
I. virginica	Southern blue flag
Sisyrinchium albidum	Pale blue-eyed grass, white blue-eyed grass
S. angustifolium	Stout blue-eyed grass
S. atlanticum	Eastern blue-eyed grass

Liliaceae (Lily Family)

The lily family is one of the most important families of plants in our spring flora. Made up of nearly 4,000 species in 280 genera, they are mostly herbs with a few shrubs and vines. The flowers typically have 3 sepals and 3 petals colored alike, so that they are all often referred to as tepals or segments. A notable exception to this rule is the genus *Trillium,* in which the sepals and petals are easily distinguished. The family includes many important horticultural plants, with ornamentals such as tulips, daylilies, lilies, hostas, and hyacinths; and vegetable-garden plants like asparagus, onions, and garlic.

Aletris farinosa	Colic root
Allium canadense	Wild garlic
A. cernuum	Nodding wild onion
A. tricoccum	Wild leek, ramp
Camassia scilloides	Wild hyacinth
Chamaelirium luteum	Devil's bit, fairy wand
Clintonia umbellulata	Speckled wood lily, white clintonia
Disporum lanuginosum	Yellow mandarin

D. maculatum	Spotted mandarin
Erythronium albidum	White trout lily
E. americanum	Yellow trout lily
Lilium canadense	Canada lily
L. michiganense	Michigan lily
L. philadelphicum	Wood lily
L. superbum	Turk's cap lily
Maianthemum canadense	Canada mayflower
M. racemosa	False Solomon's seal
Medeola virginiana	Indian cucumber-root
Nothoscordum bivalve	False garlic
Polygonatum biflorum	Smooth Solomon's seal
P. pubescens	Downy Solomon's seal
Trillium cuneatum	Southern sessile trillium, sweet betsy
T. erectum	Red trillium
T. flexipes	Bent trillium, nodding trillium
T. grandiflorum	Large white trillium
T. luteum	Yellow trillium
T. nivale	Snow trillium
T. pusillum	Ozark trillium
T. recurvatum	Recurved trillium
T. sessile	Sessile trillium
T. sulcatum	Southern red trillium
T. undulatum	Painted trillium
Uvularia grandiflora	Large-flowered bellwort
U. perfoliata	Small-flowered bellwort
U. sessilifolia	Sessile-leaved bellwort

Orchidaceae (Orchid Family)

One of the largest families of plants, with about 750 genera and 18,000 species, orchids are found all over the world. The majority of species are epiphytic plants growing in the crowns of trees in tropical forests, and as many as 25 percent of orchid species are in danger of extinction due to habitat destruction.

A typical orchid flower has 3 sepals and 3 petals. One of the petals is enlarged and may differ dramatically from the other 2 in size, shape, and color. Another peculiar structure within the orchid flower is the column formed by a joining of the pistil and stamen. Most orchids have a single stamen, an exception being our lady's slippers.

Orchids are known for their phenomenal adaptations to facilitate insect pollination. They are also highly valued for their spectacular flowers and are one of the most popular families among ornamental gardeners. All of our native orchids have symbiotic relationships with mycorrhizal fungi, making them doubly difficult to successfully transplant from the wild. Garden soil must be suitable for the fungus that lives on and in the orchid's roots, or else the transplant is ultimately doomed. Orchid growers, however, make up a huge industry in the United States and many other countries, and new hybrids of tropical species are constantly being developed. *Vanilla planifolia* is one of the few species grown for human consumption.

Aplectrum hyemale	Puttyroot
Calopogon tuberosus	Grass pink
Cleistes divaricata	Spreading pogonia
Corallorhiza maculata	Spotted coralroot
C. odontorhiza	Fall coralroot
C. wisteriana	Spring coral root
Cypripedium acaule	Pink lady's slipper
C. candidum	White lady's slipper, prairie lady's slipper
C. kentuckiense	Kentucky lady's slipper
C. parviflorum	Small-flowered yellow lady's slipper
C. pubescens	Yellow lady's slipper
Galearis spectabilis	Showy orchid
Goodyera pubescens	Rattlesnake plantain
Hexalectris spicata	Crested coralroot
Isotria verticillata	Whorled pogonia
Liparis liliifolia	Lily-leaved twayblade
L. loeselii	Loesel's twayblade
Malaxis unifolia	Green adder's mouth orchid
Platanthera ciliaris	Yellow fringed orchid
P. clavellata	Club-spur orchid
P. cristata	Crested fringed orchid
P. flava	Green orchid
P. lacera	Ragged fringed orchid
P. peramoena	Purple fringeless orchid
P. psycodes	Purple fringed orchid
Spiranthes cernua	Nodding ladies' tresses
S. lacera	Slender or green-lipped ladies' tresses
S. lucida	Shining ladies' tresses
S. magnicamporum	Great Plains ladies' tresses
S. ovalis	Oval ladies' tresses
S. tuberosa	Little ladies' tresses
S. vernalis	Spring ladies' tresses
Tipularia discolor	Crane-fly orchid
Triphora trianthophora	Three-birds orchid

Pontederiaceae (Water Hyacinth Family)

This family consists of 34 species of herbaceous plants in 9 genera. They are chiefly found growing in wet soils, mostly in tropical areas. The namesake of the family is *Eichhornia crassipes,* the water hyacinth, a native of subtropical regions that has been introduced into the temperate zone, including far western Kentucky, becoming one of the most troublesome weeds in the entire world.

Heteranthera dubia	Water stargrass
Pontederia cordata	Pickerel weed

Smilacaceae (Catbrier Family)

Another family that is closely allied to the lilies, this group is made up of 10 genera and 375 species of herbs, shrubs, and woody vines. Nearly 350 of those species are in the genus *Smilax.* They are most common in tropical and subtropical regions of the Southern Hemisphere.

Smilax ecirrhata	Erect carrion flower
S. herbacea	Carrion flower vine

Sparganiaceae (Bur Reed Family)

The bur reeds consist of about 15 species of aquatic plants in a single genus. Related to the cattails, these are plants of temperate and arctic regions in the Northern Hemisphere, growing from underwater rhizomes and standing erect with sheathing, linear leaves in 2 rows. The flowers are unisexual, arranged in 2 separate rounded heads on a single plant: male flowers above, the female flower head below. Bur-reeds are recognized as important food and cover plants for migratory waterfowl.

Sparganium americanum	American bur reed
S. androcladum	Branched bur reed

Typhaceae (Cattail Family)

The cattails are a group of 15 species of perennial herbs in 1 genus that is widely distributed around the world in shallow freshwater. The tiny flowers are crowded together at the tip of a flowering stem, with male and female flowers separate on the same plant.

Typha angustifolia	Narrow-leaved cattail
T. latifolia	Common cattail

BIBLIOGRAPHY

Beal, Ernest O., and John W. Thieret. *Aquatic and Wetland Plants of Kentucky.* Scientific and Technical Series 5. Frankfort: Kentucky Nature Preserves Commission, 1986.

Braun, E. Lucy. *An Annotated Catalog of Spermatophytes of Kentucky.* Cincinnati, Ohio: John S. Swift, 1943.

Browne, Edward T., and Raymond Athey. *Vascular Plants of Kentucky.* Lexington: University Press of Kentucky, 1992.

Carman, Jack B. *Wildflowers of Tennessee.* Tullahoma, Tenn.: Highland Rim Press, 2001.

Case, Frederick W., Jr. *Orchids of the Western Great Lakes Region.* Bloomfield, Mich.: Cranbrook Institute of Science, 1987.

Case, Frederick W., Jr., and Roberta B. Case. *Trilliums.* Portland, Ore.: Timber Press, 1997.

Chester, Edward W., and William H. Ellis. *Wildflowers of the Land between the Lakes Region, Kentucky and Tennessee.* 2nd ed. Clarksville, Tenn.: Center for Field Biology, Austin Peay University, 2000.

Correll, Donovan Stewart. *Native Orchids of North America.* Stanford, Calif.: Stanford University Press, 1978.

Cranfill, Ray. *Ferns and Fern Allies of Kentucky.* Scientific and Technical Series 1. Frankfort: Kentucky Nature Preserves Commission, 1980.

Duncan, Wilbur H., and M. B. Duncan. *Wildflowers of the Eastern United States.* Athens: University of Georgia Press, 1999.

Duncan, Wilbur H., and Leonard E. Foote. *Wildflowers of the Southeastern United States.* Athens: University of Georgia Press, 1975.

Fernald, Merritt Lyndon. *Gray's Manual of Botany.* 8th ed. New York: D. Van Nostrand, 1950.

Gleason, Henry A. *The New Britton and Brown Illustrated Flora of the Northeastern United States and Adjacent Canada.* New York: New York Botanical Garden, 1952.

Gleason, Henry A., and Arthur Cronquist. *Manual of Vascular Plants of the Northeastern United States and Adjacent Canada.* 2nd ed. New York: New York Botanical Garden, 1991.

Haragan, Patricia D. *Weeds of Kentucky and Adjacent States.* Lexington: University Press of Kentucky, 1991.

Hemmerly, Thomas E. *Appalachian Wildflowers.* Athens: University of Georgia Press, 2000.

Heywood, V. H., ed. *Flowering Plants of the World.* London: Croom Helm, 1978.

Key, James S. *Field Guide to Missouri Ferns.* Jefferson City: Missouri Department of Conservation, 1982.

Lawrence, George H. M. *Taxonomy of Vascular Plants.* New York: Macmillan, 1951.

Luer, Carlyle A. *The Native Orchids of the United States and Canada.* New York: New York Botanical Garden, 1975.

McFarland, Frank T. "A Catalogue of the Vascular Plants of Kentucky." *Castanea* 7 (1942): 77–108.

Medley, Max E. "An Annotated Catalog of the Known or Reported Vascular Flora of Kentucky." Ph.D. diss., University of Louisville, Ky., 1993.

Meijer, Willem, ed. "Herbaceous Spring-Summer Flora of Kentucky." University of Kentucky, Lexington. Photocopy. 1992.

Radford, Albert E., Harry E. Ahles, and C. Ritchie Bell. *Manual of the Vascular Flora of the Carolinas.* Chapel Hill: University of North Carolina Press, 1968.

Seymour, R. *Wildflowers of Mammoth Cave National Park.* Lexington: University Press of Kentucky, 1997.

Shaver, Jesse M. *Ferns of Tennessee.* Nashville, Tennessee: George Peabody College for Teachers, 1954.

Smith, Richard M. *Wildflowers of the Southern Mountains.* Knoxville: University of Tennessee Press, 1998.

Strausbaugh, P. D., and Earl L. Core. *Flora of West Virginia.* Grantsville, W.Va.: Seneca Books, 1977.

Wharton, Mary E., and Roger W. Barbour. *The Wildflowers and Ferns of Kentucky.* Lexington: University Press of Kentucky, 1971.

———. *Trees and Shrubs of Kentucky.* Lexington: University Press of Kentucky, 1973.

Wofford, B. Eugene. *Guide to the Vascular Plants of the Blue Ridge.* Athens: University of Georgia Press, 1989.

Wyman, Donald. *Wyman's Gardening Encyclopedia.* New York: Macmillan, 1971.

Zomlefer, W. B. *Guide to Flowering Plant Families.* Chapel Hill: University of North Carolina Press, 1994.

INDEX